THE
PERSONNEL
JOB

in a Changing World

Edited by Jerome W. Blood

AMERICAN MANAGEMENT ASSOCIATION

THE
PERSONNEL
JOB *in a*
Changing
World

CONTRIBUTORS

Douglas W. Bray

Donald W. Devine

Robert J. Doolan

Richard A. Dunnington

Lyle H. Fisher

Felician F. Foltman

George Frank

Marjorie W. Geerlofs

Saul W. Gellerman

Robert F. Groves

George E. Gullen, Jr.

Spencer J. Hayden

John R. Hinrichs

Edgar F. Huse

Emanuel Kay

A. D. Kellner

Arthur H. Kuriloff

Pres Lancaster

H. C. LaParo

R. Heath Larry

Frank D. Leamer

E. D. Mairs

Russell C. McCarthy

Robert McCoy

Leon C. Megginson

Joseph E. Milano

Harold L. Moon

W. R. Munns

Robert A. Neiman

Orden Oechsli

Charles H. Parcells

Robert F. Pearse

Mark Priceman

Dallas G. Rayl

Roy R. Reynolds

George Schermer

John I Snyder, Jr.

Benson Soffer

Richard E. Swanson

Ralph W. Walker

John K. Wolfe

EDITOR

Jerome W. Blood

THE

PERSONNEL

JOB *in a*

Changing

World

AMERICAN MANAGEMENT ASSOCIATION
NEW YORK

This is No. 80 in the series of AMA Management Reports. It has been distributed without charge to AMA members enrolled in the Personnel Division. Those who are enrolled in other divisions, or who wish extra copies, may order the Report in a hardcover edition at $6.00 per copy. Price to nonmembers, $9.00.

Library of Congress catalog card number: 64-22059

CONTENTS

SECTION I

Automation and Unemployment

The effect of automation on employment is a problem which touches almost all types of workers: blue collar, white collar, skilled and unskilled, and even some managers. Its principal effect has been felt, however, on the blue-collar workers. The first two chapters in this section outline the problem; the remaining chapters discuss three proposed solutions: extended vacation programs, job security programs, and retraining programs.

AUTOMATION AND UNEMPLOYMENT: MANAGEMENT'S QUIET CRISIS •

JOHN I SNYDER, JR.

D AVID ROCKEFELLER HAS OBSERVED that "the one thing automation cannot do is solve the problems it is creating. This is something that only human brains can accomplish."

That automation poses problems of great magnitude has been recognized for some time. But not nearly enough of us realize that we are living through a technological countdown at this very moment—that these problems of automation can no longer be consigned to "the long run," considered at leisure in symposia devoted to long-range economic problems and cerebrally probed from time to time in articles on "The Social Responsibilities of the Businessman"—articles which, I suspect, are rather little read because the problems they deal with appear to be so comfortably lacking in immediacy.

Automation is not a problem of "tomorrow." Automation is moving like a grass fire throughout the United States economy right now. It has been estimated that each week 40,000 jobs are eliminated as a direct consequence of automation. Thus the impact of automation—on jobs, on purchasing power, on management operations—is enormous. It is moving far too quickly for us to await the rescue of long-term solutions. Nobody denies that over the long term automation may work wondrous miracles for man's well-being, that we may reap from it far greater benefits than

---

JOHN I SNYDER, JR. is Chairman and President, U.S. Industries, Inc., New York, New York.

we dare dream of. This, however, is the short run. And the problems of the short run are upon us—at a moment in history that Dickens seemed to be describing in the opening of *A Tale of Two Cities*: "It was the best of times, it was the worst of times." Dickens, of course, was writing about the time of the French Revolution, but he could have been setting the stage for a thesis on the automation revolution.

On the one hand, Americans are unquestionably earning more, spending more, and enjoying more material wealth than any other people in the history of the world. In 1963, for example, personal income in the United States reached an incredible $452.5 billion—$23.5 billion more than the year before. We spent the staggering sum of $240 billion. Our total assets were well over one *trillion* dollars—or the equivalent of more than $5,800 for every man, woman, and child in our country. In all these respects, we are living in "the best of times."

On the other hand, some four million of our people—or 5.5 per cent of our labor force—are without jobs. More than two and a half million have completely exhausted all their unemployment benefits. At least one in every five persons working today will almost certainly be unemployed some time during next year, and upward of another two and a half million will have to settle for part-time jobs because no full-time work will be available to them. In our 30 major cities, 1 in every 11 workers will continue to look for work that doesn't exist. For these people, it is "the worst of times."

The fact is that partly as a result of automation and technological change, our economy cannot generate new jobs at a rate anywhere near the rate at which our labor force is growing. It is no wonder, therefore, that the new technology is feared. We have gone through four recessions in the last decade, and unemployment is still rising; and although manufacturing output has risen 17 per cent since 1953, employment has dropped more than 5 per cent.

FACTORS AGGRAVATING THE PROBLEM

We cannot overlook certain factors of broad significance that underscore and intensify the problems resulting from automation. They are coming at the worst possible time because they are creating pressures on our society to provide additional jobs at the very moment when the supply of jobs is rapidly shrinking.

First of all, the bumper postwar baby crop is out of school and seeking jobs. As of April 1963, Secretary of Labor Willard Wirtz estimated, about one million people between the ages of 16 and 21 were looking for work and unable to find it. The percentage of young people out of work was roughly 15 per cent of those available for work. These, however, are dry statistics: their meaning is clearer if we realize that this is the same as if there were not a single job opportunity for any boy or girl between 16 and 21 in New York, Chicago, Philadelphia, or Los Angeles. In addition, the rate of high school dropouts is rapidly accelerating, which means that vast numbers of unskilled young people are looking for work at the very time when unskilled jobs are disappearing.

Second, we are in the midst of a social revolution. Our headlines have been dominated by news of the racial conflicts that have convulsed one American city after another. Few would quarrel with the observation that the Negro's drive for redress of his long-standing grievances has as much an economic basis as it does a social or legal basis. The goals are legal and social equality but, even more, economic equality. We are again facing a dilemma here because this drive for economic opportunity comes at the very moment when *all* job opportunities are rapidly shrinking. Meanwhile, the proportion of minority groups without jobs is just about double that of the work force as a whole. About 12 per cent of Negroes of working age are looking for work; and for Negroes under 21, the figure is over 20 per cent.

The third factor is intensified competition for the consumer's dollar. We have seen an increasing competition by foreign products for the American consumer's dollar. On the one hand, this represents a strong argument for further automation to strengthen our ability to produce goods at competitive prices. But at the same time we must ask ourselves what is becoming of the purchasing power of the people who are joining the ranks of the unemployed week after week. The dilemma here is that we are faced with greater competition for the American consumer's purchasing power at the very time when increasing numbers of Americans are losing their power to purchase or, in many cases, their ability even to subsist unaided.

Finally, we are experiencing pressures for faster automation. As David A. Morse, director general of the International Labor Office, has pointed out, Federal action taken in the interest of fostering long-term economic growth will compound, during the short term, the problems of unemployment growing out of increased automation. Tax credits for the purchase of new capital equipment and depreciation allowances approved in the

United States and Great Britain are examples of such action. Industry is fooling itself if it ignores the short-term consequences of such action and the immediate effects upon employment and purchasing power. The funds made available to industry as a result of such measures will be used for "modernization"—which is to say, automation. And in speeding up automation they will displace more workers faster than they would otherwise have been displaced.

It should be emphasized that actions such as these, which are economically sound and desirable for the long term, should not be delayed or suspended because they create immediate problems. But we are deluding ourselves if we reason that such measures will, in the short run, create more jobs. We cannot have it all ways. Such measures will not create more jobs: They will do the opposite.

MISCONCEPTIONS ABOUT AUTOMATION

Albert Camus once said, "Truth, like light, blinds. Falsehood, on the contrary, is a beautiful twilight that enhances every object." A corollary to this is that it is much easier to seek proof that a problem does not exist than to admit its existence and move to solve it. Thus a number of misconceptions about automation have arisen.

The first is that automation is just another phase of the Industrial Revolution and that the problems are essentially the same as problems faced and solved in the past. The analogy is false. People were hurt by the Industrial Revolution because countries broke out of an agrarian society, but they replaced it with an industrial society that created jobs. Today we live in that industrial society, but with automation we are making obsolete not only our conventional machines but hundreds of thousands of modern men as well. The Industrial Revolution created jobs; our sophisticated machines are now destroying jobs.

Many of us fail to understand the nature and extent of the thrust of this technological revolution. Change can be measured in "orders of magnitude," meaning a factor of ten times as much. It is a common observation that a change of an order of magnitude produces entirely new effects. Jet planes are about one order of magnitude faster than the first airplane; missiles are at least two orders faster. Automobiles are one order of magnitude faster than a horse and wagon. The computer—which along with automatic machinery makes up an automated system—is in its processes some six orders of magnitude faster than man.

The effects of the Industrial Revolution cannot be equated with the effects of automation, for we are not substituting machines for men on a one-to-one, a one-to-five, or even a one-to-ten basis. The number of men who can be displaced by automated equipment in a given plant may range from 60 or 70 or 100 to several hundred or more. The problems we face now, as against those faced during and since the Industrial Revolution, are so quantitatively different that they have become qualitatively different as well. And they will call for different solutions.

A second misconception is that automation is not going to eliminate many jobs. This argument ignores the evidence that automation is a major factor in eliminating tens of thousands of jobs a week. It is displacing people not only directly but indirectly, through the "silent firings" of workers who would have been hired had their jobs not been eliminated by automation. There are also workers who lose their jobs through vertical integration due to automation, as was the case in a company that formerly supplied a third of the body parts used by one large automobile manufacturer. When the manufacturer automated his stamping plants, none of his own employees were displaced, but 5,000 employees of the supplier company were taken off the payroll.

Third, there is the idea that automation will create jobs for workers not only in running the machines but in maintaining and building them. The hard truth is that modern automated equipment requires very little maintenance. If it did not, it would not pay to operate it; and if the equivalent number of workers replaced by automation were required to build the machines and systems, there would be no point in automating.

Fourth, some people contend that those who lose their jobs to automation can be retrained and put into other jobs requiring higher skills and paying more money. Studies have shown that automation is more likely to reduce than to increase the number of jobs requiring high skills and aptitudes. Besides, many people are just not retrainable because of their levels of intelligence, education, and age.

Still another misconception is that workers displaced by automation in one part of the country can find jobs in other areas. The truth is that the workers thrown out of jobs are usually those least able to move. They are the lower paid, the older, the unskilled. Either they cannot afford to move from an economic standpoint, or they are psychologically incapable of beginning a new life in a strange area.

Finally, there is the common tendency to think of automation primarily as it affects factory jobs. We know that the ratio of white-collar to blue-collar jobs in the United States has changed and that the service industries are growing in economic importance year by year. And many of us seem to accept implicitly the groundless reassurance that workers displaced from factory jobs can, to some extent, be absorbed into the white-collar workforce or into the service occupations.

Those inclined to go along with this theory should consider for a moment a typical series of events in the life of John Doe, a middle manager (still employed), as he and his wife go about their Saturday chores. Leaving their apartment house, he and Mrs. Doe descend to the garage of the building in an elevator that has recently been converted to self-service operation. Mr. Doe passes the milk-vending machine and pauses to buy cigarettes from a machine near where his car is parked. As he drives out, no attendant assists him in opening the garage door, for that has long since been operated by an electric-eye system.

Dropping his wife off at the laundromat, which is attended by only one employee (it operates around the clock and at night is attended by no one), he pauses before a machine that makes change automatically, because he knows he will need more silver at their next stop—the automatic dry-cleaning plant, completely coin-operated and manned by only one attendant during the day and by no one at night. Within an hour, he and his wife and the machine will have done 24 pounds of dry cleaning that a few years ago would have kept a number of people "in the service occupations" busy for several hours. The next stop is at an enormous supermarket, crowded with customers and almost devoid of personnel. Here, the Does will select their groceries and other soft goods with the help and blandishments of no salesmen other than the packages on the products that have been designed to sell themselves.

Before they start home, Mr. and Mrs. Doe may pause before a vending machine for a soft drink. Going home, they may pass over a toll bridge, also unattended, which will collect the toll from Mr. Doe when he pays it or report him if he does not. Later at home, he may make a long-distance telephone call, dialing directly unaided by any human telephone operator. Afterward, he and his wife may go out to dinner and be served frozen vegetables and other foods that were processed by automated machinery before they ever reached the restaurant—thanks to which the proprietor of that restaurant has been able to make drastic reductions in his kitchen staff. And these vegetables in all likelihood will have been picked and processed on automated farms employing considerably fewer people than they employed a year ago.

These are just a few examples of automation in the service and farm industries, and such obvious ones that they are old hat to most of us. There will be many, many more—and more exotic ones—in the years to come. But they should at least give us pause about the much-vaunted employment opportunities in the service and supporting industries. This does not mean that new kinds of services will not come into being in the future and that services will not expand, creating some new jobs. But we do not have those unfilled jobs *now,* and none of us can be sure how many of them we will have a year or two years from now. For the short run, we cannot look to the service industries for a solution.

A SEARCH FOR SOLUTIONS

What does all this mean for American management? It means that those in business will have to face up to the fact that continued mass unemployment and the resultant loss of purchasing power by millions of citizens will eventually hurt not only individual businesses but the national economy as well. There is a basic economic law that must be applied here—that reduced purchasing power equals unsold goods equals further unemployment equals still less purchasing power.

The human brain power that alone can solve the massive problems of automation will have to come in large measure from management, even though their solution will, of course, depend on the brain power and action of other groups in our society as well. The trouble is that the problems, where they are recognized by managers at all, are too often viewed abstractly. The consequences of automation are theoretical problems removed from the immediate, day-to-day, pressing, "real" problems of business.

Where within our corporations today has the responsibility been fixed for doing something about them? On how many company meeting agendas do they appear? In how many companies are they viewed as specific and immediate operating problems of the business, as pressing as, say, the overnight loss of thousands of customers or the sudden drying up of prime markets for the company's product? I venture to say in few.

I suspect that many managers feel that automation does not and will not pose any real problems, either for their own business or for the economy as a whole. They feel that somehow everything will shake out and settle itself. Many are fearful of looking at the "gloomy" side of automation, because they do not want to appear to be obstructing progress, they do not want to appear to be clinging to the *status quo*. Worrying about the consequences of automation puts them on the side of the skeptics and "pessimists" who have always resisted and bemoaned progress. And what business executive today can afford to be in such company? Others fear that, if they acknowledge the problem—which is so massive, so overwhelming—they won't know where to begin to solve it. And besides, they reason, their first job is to meet their specific management responsibilities by running the business and showing the tangible results of their efforts on the company profit and loss statement.

Even among businessmen who do see the gravity of the situation, there seem to be two conflicting tendencies: One is to protest Government's entry into the picture—to tell Government to keep hands off; the other is to rely completely on Government to produce the magic solution to all our problems. In my view, both are quite wrong. Industry alone won't be able to solve the enormous problems that technological change is creating and will continue to create in coming months and years. The task is just too big and too tough for the business sector of our economy to handle alone. The same can be said of Government and such efforts as are represented by the Manpower Development and Training Act and the Area Redevelopment Act. If we are to find solutions, labor, industry, and Government are going to have to work more closely together than they have ever done before. Moreover, they are going to have to focus greater imagination upon their task.

Genuine innovations, really new sociological and economic ideas, are going to be needed if we are to solve the problems we face in this area. We shall have to recognize that our present ways of thinking may be seriously out of phase with today's march of events. Perhaps we need to establish new concepts with regard to some of our basic institutions and beliefs if we are to find satisfactory solutions to some of our present problems. This could apply to the whole spectrum of our social existence, but it applies particularly to our attitude toward work.

If I were asked, "Is it ethical to make a man sit in a labor pool, however well paid he is, and not give him any satisfactory work?" my answer would be that it is ethical if you have no work for the man to do; and it is certainly more ethical than sending the man out the gate because he has been displaced by a machine. This view always causes dissent and discussion because of our traditional moral concept of work. It is almost sacrilegious to suggest that the old precept of an honest dollar for an honest day's work doesn't *always* apply or that a day may come when our standards have so changed that it might not apply at all.

In fact, it has already been suggested that work and income may have to be separated altogether, with the pay a person receives having little relationship to the work he does or does not do. This suggestion has come not from labor spokesmen but from people who have been identified closely with management and whose views are respected by management. We may not agree; we may not see the necessity for ever separating work from pay; and we may take strong exception to a lot of other theories we'll be hearing. But we will not be able to evaluate these theories or come up with better ones unless we learn to view our problems within the context of the times rather than in relation to old and perhaps outmoded ideas.

U.S. Industries, in cooperation with the International Association of Machinists, has established the American Foundation on Automation and Employment. The Foundation is financed by monthly "dues" paid into the fund by U.S. Industries on the basis of the lease or sale price of each automated machine purchased from our company. Funds from the Foundation are supporting studies of such critical problems as the effectiveness of the shorter workweek as a solution to the unemployment caused by automation, the retraining of adult workers displaced by automation, and the effects of automation in the Common Market countries. The Foundation seems to be working; but when we first proposed it, neither the unions nor anybody else thought it was a very good idea. It was too much out of phase with traditional approaches. Now other companies have foundations.

Labor unions, of course, have a big responsibility here, too. Their obligation and practical stake are no less than those of management in easing the impact of automation on workers and seeking ways to provide a living for those whose jobs are lost to machines. Many labor unions have not been particularly inclined to shoulder their share of the responsibility in working out long-run solutions to the problems of technological displacement. What moves many unions have made have been with the narrow objective of making short-run agreements that protect current members but toss future workers out on their own.

It is the moral obligation of both labor and management to devote a greater share of their time, energy, and financial resources to the solution of purely human problems. They must make a substantial contribution to the advancement of the social sciences—the study of man himself—so the techniques of the physical sciences, which have raced so far ahead, can be devoted to the solving of human problems. For scientific progress without human progress is no progress at all but an invitation to disaster.

There is absolutely no doubt that automation will change the world. But its ultimate effect on the well-being of people in all social and economic groups—whether it will be for better or worse—has not yet been determined. That decision, happily, is still ours to make.

AUTOMATION AND UNEMPLOYMENT:
WHAT CAN BE DONE •

RUSSELL C. McCARTHY

SINCE THE BEGINNING OF THE INDUSTRIAL revolution in the United States, technological progress has always meant more jobs as well as increased productivity. In fact, the industrial growth and expansion that have taken place in this country during the past century have been primarily the result of the technological progress that has been achieved. It is true that from time to time there was temporary displacement of people, but in the economy as a whole the result was greatly increased overall employment.

It is only in recent years—perhaps the past five or six—that we have become really alarmed about the impact of technology on our work force. We have seen more technological change in the past decade than we had in the previous 30 years, both in manufacturing and office operations. During the first several years of this accelerated technological period, most observers seemed to feel that we were experiencing a natural postwar development—a sort of pent-up demand that would run its course and would soon level off into a more "normal" situation. We know now that this did not happen. The period of rapid change has shown no signs of abating, and there is a considerable amount of evidence to support the contention that the accelerated pace of automation and technological

---

RUSSELL C. McCARTHY is Manager, Industrial Management Council of Rochester, Rochester, New York.

advancement has accounted for the displacement of an abnormally large number of employees, many of whom have been unable to find other employment.

The four major types of automation that have been growing rapidly in the past few years are as follows:

1. *Computers,* which involve automatic handling of information by the use of electronic systems.
2. *Detroit automation,* which is the integration of machines by means of automatic transfer devices.
3. *Process-control systems,* which are computer and integrated control systems for the operation of process plants, as in the oil, chemical, and atomic industries.
4. *Numerical control,* which is the use of tape and other automatic control devices to direct the operation of machines and machine systems.

There are a number of reasons for the acceleration in the pace of such automation. One is high annual wage increases, which have created abnormally high labor and materials costs. There has not been a year in the postwar period when we haven't had wage increases averaging about 5 per cent. Corporate profits have increased about 8.5 per cent since 1950, compared with an increase of 90 per cent in labor costs. Faced with such rapidly growing costs, management has been turning to increased mechanization and automation in order to stay in business.

The second reason for the increased pace of automation is simply increased competition, both foreign and domestic. After the immediate postwar period, when there was a terrific demand for everything, competition grew increasingly keener and more and more companies found that they had to cut costs in order to remain competitive.

A third reason is to be found in the threat of obsolescence. Companies that have modernized, built new plants, added new equipment, and introduced cost reduction programs have continued to be competitive; those that did not have fallen behind and are losing out. It has been estimated that industry spent $40 billion on new plants and equipment in 1963. Of this amount, only 25 per cent was for expansion, and the rest was invested in the mechanization and modernization of existing plants and equipment owned by companies.

Finally, $12 billion has been spent annually for the past ten years on research and development, and this tremendous expenditure of effort and money has inevitably resulted in an acceleration of change.

THE IMPACT OF AUTOMATION

Although it is extremely difficult to determine the amount of unemployment that has been caused by automation, the U.S. Labor Department estimates that 1.5 million of the 4 million persons currently unemployed have been replaced by machines. The very fact that over the past 10 or 12 years the nation's manufacturing work force has remained fairly constant while industrial production has increased 30 to 40 per cent is evidence of the magnitude of the effect that automation has had on manufacturing employment.

Some of the nation's major industries provide more specific evidence of this effect. The coal industry, for example, is producing 45 million more tons of coal a year with 200,000 fewer miners than were employed ten years ago. Production in the electrical machinery industry is 25 per cent higher than it was ten years ago, and 80,000 fewer workers are employed. The steel industry is producing 20 per cent more steel with 80,000 fewer workers. The automobile industry has the capacity to produce ten million new cars with 200,000 fewer workers than in 1953. Nor is this effect limited to manufacturing industries: Automatic elevators, for example, have displaced 40,000 operators in New York City alone; and the telephone industry, which has had a 25 per cent increase in business in the past seven years, employs 30,000 fewer people.

Such figures as these convincingly illustrate the impact that automation has had on employment in some of the key areas of the economy. This impact has been felt most severely in cities or areas in which a particular industry has dominated employment, such as the auto industry in Detroit, steel in Pittsburgh, textiles in New England, and coal mining in Pennsylvania and West Virginia. The more highly diversified industrial areas seem to have fared much better during this period of accelerated automation.

Moreover, certain occupations have borne the brunt of the unemployment; in others, employment has been unchanged or has even increased. A look at what has happened to the structure of the manufacturing work force over the past ten years is most revealing and is indicative of the trend that will continue throughout the 1960's. During the past ten years, while total manufacturing employment remained fairly constant at approximately 16 million, the number of production workers declined by 1.5 million while the number of technical, supervisory, and clerical employees increased by the same amount. This will be a continuing trend for the next decade. A recent study of occupational trends by the U.S. Department of Labor indicates that employment of professional and technical manpower will increase by 40 per cent between 1960 and 1970, leading all other occupations, while employment of managerial personnel and skilled employees will show a 25 per cent increase.

There will be increasing opportunities for professional, technical, and skilled personnel to design, install, program, operate, and maintain new machines and equipment. Computers alone in years ahead will require thousands of specialists in programing. There can be no doubt that the demand for high skills will continue to accelerate while the demand for unskilled labor will continue to diminish.

ATTEMPTS TO DEAL WITH THE PROBLEM

The growth of automation has provoked a number of responses from both management and labor. Most of the serious labor-management controversies of the past few years have occurred when companies installed automated equipment, closed obsolete plants, and replaced these plants with new and modern ones, often in a new and more advantageous location.

For its part, labor has become increasingly concerned with the so-called noneconomic issues involving job security rather than those of higher wages and fringe benefits. Unions now feel they have a stake in maintaining the status quo—at almost any cost. They have been trying to control or even prevent change. Thus unions have resisted changing work rules and featherbedding provisions such as those which have caused so much trouble in the railroad industry. They have struggled to retain seniority rules which have denied to management flexibility in the use of the work force.

Management, on the other hand, has been able to overcome these obstacles and decrease employment. It has sometimes had first to contend with union demands for some measure of control over the rate at which automated equipment is introduced and employees terminated or over the reclassification of jobs and of rates of pay for new jobs. But in the end jobs have been lost although the blow has been softened through attrition, severance pay, supplementary unemployment benefits, or provisions for early retirement.

Neither labor's demand to retain obsolete jobs nor management's softening the blow of losing jobs are ideal solutions to the problem of unemployment caused by automation. They are essentially stop-gap methods. In some cases, such as between the Western Council of Cannery and Food

Processing and a Teamsters union and between the Pacific Maritime Association and the Longshoremen, labor and management have reached agreement on preserving the jobs of present employees through the establishment and use of automation funds.

Another short-range solution is to be found in the extended vacation programs of such companies as American Can Company, Aluminum Company of America, Timken Roller Bearing Company, and the major steel companies. These programs are essentially in the category of those share-the-work measures which also include proposals for the reduction of overtime and the shortening of the work week.

More long range in nature as solutions to the automation problem are the proposals for greater education and training of future employees and for retraining present workers displaced by automation.

Accelerated technology has created demands for skilled and technical manpower far in excess of the supply the nation's educational institutions have been able to produce. Many of our industries, not having the necessary manpower to operate and service their modern equipment, have been faced with major retraining programs of their own. Moreover, technological advances have been so rapid that engineering graduates, for example, soon become "obsolete" unless they continue their education after graduation and while employed.

Dr. Thomas Stelson, the head of the civil engineering department at Carnegie Tech, says this: "With modern technology advancing so rapidly, the indications are that the experienced man may have to devote about a third of his time to self-education. The decline in value, or obsolescence, of engineering personnel may likely become an increasingly serious problem in modern technology unless professional societies, employers, and educational institutions recognize its importance and develop suitable remedies." He also says that unless a graduate of ten years ago spends 10 per cent of his time developing his knowledge beyond the level of his collegiate training, he cannot compete in value with a recent college graduate.

In order to prevent engineering obsolescence, IBM has arranged to have Syracuse University conduct in-plant training and retraining programs, not only for the engineers who have been with the company for some time, but for new engineers who come to IBM and who want to take courses that are of benefit to IBM as well as to themselves.

The rapid rate of skill obsolescence as the result of the continuing rapid rate of technological changes points up the expanded need for such retraining programs, both in plants and in our educational institutions. Educational institutions and professional societies must provide opportunities for those who were educated and trained in an earlier period to obtain refresher training and keep up with modern technology. This is the kind of educational effort that will become increasingly important as time goes on.

In addition, educational institutions themselves will have to face up to some of the demands of an increasingly automated economy. With the continuing rapid pace of technological change, there is danger in stressing highly specialized training. The more specialized the training, the greater is the likelihood of the early obsolescence. Automation emphasizes the desirability of providing sound basic education and training that can contribute to the future flexibility of members of the labor force by enabling them to shift more readily to new types of work. Greater emphasis should be placed on sound grounding in mathematics. Guidance and counseling services need to be strengthened—not only in high school, but a grade or two below the high school level. Industry and education must work together in order to accomplish the most effective results in the development and utilization of our manpower resources.

Much discussion and some experimentation have taken place in attempts to retrain persons who have been displaced by machines or who have been terminated because of plants closing or moving. The Federal Government has taken steps in this direction with the Manpower Training and Development Program. Although some good has resulted from these efforts, the number of people who have really benefited from such training has been very small in proportion to the number that have been displaced or terminated. Success depends on the ability of employees to absorb further training. Today's electricians will have to learn electronics; pipefitters will have to learn hydraulics; skilled workers who formerly measured with calipers and now use micrometers will soon have to work with tolerances measured in light waves. Most skilled craftsmen, with special instruction, can keep pace with technological advances in their own field.

The reason for the limited success in retraining programs generally is the fact that the great majority of persons displaced by technology are unskilled and have had very little basic education. Many of them lack capacity or aptitude to absorb any type of training.

In its last collective bargaining agreement, Armour & Company agreed to set aside half a million dollars and to select a committee headed by Clark Kerr, the chancellor of the University of California, to handle this fund, which was to be used largely for retraining unemployed or displaced persons in Armour. One of the first experiments resulted when the company closed its plant in Oklahoma City, idling 433 people. Of these, 170 applied for retraining programs. The committee set up a series of tests, and of the 170 tested, only 58 qualified for any kind of a retraining program. They were trained in typing, upholstering, blueprint reading, meatcutting, welding, real-estate selling, electronics, auto mechanics, and so on. However, only a few of the trainees found jobs after retraining.

Much more successful are the many in-plant retraining programs being conducted by the nation's major industries. Ford last year retrained 3,000 employees to handle more advanced hydraulic equipment. General Motors, in addition to its apprentice programs, retrains about 7,500 employees per year. IBM retrains 100,000 workers each year to operate the computers and other equipment it sells and leases. And many industries that have installed modern equipment have retrained their own employees for new types of occupations.

The retraining problem is not so difficult where the individual has had an allied experience or has the basic education and aptitude. The real problem lies with the large mass of unskilled workers who have had little or no education and who have neither the ability nor the aptitude to absorb the required training. Nationally, this number is quite significant, and it accounts for a high percentage of the continuing hard-core unemployed.

Mechanization and automation will and must continue; they are the means by which industry maintains its efficiency and its competitiveness. But technological progress need not be a serious barrier to greater employment. Mechanization over many years has been responsible for increased employment opportunities. Given the right climate, investment in modern machinery can provide more and better jobs. Labor may be expected to press its case for greater security for the worker, and management should be fully conscious of its obligation to maintain job security. There are signs that the type of statesmanship required to study and to find a solution to these current problems, both social and economic, may be emerging. Time, however, is wasting, and sound and unselfish thinking on the part of government, labor, and management is urgently needed if we are to get back on the right track.

EXTENDED VACATION PROGRAMS •

I. The Plan at Alcoa

E. D. MAIRS

FOLLOWING THE 1962 STEEL settlement, Alcoa and the majority of the other major aluminum producers agreed to a supplemental vacation plan (SVP) to be financed by a company contribution of three cents per hour. This provided for an extra week of vacation for approximately one-half of the work force. In addition, the financing of our supplementary unemployment benefits (SUB) plans was increased from five cents per hour to nine and one-half cents per hour, with a provision providing for "spillover" up to four and one-half cents from this fund of monies not needed for SUB purposes. The spill-over was to be added to the three cents for SVP to provide additional vacations over and above those financed by the three cents per hour. While some of our financing arrangements and other details were different from those negotiated in the basic steel industry, the benefits were the same except that we permitted up to one week of supplemental vacation per year as compared to the one week every other year permitted in steel.

The experience with SUB in the aluminum industry was better than in most steel companies; and, as a matter of fact, one of the smaller aluminum

---

E. D. MAIRS is Vice President—Personnel and Industrial Relations, Aluminum Company of America, Pittsburgh, Pennsylvania.

companies was spilling over the full four and a half cents by the end of 1962, therefore adding this amount to the SVP accrued for additional vacations in 1963. Alcoa began to spill over in 1963. If our experience had continued in that pattern, we would have been spilling over the full four and a half for the 1964 financing of SVP vacations had this plan and the SUB remained unchanged.

THE 1963 NEGOTIATIONS

Although we cannot, of course, speak for the steel industry, it is our understanding that it came to the conclusion early in the 1963 negotiations that extended vacations were earnestly desired by the Steelworkers Union and that if it wished a reasonably inexpensive settlement, this was the route it would have to go. Conversely, if it resisted this concept, the union would undoubtedly put a much higher price on another type of settlement. Certainly, it is true that this was quite apparent to us as we began our negotiations in aluminum. I have no doubt that the complex economic philosophies involved were thoroughly explored in the long and earnest steel negotiations.

The steel settlement provided that the 13 weeks of extended vacation would apply to 50 per cent of the work force and would be accompanied by a continuation of the extra week or weeks of vacation under the SVP for the so-called junior group of the work force. The program was to be financed at a rate of nine and a half cents per hour plus three cents from the old SVP, and it is our understanding that this financing method was ultimately adopted to insure the same costs to all of the companies participating in these negotiations.

When we opened our negotiations with the Steelworkers, this was the program (the financed plan) which was proposed to us, and certain objectionable points early became apparent. First of all, for several reasons we did not like the idea of splitting the work force into senior and junior groups. If this splitting were done on a companywide basis, certain of our older plants would have all of their employees covered by extended vacations, while some of the newer plants would have none eligible in the beginning of the program. On the other hand, if we went the plant-by-plant route and split the work force into senior and junior groups by plants, at some of our newer plants employees with five years or less of service would be eligible for extended vacations, while employees with 20 years or more at some of the older plants would not be eligible.

In the second place, particularly in light of the SUB experience in aluminum with the spill-over then occurring, it appeared that nine and a half cents plus three cents was more money than was needed to provide 13 weeks of extended vacation to 50 per cent of the work force, whether taken companywide or on a plant-by-plant basis. This, of course, was obvious to the union negotiators, and they therefore began to talk in terms of providing extended vacations of 13 weeks for more than 50 per cent of the work force. We felt that if we adopted the financed plan, we should not be expected to provide extended vacations of 13 weeks for more than 50 per cent of the work force, as this would create a greater impact, from the standpoint of scheduling and disruption, in aluminum than had been created in steel.

Frankly, while we were still considering the financed-plan approach, we were thinking in terms of limiting the finances for extended vacations so as to provide such vacations for not more than 50 per cent of the work force, recognizing that the union would then claim that our package was less than the one it had negotiated in steel and that we no doubt would have had to find some way to spend more money in other areas to come up to the steel package. We never got into this area in our negotiations with the union, however, because the picture changed rather dramatically.

It was at this point that the union proposed that we approach the matter of extended vacations from a "benefit" standpoint. As we pursued this approach, it took on some appeal to us, even though it contained some element of a gamble. But if our SUB experience was to continue as it had for the past few years, it looked like a good gamble. We then began to discuss seriously an extended vacation plan which would be a modification of and, in some respects, quite different from any previously negotiated by the Steelworkers.

Tied in with the negotiations of the extended vacation plan and very important to it was the full elimination of the SVP negotiated in 1962 and financed at a firm three cents per hour. Our SUB plan was changed to eliminate spill-over completely. Money not needed to finance basic SUB benefits is, therefore, not spent on any other employee benefit; so when we reach maximum financing in the SUB plan, our only obligation is to pay benefits. We do not have to continue pumping company money into a fund either for SUB or additional vacations. This was most important in our considerations of the extended vacation plan, because this eliminated certain monetary commitments made by the company in the 1962 negotiations. If we had not had the opportunity of recouping this money (three cents from SVP plus up to four and a half cents from SUB), the union's benefit approach on extended vacations would have had no appeal whatsoever.

Another item which had some appeal was that instead of having to take the entire impact of 13 weeks among a limited portion of the work force—for example, 50 per cent—our approach spreads the impact through 10-week vacations (with 13 weeks' pay) over the entire work force, and our method and rate of vesting gives us a large base from which to schedule people. We hope this will prove beneficial. The plan that evolved, therefore, has no cents per hour attached to it but is approached entirely from a benefits standpoint.

THE EXTENDED VACATION PLAN

The plan provides for the granting to each employee who becomes vested of ten consecutive weeks of time off with thirteen weeks of vacation pay once in each five-year period, beginning January 1, 1964. The extended vacation in any calendar year includes the regular vacation for that year. Essentially, all employees who qualify for a regular vacation—that is, have one or more years of service—will at some time during the five-year period qualify for one extended vacation.

The vesting of extended vacations is as follows:

1. Fifty per cent of all those employees at each plant, in order of seniority, who are eligible on December 31, 1963, for a regular vacation in 1964 shall become entitled to (vested) an extended vacation on January 1, 1964.

2. Fifty per cent of all those employees at each plant, in order of seniority, who are eligible on December 31, 1964, for a regular vacation in 1965, exclusive of those who vested in 1964, shall become entitled to (vested) an extended vacation on January 1, 1965.

3. All employees who are eligible on December 31, 1965, for a regular vacation in 1966, exclusive of those who vested in 1964 or 1965, shall become entitled to (vested) an extended vacation on January 1, 1966. This means essentially that 50 per cent of the work force at each plant vests for an extended vacation on January 1, 1964, the effective date of the plan; another 25 per cent one year later; and the remainder at the beginning of the third year. This provides a

broader base or group of people for scheduling during the early years of the plan than is provided in other extended vacation plans.

4. The plan also provides for the vesting of extended vacations for those employees who did not vest as per the above because they were not eligible for a regular vacation on the vesting date but later become eligible for a regular vacation.

5. In addition, an employee who retires on pension, except a deferred vested pension, on or after December 31, 1963, and who has not previously vested, becomes vested upon such retirement.

The weekly amount of 13 weeks of extended vacation pay is calculated on the same basis as the regular vacation pay.

As regards partial benefits, those retiring after having vested for an extended vacation receive, in addition, a partial benefit equal to one week of vacation pay for each six months between the vesting date and the date they become eligible for normal retirement or otherwise retire, whichever date is earlier. On the other hand, those who are terminated by reason of quit or discharge before vesting for the extended vacation receive one week of vacation pay for each six months of seniority accumulated after January 1, 1964, or when eligible for a regular vacation, whichever is later. Finally, those who go on layoff or sick leave after July 26, 1964, (effective date of agreement) and remain on such layoff or sick leave for more than two years, or who die after July 26, 1963, after having accumulated five years of seniority and before becoming vested, shall receive (or their proper legal representative shall receive) the greater of one week of vacation pay for each six months after January 1, 1964, or six weeks of vacation pay.

SCHEDULING PROVISIONS OF THE PLAN

At Alcoa, the period for regular vacations as well as extended vacations is the entire calendar year, January 1 to December 31. This helps to level out the scheduling so that we are able, to some extent, to avoid the peaks and valleys. More and more in recent years we have followed the practice of scheduling all vacations over the 12-month period.

The 1963 agreement provides for negotiations between the local union and local management on vacation scheduling practices with the object of arriving at mutually satisfactory scheduling arrangements for the five-year period. These local negotiations were to be concluded by September 15,

1963. In these negotiations, the parties were to "endeavor to accommodate the wishes of the employees as to desired vacation periods in an equitable manner, giving consideration to operating requirements and the desire of employees to take their extended vacations and their regular vacations at times most appropriate to their individual situations."

It was provided that if the local parties could not agree, then a master contract provision would apply: "The employee shall take his vacation as scheduled by the management . . . The employee's wishes as to the time his vacation is to be scheduled will be given consideration, but such scheduling will necessarily be governed by the operating requirements of the plant." In the majority of cases, however, the local unions and the local managements were able to agree on the scheduling procedures in the time provided.

It was agreed that extended vacations are to consist of ten consecutive weeks. In addition, the company, to the extent practicable, may schedule employees for extended vacations in approximately equal numbers each year. The company may schedule at an accelerated rate so as not to be jammed up at the end of the five-year period with a number of eligible people still to be scheduled. The company, to protect itself against undue dilution of experienced employees in a classification, department, or subdivision, may limit scheduling of such employees to not more than 20 per cent to start extended vacations in any one year. In cases of substantial increase in employment at any plant, the time for scheduling extended vacations may be extended past December 31, 1968, to insure orderly operation of the plant. Also, those becoming entitled in 1968 may be scheduled in 1969.

Employees scheduled for extended vacation are to be notified at least 90 days in advance, and no change can be made without 60 days' notice unless the employee agrees. Employees on layoff or sick leave, after exhaustion of sickness and accident benefits, may elect to take extended vacation, if entitled, with the approval and under conditions set forth by local plant management. An employee 63 years of age or older at the time that his extended vacation is scheduled (provided it is scheduled within two years of his vesting date) may at his option (1) take the vacation as scheduled, (2) elect to take it during the ten weeks prior to his retirement, or (3) take a lump sum payment at retirement.

No particular reference has been made to our extended vacation plan with the Aluminum Workers' International Union, where the only significant difference is that three weeks' pay of the extended vacation pay of

13 weeks goes into individual trust accounts which the employee receives upon retirement or other termination of employment. He receives 10 weeks' pay for his extended vacation as such.

We believe our administrative procedures have been simplified to the maximum by the type of plan we have. Since there is no financing involved to determine when people become eligible to vest, the determination is a straightforward one which can be made at the local plant level and does not require elaborate home office procedures. The plants are able each year to determine in advance those eligible both for extended vacations and for regular vacations and to relate these eligibilities to planned manning requirements. In other words, administration is done chiefly at the local plant level and is principally a matter of scheduling.

While we have been involved in the problem of determining those who are eligible or those who will vest for extended vacations as of January 1, 1964, and in all the problems relating to scheduling, we have not as yet encountered any particular "special problems." As we get more experience under our belt, these problems may, of course, develop.

APPLICATION TO SALARIED PEOPLE

Alcoa has instituted a program of comparable benefits for all salaried personnel with the exception of principal officers of the company. The plan became effective January 1, 1964, for a five-year period.

Briefly, the program provides alternate choices to our salaried people. First, we amended our savings plan for salaried employees to provide that the individual employee may elect to have added to his savings plan account an additional company contribution of 1.6 weeks of pay each year during the five-year period. If he does not elect to have this additional contribution made into the savings plan account, he may take advantage of a plan of additional vacation benefits which also provides him with a choice. He may elect to receive 1.6 weeks of additional salary each year during the five-year period at the time when he takes his regular vacation, or he may elect to take additional time—up to three weeks— over the five-year period. The latter provision enables him to take from one to three weeks—either a separate week at a time or as much as three weeks at one time—during the five-year period in addition to his regular vacation. For each week of additional time off, he receives .6 week's pay in addition to his regular pay. For weeks not taken as time off under the latter option, he receives 1.6 weeks of extra salary.

Since our extended vacation plan is tied in with the elimination of the SVP of three cents per hour and the SUB spill-over, which could have been as high as four and a half cents, we cannot, in honesty, accurately put a cost on our extended vacation plan. Neither we nor the unions have published a cost figure for the plan. Only experience will indicate what the cost will be.

It is also too early to give an accurate appraisal of the impact of the extended vacation program. We need more experience with its actual operation. Obviously, there will be some impact on work scheduling, training of replacements, and upgrading of personnel; there will be disruption of work arrangements, and the upsetting of crews. However, it is much too early to speculate on the extent of the impact.

Employee reaction to the program was surprising. Some of us thought this was an "organization" program, sponsored by the union with very little enthusiasm on the part of the employees, but employee acceptance has generally been good. Either the union did an excellent job of selling the program and its objectives, or some of us misjudged employee reaction.

Again, it is too early to predict with any accuracy the effect of the extended vacation program on our employment situation, on that of the aluminum industry, or, certainly on that of industry in general. The outcome is wrapped up in how well the levels of production fare, how universal such vacations become, and how fully they are paid for by changes in productivity.

II. The Experience of American Can Company

ORDEN OECHSLI

CANCO, A DIVISION OF THE AMERICAN Can Company, and Continental Can Company were pretty much the ground breakers for extended leaves in the United States. Canco negotiated, in the fall of 1962, a five-year extended leave plan which was built into a two-year, nonreopenable labor agreement between the majority of plants in the Canco division of American Can and the United Steelworkers of America. Shortly afterward, we negotiated the same plan with the machinists' union. Agreements with these two unions are our two largest national contracts. Between them they represent about 80 per cent of the hourly rated employees in the Canco division.

At the same time that the plan for the hourly rated employees covered by these two primary union groups went into effect, we announced a plan for all nonorganized, hourly rated employees. This plan is much the same as the one for all of our hourly rated people, unorganized and organized, except for a few specialized area craft people such as lithographers and teamsters.

An employee is eligible to take a vacation under this plan when he has 15 years or more of accredited service with the company. He is then entitled to a 13-week vacation with pay once each five years. Within the year in which he takes the extended vacation with pay, the 13 weeks include the regular annual vacation that he is entitled to under the vacation plan. It is not a pyramiding situation. It's 13 weeks of vacation for that particular year.

The considerable backlog of our people who've had 15 years or more of accredited service are now eligible to take a 13-week extended leave

---

ORDEN OECHSLI is Manager of Communications, Industrial Relations Department, Canco Division, American Can Company, New York, New York.

some time during the five calendar years. For these people the process repeats every five years during their continued work with the company up until their retirement. As new people reach the initial 15 years of service, the process begins and continues for them.

When an employee earns his first extended leave by reason of his coverage under the plan and 15 years of service, it becomes a vested benefit for him. He gets the time off all in one piece. Neither he nor the company is in a position to defer it, cash it out, pass it up, trade it off, or do anything else with it. It's a chunk of time that he gets. If he quits or if he's fired after he's earned an extended leave and before he can take this time off, he cashes it because he doesn't have a chance to take it as time.

The retiring employee gets an additional benefit in the plan. When he retires, he picks up in many cases, in addition to whatever vested leave benefit he may have accumulated, some money which is proportionate to the amount of time that he's worked during his current five-year cycle. In other words, he hasn't finished the five-year cycle, and rather than take another 13 weeks if he retires in the midst of such a cycle, he cashes it out. Under our pension plan hourly rated people are not required to retire at age 65, 67, 68, or at any other time. They have the option to continue working. But an employee who continues working past 65 for purposes of his extended leave plan is not going to build up any additional credit in time or money for this time. As a matter of fact it starts running backward. If he works as much as two or two and a half years after he's 65, the extra partial benefit washes out entirely. So the employee is encouraged to cast off his accounts and take a little extra money out of this package by retiring soon after he's 65.

One of the most important features of the extended leave plan is the vested right that management retains to determine who takes extended leave and when he takes it. In other words, we fit our extended leave schedules into the operating requirements of our business, and our business requires us to operate in all respects as economically, efficiently, and profitably as possible.

The manager of a plant or office whose people are covered by this plan has to look and plan ahead. It's a complicated task, but to the best of his ability he must do it. Then he schedules the actual vacation period so that he can maintain efficient operations, and he does this with respect both to the numbers of people who can be away from his operations during a particular three-month period and to the skills and experience that he has to have in his shop at a given moment in order to operate effectively.

We do everything that we reasonably can to let employees take three-month extended leaves as near as possible to the time they would like to take them. We do this partly because it's written into the contract and we are expected to pay reasonable attention to employee preferences within the framework of efficient operations and partly because even if this was not written into the contract it would be shortsighted on our part if we didn't do everything that we reasonably can to balance out the desires of employees with the requirements of the business.

We have pretty much the same plan for salaried employees. On the day we first announced that the hourly plan would become effective, every salaried employee in the Canco division from the top executive on down had a letter in his hands telling him that he was going to receive the same kind of an extended benefit that had just been announced as having been negotiated with the hourly rated people.

Ninety per cent of our nonsupervisory salaried employees are not represented by any union. We do have six or seven small clerical collective bargaining groups, mostly in the Steelworkers, and they fall under the regular negotiated Steelworker extended leave plan.

Soon after the initial announcement we added an extra benefit for unorganized salaried employees. It's a personal option. The salaried employee can take his 13-week extended vacation every five years if he wants to. If he doesn't want to, he has the option of deferring, of laying aside unused, this vested time as it accumulates. Then when he retires he can trade in each of the extended leave periods he has accumulated and deferred for an extra cash retirement benefit. It figures out to a bit better than a couple of months regular pay for each of the periods that he has chosen to defer. He obtains this money in monthly installments during his first two years of retirement.

THE BACKGROUND OF EXTENDED LEAVES

In approaching our negotiations in 1962, we took into account the economics of our own business, and we looked very carefully at the labor-costs arithmetic of our own business. Why did we decide on extended leaves?

First, we looked ahead to what seemed to be a swelling of interest on the part of unions, workers generally, and politicians in a number of schemes that have the theoretical effect of spreading available work among more people and maintaining pay levels while decreasing the amount of time worked. We saw that sooner or later we were going to be approached with what looked to us to be less practical, more complicated, more distasteful, and more expensive propositions than this particular plan, which at that time was an innovation in this country. Second, we knew that employees—and I mean people on the job, not just the committee over the bargaining table—would rate this type of extended vacation plan as a practical and valuable benefit attaching to their jobs. Last but by no means least, we knew this was a plan that we could devise for ourselves; we would have some idea of how it would work and affect the business; it would be a plan based on the conditions of our business, not somebody else's, and on what we thought to be sound considerations of management interests as well as employee interests. We thought this was a practical way and a practical time to approach the situation, and we hoped that it would be a marketable bargaining-table proposition. We had the advantage of having the time between the first of October 1962 and the first of January 1963 to look at this package and see how to make it work most effectively.

Advance planning was important for two reasons. First, our plan provides a very specific and very fixed amount of benefit to employees who meet the eligibility conditions. In other words, it's a variable cost plan. It promises a degree of benefit, and its cost can fluctuate widely depending on how well we are capable of administering the plan in relation to the condition of our business from day to day and year to year.

Second, most of our plants are relatively small. They have 500, 400, or 300 people in most locations. Many of these plants have a considerable degree of seasonality, peaks and valleys dictated by crop seasons. And certainly in our business, every local man has to be totally sensitive to the variations of customer schedules, customer problems, and the aggressive efforts of competitors who are out to take business away from us.

We took detailed local manpower inventories plant by plant. We arranged them by skill, experience, training, development potential, seniority, and all the other facts we could line up. We projected this manpower inventory against each plant's total business plan for five years ahead and for each of those years. In other words, we pulled into our extended vacation planning everything we could lay out—every year with respect to capital investment, market research, market approaches, new technology, operating innovations, the growing competition, and all the rest.

We took all the factors that are used to plan other aspects of our business and tried to project our extended vacation plan against that kind of a back drop. This made it possible for us to make an estimate, at least, of the number of people, skills, and experience we thought we'd need for each of the five years ahead. Again this was plant by plant, season by season, and skill by skill. We couldn't wait until people started signing up for their vacations to find out what their choices and preferences would be, and so we had to do some forecasting.

Finally we checked our then current manpower inventories against this entire projected drainoff of people and skills by the new plan, balanced this out with the five years ahead, and anticipated total manpower and skill requirements. In this way we were able to make a reasonable projection of how many additional people, how much additional training, and how many skills we were going to have to invest in.

HOW THE PLAN HAS WORKED

About 15,000 people from the Steelworkers' group are potentially eligible for extended leaves. About 6,000 of them were eligible to take a 13-week extended leave at some three-month period during the first five years. Of those already scheduled nearly half, or about 47 per cent, got their first choices. Approximately 10 per cent got their second choices, and another 10 per cent got their third choices. This means that about two-thirds of those already scheduled got their first, second, or third choices. We think these figures illustrate the kind of planning that can be done on this.

The option that our salaried employees have takes practically all the pressure off the problem of scheduling them. We didn't know beforehand how this would work out, but we find in practice that most of our salaried people choose the deferment option. We have about 3,000 salaried employees in the Canco division who are eligible for an extended vacation during the five-year cycle. Of the exempt group in that 3,000, about three out of four have chosen deferment. Even in the nonexempt group, about two out of three have chosen deferment. We don't know how to read that for the long-range future, but that's the way the experience is running.

There's a great deal more we *don't* know about the operation of this plan than we *do* know. One of the things we don't know is what our people are going to do with their three-month sabbatical vacations. The reason we don't know is that we haven't asked, and we haven't asked because we don't think at this point that it's any of our business. This does not mean that we are unaware of the long-range social considerations of this type of situation but only that we're not deep enough into it yet to have any firm ideas about it.

Also, since ours is a fixed-benefit cost program and since only experience and effectiveness of operation will tell what our costs are going to be, we don't know precisely what the program is costing us or is going to cost us. We do know certainly that the effectiveness of our administration is going to have the biggest single thing to do with whether the cost is in line with reasonable efficient operations or whether it will be excessive. We know it would be very easy to let costs get out of line.

For these same reasons we don't know how many additional jobs the plan has created or will create. We don't know the extent to which these jobs will be filled by new people coming in, and we don't know the extent to which they will be filled by people who might otherwise be on layoff.

III. The Agreement at Timken Roller Bearing

DALLAS G. RAYL

A N EXTENDED VACATION BENEFIT agreement was negotiated between The Timken Roller Bearing Company and the United Steelworkers of America in September 1963 and became effective January 1, 1964. The benefits provided by this agreement consist of five weeks of extended vacation time off with seven weeks of vacation pay to eligible employees once in each five-year period. In order to be eligible for extended vacation, an employee must have five years of continuous service on or prior to any calculation date during the life of the agreement. The vacation benefit provided under this agreement is in addition to all other vacation benefits to which an employee may be entitled.

The amount of extended vacation pay which an employee receives under this plan is equal to 280 hours at the employee's average hourly rate during the first two of the last four pay periods in which the employee worked prior to the date on which he starts his extended vacation. In order to receive his extended vacation pay, an employee must take his extended vacation time off. He is also required to take any regular vacation allowance to which he is entitled in the vacation year in which he takes his extended vacation. Employees receive their extended vacation pay in a lump sum payment on the last day worked before starting their extended vacation.

The first calculation date under the plan was January 31, 1964, and calculation dates occur monthly thereafter. Approximately one-sixtieth of the employees covered by this agreement must become entitled to extended vacations on each calculation date. Employees are scheduled for extended vacations in about equal number each month and, insofar as possible,

DALLAS G. RAYL is Director of Labor Relations, The Timken Roller Bearing Company, Canton, Ohio.

in the order of their continuous service unless this causes too many experienced employees in any seniority unit to be on extended vacations during any given year. In this case, the company may at its discretion schedule these vacations over the entire five-year period covered by the agreement. The final right to schedule extended vacations is reserved exclusively to the company to enable it to provide for efficient operation, subject to the following qualifications:

1. An employee scheduled for an extended vacation must be notified at least 60 days before the start of such vacation.
2. A scheduled extended vacation shall not be changed without at least a 25-day notice to the employee unless he consents to shorter notice.

An employee who is 60 years of age or older at the time he becomes entitled to an extended vacation may defer such vacation until immediately before retirement, or he may elect to receive extended vacation pay immediately following his retirement without taking an extended vacation.

Partial benefits are provided for employees who retire or die before becoming entitled to extended vacations. The amount of this partial benefit is equal to 40 hours of pay for each eight months (or major fraction thereof) in which such employee retains continuous service during the term of this agreement.

A general coordinator has been appointed to supervise the overall administration of extended vacations. Numerous reports are prepared under the direction of the general coordinator for the purpose of determining which employees have become entitled to extended vacations and to assist plant vacation coordinators and operating supervisors in carrying out their responsibilities under the extended vacation plan.

In order to facilitate the scheduling of all types of vacations (regular, supplemental, and extended) to which employees are now entitled, plant vacation coordinators have been appointed for each company plant. These men function as a liaison between the general coordinator of vacations and the individual operating supervisors. The general responsibilities of the plant vacation coordinator are to make sure that all vacations are scheduled and taken in a manner which fulfills company contractual obligations and minimizes disruptive effects on company operations.

The general coordinator maintains a master list of all employees in continuous-service order. As employees become entitled to extended vacations, notification of such entitlement is provided to the plant vacation coordinator by the general coordinator. The plant vacation coordinator is also provided with a master list of employees in his plant and various other reports which will assist him and operating supervisors in the administration of employees' vacations. These reports include such information as the amount of regular and supplemental vacation due to each employee in the given plant, the amount of completed vacation for each employee (regular, supplemental, and extended), and the number of extended vacations which must be scheduled each month in order that scheduling requirements may be fulfilled.

The plant vacation coordinator notifies individual operating supervisors when employees in their departments have become entitled to extended vacations. The operating supervisors advise the plant vacation coordinator which of these employees may be scheduled for immediate vacations, which employees' vacations must be postponed, and, for employees over age 60 at the time of their entitlement, which option has been elected. Using this information, the plant vacation coordinator determines how many additional employees must receive accelerated entitlements in order for his plant to meet its monthly vacation schedule quota. The plant vacation coordinator and operating departmental supervisors then must collaborate to determine where accelerated entitlements may best be made in order to minimize detrimental effects on production.

In general, employees become entitled to extended vacations in the order of their continuous service with the company. On the master list of all employees having five or more years of continuous service, employees are listed in descending order of continuous service. At the end of each month during the five-year term of the extended vacation benefit agreement, the names of all new employees who have completed five years of continuous service during that month are added to the list.

On each calculation date—that is, the last day of each month—a certain number of employees on this list automatically become entitled to extended vacations. Under a formula specified in the contract, the exact number who become entitled is determined by dividing the number of employees who are eligible for and have not yet become entitled to extended vacations by the number of calculation dates remaining under the agreement. The quotient always equals approximately one-sixtieth of the company's work force, or 150 employees.

For example, on the first calculation date under the agreement, the number of employees eligible for an extended vacation is 9,000. The number of calculation dates remaining under the agreement is 60. The number of employees entitled for extended vacations, therefore, is 150, or 9,000 divided by 60. On the second calculation date, the number of employees eligible for extended vacations is 8,850, or 9,000 reduced by the previous entitlements. The number of calculation dates remaining under the agreement is 59. The number of employees entitled to extended vacations, therefore, is 150, or 8,850 divided by 59.

The plant vacation coordinator tries to schedule as many of these 150 employees as possible for an immediate extended vacation (subject to the notice provisions of the contract). However, it is unlikely that all of these employees may be scheduled for immediate vacations since several of them may be employed in the same seniority unit or even in the same occupation, and this would create serious operating difficulties. Therefore, it is necessary to postpone extended vacations for some employees.

Although most employees become entitled to extended vacations in the manner discussed above, the company may entitle additional employees on any calculation date by a procedure called "acceleration." Acceleration simply means that an employee who would not otherwise be entitled to an extended vacation under the previously described formula may, at the sole discretion of the company, become entitled for the purpose of expediting entitlement to and scheduling of extended vacations. Accelerated entitlements are made only for the purpose of scheduling employees for immediate vacations. Determinations as to which employees will be accelerated are made on the basis of the following:

1. Operating conditions, that is, which employees can most easily be excused at a particular time.
2. Prevention of later scheduling problems in any department which may have a large number of younger service employees.
3. Continuous service, that is, where possible senior employees are accelerated before junior employees.

In order to meet the scheduling requirements of the extended vacation plan, it has been determined that 150 extended vacations must be scheduled each month on a companywide basis. This total is broken down on a plantwide basis as follows:

1. Plant *A*—62 extended vacations each month.
2. Plant *B*—46 extended vacations each month.
3. Plant *C*—38 extended vacations each month.
4. Plant *D*—4 extended vacations each month.

The individual plant vacation quotas reflect the percentage of all bargaining-unit employees working in that individual plant. The accompanying table illustrates how these quotas are attained on a companywide basis

Company basis:

Number entitled under formula	150	Number to be scheduled (monthly quota)	150
Number who may be scheduled for immediate vacations	120	Number of those entitled who are scheduled for immediate vacations	120
Number to be postponed	30	Number short of monthly quota	30
		Number to be accelerated	30

Plant basis:

Number entitled under formula	89	Number to be scheduled (monthly quota)	62
Number who may be scheduled for immediate vacations	53	Number of those entitled who are scheduled for immediate vacations	52
Number to be postponed	36	Number short of monthly quota	9
		Number to be accelerated	9

and on a plantwide basis. The table shows how the plant vacation coordinator ascertains the number of accelerated entitlements to be made each month.

Plant vacation coordinators and operating supervisors work from a vacation planning sheet in scheduling employees for vacations. This report lists each employee in the department and the number of weeks of regular, extended, and supplemental vacation to which he is entitled in a given year. This form is prepared at the beginning of each year; and as employees in the department are scheduled for vacations during the year, an entry is made after their names in the appropriate columns for the particular weeks they will be on vacation. There are 52 columns on this form, one for each week of the year. The letters *R, E,* and *S* are used to designate which type of vacation is being scheduled (regular, extended, or supplemental). By using this form, it is possible for a supervisor to readily ascertain which weeks during the year may be available to any given employee for vacation purposes.

The plan has application only to bargaining-unit employees. However, for salaried employees, the company has initiated a separate and different extended vacation program. This program provides an extended vacation of seven weeks over a five-year period in addition to regular vacation. This extended vacation vests and is allowed at the rate of seven days per year in accordance with these rules:

1. Starting January 1, 1964, and on January 1 of each year thereafter, an extended vacation of seven days is vested for each employee who has had continuous service during the previous year.
2. Once the vacation has vested, each employee must dispose of it be either (*a*) electing to take time off with pay some time during the calendar year in which vesting occurs or (*b*) electing to take a cash payment and no extended vacation time off.
3. The election must be made by January 31 of each year. If no election is made by that date, the employee is assumed to have elected the option of a cash payment without time off.
4. Where an employee elects to take time off with pay, he must schedule his time off as one continuous vacation period between January 31 and December 31.

The successful administration of the extended vacation plan or any other type of vacation depends on the cooperative efforts of many individuals at various management levels in operating and nonoperating divisions of the company. Extended vacation plans are late arrivals on the industrial relations scene. They present management with an entirely new area of problems and challenges. It is hoped and anticipated that this plan will be flexible enough to adapt to any unforeseen or unusual situations that may develop and yet rigid enough to insure sound administration and complete compliance with the letter of the extended vacation benefit agreement.

ONE APPROACH TO
EMPLOYMENT SECURITY •

ROY R. REYNOLDS

THE LONG-RANGE SHARING PLAN developed by Kaiser Steel Corporation and the United Steelworkers of America is designed to eliminate periodic negotiations and possible strikes over the basic economic aspects of our union contracts through an equitable sharing of savings in manufacturing costs on a continuing basis. In order to encourage employees to make a maximum contribution to this cost-reduction effort, they have to be given some assurance that their individual employment and income will not be jeopardized in the process. The employment-security provisions of the sharing plan give them this assurance. It should be kept in mind, however, that these provisions are only a part of the entire program.

No program in the field of industrial relations originates or exists in a vacuum. The concept of the sharing approach can be traced directly to the lengthy 1959 strike in the steel industry, in which Kaiser Steel was a participant. When George W. Taylor, appointed to head the Taft-Hartley Board of Inquiry established to review this dispute, saw the bitterness and recriminations which had developed on both sides, he expressed his profound conviction that the parties *had* to find a better way to resolve the issues involved in this situation. Both Edgar Kaiser and David J. McDonald shared this conviction, and when Kaiser Steel and the Steelworkers finally sat down to reach a separate settlement they were both firmly committed to search for a solution to this complex problem. Both recognized, however, that no solution was likely to be developed in the time available or under the pressures involved in the 1959 settlement. Instead, they agreed to appoint a committee to study the whole subject and arrive at a satisfactory program which could be recommended to the parties.

ROY R. REYNOLDS is Director, Industrial Relations Planning, Henry J. Kaiser Company, Oakland, California.

The Long-Range Committee, as this group has come to be known, is a tripartite body made up of three public, three company, and three union members. George W. Taylor is chairman, and John T. Dunlop and David L. Cole are the other public members. The Kaiser Steel members are Edgar F. Kaiser, chairman of the board; E. E. Trefethen Jr., vice chairman of the board; and C. F. Borden, executive vice president. The original Steelworker members were President David J. McDonald; General Counsel Arthur Goldberg; and Charles J. Smith, district director for the Western states. When Arthur Goldberg was appointed Secretary of Labor, his place was taken by Marvin J. Miller, assistant to David McDonald.

The stated objective of the Long-Range Committee was initially expressed as: "The establishment of a long-range plan for equitable sharing between the stockholders, the employees, and the public of the company's future economic progress." This objective was further elaborated in the following more specific guidelines for any such plan:

1. To promote stability of employment.
2. To safeguard employees against increases in the cost of living.
3. To provide for equitable sharing of increased productivity.
4. To encourage the necessary expansion of the company.

Even at this point the idea of "sharing" carried with it a strong commitment to the concept of economic and employment security for the employees affected.

Once the Long-Range Committee actually began to function, it identified a number of subjects which appeared to warrant study, much of which was accomplished by the appointment of subcommittees. One of these subcommittees, made up of two union and two company representatives, was assigned responsibility for studying possible approaches to the committee's basic economic objective and for recommending a program. This subcommittee, assisted by other union and company staff personnel, explored a wide range of alternative ideas over a two-year period before they were able to develop and present a complete program for the approval of the committee.

Employment security was early recognized to be a vital and, in fact, key consideration in any program that might be proposed. The union representatives felt very strongly that they could not propose and endorse a program to their membership that jeopardized either the job or income security of individual employees. At the same time all agreed that it would be unrealistic to assume that employees would cooperate wholeheartedly in any program that might cost them their jobs. On the other hand, the fact remained that the company could not agree to any employment guarantee which eliminated the possibility of future improvement in labor costs or obligated them to hire or retain unnecessary employees in the face of changes in the level of operations. The search, therefore, was for a program which balanced the need of the individual employee for a reasonable degree of security against the need of all parties for a continuing improvement in labor-cost performance. This was obviously one of the knottiest problems faced by the subcommittee in its lengthy deliberations.

Everyone concerned recognized the need for careful consideration of alternatives and decided at an early stage that no artificial deadlines should be established. Although the Long-Range Committee was consulted and asked to give assistance at various stages during this period and was regularly kept informed on the course of discussions, it was only after the entire subcommittee had reached agreement on the plan that it was formally presented to the full committee for review. The Long-Range Committee recommended acceptance of the Long-Range Sharing Plan, and it was adopted by the parties—subject only to a vote of the covered employees— on December 16, 1962.

After approval had been given, the committee held mass meetings of the employees and their families to give them a broad outline of the program. The union then held a series of small group meetings for all employees to explain the details more fully and to permit questions on all aspects of the proposal. The Long-Range Sharing Plan was then submitted to a vote by the covered employees on January 11, 1963, and was accepted by a three-to-one margin for installation effective March 1, 1963.

The Long-Range Sharing Plan was developed to cover all employees represented by the Steelworkers at Kaiser Steel's basic steel mill at Fontana, California. As such, it covers about 6,200 members of the production and maintenance bargaining unit and 475 in the clerical and technical unit. It does not cover Steelworker employees in the company's fabricating operations or any other groups at other locations.

The basic provisions of the sharing plan are divided into three sections:
1. The employment-security section, which provides for employment and income protection.
2. The section on sharing in cost savings, from which the plan derives its name, contains a number of detailed provisions. Basically, it calls for the employees to share to the extent of 32.5 per cent in all savings in labor and materials and supply costs in the basic manufacturing operations at Fontana. These savings are measured from

an actual base period, for which we selected the 1961 calendar year, in addition to which there are adjustments for changes in the Consumer Price Index and the Wholesale Price Index of those categories of steel products manufactured at Fontana. The employees' share is calculated monthly, a portion is set aside to cover the cost of any future wage or benefit improvements that might be adopted, and the balance is distributed in the form of cash payments to participating employees on the basis of a formula which takes historical wage relationships in the industry and company into account.

3. The section on elimination of existing incentive, which provides for the gradual transfer of group incentive workers to Sharing Plan coverage through voluntary transfer, acceptance of company offers of lump-sum payments, or, ultimately, attrition. This section was made necessary by the fact that, at the start of the Sharing Plan, approximately 40 per cent of the eligible employees were covered by standard group incentive plans which could not be eliminated immediately without endangering the earnings potential of a large group of employees.

The Long-Range Sharing Plan was adopted on a continuing basis, subject to an annual review and revision and to potential cancellation only at four-year intervals. The first four years, therefore, are regarded by the parties as a trial or pilot period, during which it is hoped that all sections of the plan may be carefully evaluated on the basis of a variety of experience. Although the experience during the first year was helpful in this regard, it was far from a complete test of many aspects of the plan.

EMPLOYMENT-SECURITY PROVISIONS OF THE PLAN

The employment-security section is one of the basic and more complex sections of the Long-Range Sharing Plan. The complexities arise, however, in an attempt to apply the more easily understood principles underlying this provision. These principles can be expressed as follows:

1. Employees should be protected from losses attributable to changes in technology or improvements in methods of production.
2. Protection offered on this basis should be consistent with the seniority practices which have been established under the basic union agreements.
3. Operation of the plan should not interfere with the reduction in numbers of employees *solely* as a result of a reduced level of operations.

4. Nothing in the plan should require the company to hire new employees to meet obligations arising under these provisions.

In general terms, therefore, it is fair to say that the intent of this provision is to protect present employees against the immediate impact of technological or methods improvements while still permitting the long-run mutual benefit of such economies to accrue through the process of attrition and business expansion.

In order to protect employees from loss of employment or earnings under such circumstances, a three-pronged approach was developed. It included the following safeguards, each designed to offer a different type of protection: (1) employment reserves, (2) displacement differentials, and (3) short-week benefits.

Employment reserves. This concept represents the most fundamental, the most complex, and in certain respects the most radical protective provision of the plan. Because it provides protection against the awesome yet often nebulous threat of technological advances, it is regarded as the very foundation of the plan by a large number of employees.

In approaching the development of this phase of the plan, the subcommittee was faced with a basic problem. It was agreed that the employee who was directly subject to layoff or downgrade as a result of a specific change in methods or technology could in some cases be identified and offered some type of assistance, but in other situations identification would be impossible as in the case of indirect employees such as maintenance or service personnel. Moreover, it was recognized that any approach must recognize the possibility of longer-range effects from "creeping change." It was agreed, therefore, that some type of "formula" approach to measuring the full impact of such changes was called for in this situation.

The original solution to this problem was incorporated in the plan as it was installed on March 1, 1963. Fortunately, there was little need for this type of protection during the first year because few changes were introduced and a high level of operations assured jobs for any who were displaced.

In the course of administering the plan, however, certain problems with this provision became evident. As worded, there was some basis for variations in interpretation, there was an indication that fluctuations of too wide a margin might occur on a month-to-month basis of calculations, and, finally, there was a conflict with certain new seniority provisions of the basic agreement. As a result, this section of the original plan was revised by mutual agreement, effective January 1, 1964.

In actual practice, there are two employment reserves established under the plan—one for production and maintenance and one for clerical and technical employees. Each of these involves the same concepts and calculations but are treated here as a single entity. The number of jobs required in the employment reserve each month is determined on the basis of two types of calculations: (1) a direct count of displacements plus (2) any positive result from the application of a productivity formula.

The direct count represents the number of employees who, in the absence of this provision, would be displaced (either by being laid off or by being transferred to other available work) as the result of a change in work practices resulting from installation of a technological improvement or a new or improved work method. This number is determined at the time of such change.

This direct obligation is subject to reduction in two ways. First of all, this number of jobs is reduced by the number of employees from the same seniority pool who terminate from active employment at a time when the obligation under the productivity-formula calculation is greater than this direct obligation or there is no one on layoff from the plant. Second, at the start of the third full month after the end of the month in which each direct obligation is created, the obligation is reduced to two-thirds of the original number or, if lower, to the reduced amount resulting from terminations. At the start of the fourth month, the obligation is similarly reduced to one-third, and it is reduced to zero at the start of the fifth month. In short, this obligation is eliminated over a maximum period of five months.

The second part of the total employment-reserve obligation is based on a productivity formula. Under this formula, the obligation for any given month is determined as follows:

1. The average actual man-hours are calculated for the three-month period covering the fourth, third, and second preceding months.
2. The average actual man-hours are subtracted from the average standard man-hours for this same period.
3. This difference between standard and actual man-hours (if positive) is divided by 173 hours to convert it to the number of jobs required under this formula.

This provision is complicated by a number of qualifying factors which can best be explained by reference to the hypothetical example shown in the accompanying exhibit. Looking first at Line 1, we have the standard man-hours established on the basis of 1961 actual performance at various levels of operations. This represents the initial determination for "standard man-hours" in the above calculations. However, the plan further provides

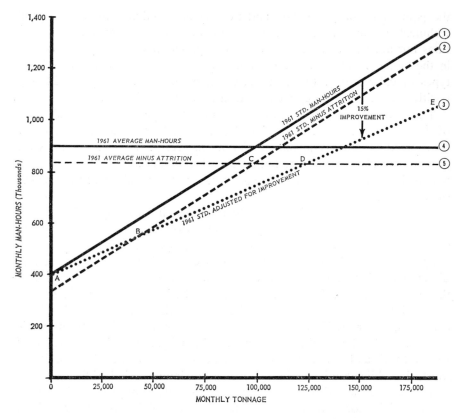

that this standard may be permanently reduced by the weighted average percentage improvement between 1961 and any consecutive three-month period after the installation of the plan in which there were no employees on layoff during the third month. For example, if there had been a weighted average improvement of 15 per cent and the average production during the three-month period had been 150,000 tons, the 1961 standard man-hours at that point would have been reduced by 15 per cent. The reduction at other levels of production would then be determined by drawing a straight line from the 1961 standard at zero production (400,000 man-hours in this illustration) through the point of 15 per cent improvement at 150,000 tons. This new line would then represent the standard man-hours for the purpose of future calculations under this formula.

Although this formula represents the long-run basis on which the employment-reserve calculation is based, there is a further provision for two alternative calculations which may provide different results during the early life of the plan.

As expressed in the plan, the lesser of the following two alternative formulas is used in determining the standard man-hours for any month in which it exceeds the calculation under the basic formula:

1. The average hours worked per month during 1961 minus 173 hours for each employee on the payroll as of December 31, 1961, who has since terminated. This is represented in the exhibit where Line 4 shows the average man-hours per month during 1961, and Line 5 shows this as adjusted for attrition.

2. The standard man-hours based on 1961 performance minus 173 hours for each employee on the payroll as of December 31, 1961, who has since terminated. In the exhibit, this is represented by Line 2, which is merely the basic 1961 standard reduced by attrition.

As shown in the exhibit, it is apparent that different calculations would be controlling at different levels of production. At the two extremes of production the basic formula would be controlling between points *A* and *B* and points *D* and *E*. In the intermediate range of output, however, the alternate formulas would be applied, with Line 2 being the lesser (and hence controlling) between points *B* and *C* and Line 5 controlling between points *C* and *D*.

In spite of the complexities introduced by the alternative calculations, a further reference to the exhibit shows that the long-run effect is for attrition to eliminate these alternatives (Lines 2 and 5), leaving the calculation under the basic formula as the ultimate controlling factor at all levels of production. In effect, therefore, this shows the alternative calculations in their true light as interim means of offering a greater degree of immediate protection to present employees without hindering the long-run operation of the productivity formula.

It is very easy in any program such as this to get so involved in the mechanics that we lose sight of the real objectives of these calculations. In the case of the plan, the application of these various formulas tells us, in the final analysis, only the number of jobs that need to be made available in the appropriate employment reserve. This leaves some basic questions yet to be answered, starting with one as to who is entitled to fill these jobs.

The intent so far as the plan is concerned is that job openings in the employment reserve be filled on the basis of plantwide seniority within the respective bargaining units. Two points are significant in this regard.

First, it is apparent from this that no individual is protected against layoff under this provision, even though displaced directly by a technological change, if there is someone else on layoff status with greater seniority. This is true even if the senior employee on layoff is there as the result of a reduced level of operations. This provision protects a certain number of jobs, therefore, but individual employees are protected on the basis of seniority. One qualifying condition is also inserted here that any employee, to receive protection by employment in the employment reserve, must have worked in 26 weekly pay periods. This leads directly to the second point, which is the fundamental principle that the company is not obligated to hire *new* employees to fill jobs in the employment reserve. The protection is offered *only* if there are present employees available who need this protection.

The issue of what use will be made of employees assigned to these jobs is a delicate one and one which will require further clarification in actual cases. In principle, however, several approaches are already defined. Employees in the employment reserve are used to eliminate overtime, to fill in for temporary absentees, and to do any other work which does not replace another employee. While this latter area is the one where definitions are difficult, it is a situation which both parties are confident can be resolved locally.

Displacement differentials. Although primary concern in the area of employee security is directed at job protection, there was naturally some concern for those employees who might suffer a reduction in earnings as a result of technological or methods changes, even though they were retained on other jobs. Therefore, it was agreed that any such employee would receive a displacement differential equal to the difference between the rate he would have received without the change and the actual rate he received after the change. For example, if an employee has been working on a Job Class 10 classification at $2.66 an hour and, because of a change in the work, is downgraded to a Job Class 6 job at $2.38 an hour, he receives a displacement differential of 28 cents an hour. If, at some subsequent point, the employee moves up to Job Class 8 at $2.52 an hour—so that the differential would then be the difference between Job Class 10 and Job Class 8, the displacement differential is reduced to 14 cents an hour.

Displacement differentials are regarded as a temporary protection for individual employees until such time as they can regain a reasonable rate level in relation to their old jobs or adjust to a lower rate expectation. They are limited on a time basis, therefore, to a maximum of 52 weekly payments, three calendar years, or until the employee regains the rate level to which he would otherwise be protected, whichever occurs first. Also, because this provision is intended to protect an employee only until he regains his expected rate level, it is canceled at any time he declines a promotion to a permanent, higher-rated job which he has the ability to perform.

As in the case of the employment reserve, displacement differentials are intended as temporary protection for individual employees who would otherwise suffer hardship as a result of long-term improvements in the utilization of the company's labor force. By granting this temporary relief, it was the expectation of the parties that the rate of improvement in cost performance could be increased to the long-run benefit of all concerned.

Short-week benefits. The other type of income loss that might be involved under the impact of technological or methods changes is that of reduced hours of work. In order to insure that the level of employment would not be held at an unnecessarily high level by means of sharing work through a reduction in hours below the standard 40-hour schedule, a further provision was required. This calls for the payment of a short-week benefit to any employee whose hours are reduced below 40 because of such a change. This payment is equal to the difference between his actual earnings and what he would have earned on a regular schedule. This is accomplished by paying him his average hourly earnings times the number of hours less than 40 for any week in which his schedule is so reduced.

There are certain qualifications attached to such benefits, although the primary one in this instance is that the employee must be available for 40 hours of work in order to be eligible for this protection. This benefit should be carefully distinguished from the other short-week benefit provided under the normal industry supplementary unemployment benefits program to cover a different set of circumstances.

DISTRIBUTION OF EMPLOYMENT-SECURITY COSTS

As might be surmised from the importance attached to employment security in the development of the Long-Range Sharing Plan, the cost of these provisions comes "off the top" of the plan. This is accomplished, in fact, in two ways, both of which have the same effect as far as the rest of the plan is concerned. Looking first at the guarantees involved in the employment reserve, to the extent that employees are retained on jobs in the reserve and thus result in a direct payroll cost, any savings under the plan are automatically lessened by that amount. Except to the extent that this amount is of interest from the standpoint of evaluating the performance of the employment reserve itself, it is no different than any other labor cost incurred in the operation of the plant.

In the case of displacement differentials and short-week benefits, actual and measurable costs are involved in the application of these provisions. These costs are deducted from any gross savings measured under the sharing plan calculations—however, *before* the employees' share is computed. The net result in each case is the same, with all of the employment-security costs being absorbed before any remaining net cost reductions are subject to sharing on the basis of 32.5 per cent going to the employees' share and the balance being retained by the company.

* * *

The formulators of the plan were faced with an obvious dilemma. On one side, they were aware that one of the major obstacles to improved performance was the resistance of employees who feared for their own future security. This had to be overcome by some offer of protection which would satisfy the employees. At the same time, any long-term freezing of labor costs at existing levels removed a major source of savings and would have rendered any plan virtually meaningless. Their search, therefore, centered on the need to achieve a balance between these two opposing forces—short-term protection for individual employees versus long-range improvements in performance of the group as a whole—and these employment-security provisions of the plan were developed to provide such a balance.

How well they will do this job remains to be seen. Both parties have already stated that these sections of the plan were not adequately tested during the first year. By their very nature, a true test requires exposure to various changes, not only in technology or methods but also in levels of economic activity. These long-range expectations cannot be evaluated on the basis of short-range performance. Even though it is true that the original mechanics of the employment reserve were found to present some problems and were subsequently revised, the basic objectives remained the same. Whether they will be achieved remains one of the fundamental questions which must be answered on the basis of future operation of the plan. At this early stage, both parties have expressed optimism that their present expectations will be fufilled through their own efforts and the collective bargaining process.

MEETING THE PROBLEM OF
AUTOMATION AND JOB SECURITY •

PRES LANCASTER

In late 1960 the stevedore, terminal, and steamship companies of the Pacific Maritime Association (PMA) signed a collective bargaining agreement with the waterfront workers of California, Oregon, and Washington on the subject of automation and job security. The workers were represented by the International Longshoremen's and Warehousemen's Union (ILWU). Management benefited from the negotiated procedures for the introduction of laborsaving devices, changes in job manning and gang structure, and revision of the longshoremen's work rules. The workers' *quid pro quo* was a $29 million fund which was to be collected over a period of five and one-half years and used for supplemental wage benefits, early retirement benefits, and death and disability benefits. The five and one-half year agreement became effective on January 1, 1961, and is to run to June 30, 1966. The programs established under the agreement will still be operating in 1969, but the expenditures are limited to the $29 million which has been provided and any earnings which may accrue.

The agreement is a multiemployer agreement. The longshoremen and other classes of waterfront workers work principally for stevedore and terminal companies. The stevedore and terminal companies work for both foreign and domestic steamship companies, who are the real parties of interest on the management side though they seldom employ longshoremen directly. Stevedore and terminal companies often work on a cost-plus basis, and, accordingly, their interest in a laborsaving contract is not the same as that of the principals, the steamship companies. The negotiation of the ILWU-PMA Mechanization and Modernization Agreement was conducted for management by steamship company representatives.

Pres Lancaster is Manager, Contract Data Department, Pacific Maritime Association, San Francisco, California.

The work covered by the agreement consists of hundreds of dissimilar operations: the loading of logs in the Pacific Northwest, the loading of lumber in packages, the pouring of grain into ships specially designed for the purpose, the handling of all the miscellany which supports the overseas military establishment. The products handled also include fresh fruit in cases, shiploads of nothing but truck-sized containers handled automatically, shiploads of automobiles, shiploads of steel, rolls of newsprint, and so on. The structure of job security rests on these diverse operations.

Any forecast of how much work will be available in any period of time is mostly pure guesswork. Any forecast of how many jobs may be eliminated by new methods is also mostly pure guesswork. New techniques and new work methods are now being made part of the operations almost daily. Some of the techniques which promised major savings when the agreement was signed have been radically transformed since, and anticipated savings now occur in different areas. The proposed changes were not planned by a central agency but, rather, competitively by the various carriers; they were naturally reluctant to disclose their thinking. These circumstances had to be subsumed in the agreement.

It was anticipated that the changes under the proposed contract would be widespread and of considerable impact. Man-hour savings in a year were expected to exceed 5 per cent of the 1960 total man-hours, and they did. A 5 per cent cut in man-hours would cover the cost of the benefits provided. Further savings would have to be achieved in order for the employers to benefit from lower operating costs. But it was not possible to predict accurately where the savings would be realized or how deep the cut in man-hours would be. These considerations turned on the nature and organization of the work force.

In 1934, on the recommendation of a panel appointed by the president, the longshoremen's work force was registered jointly by the parties. This procedure was established to give the regular, "professional" longshoreman first claim on the available work opportunity, in preference to the casual worker who was either seeking temporary or part-time employment or earnings to supplement those from another job. The registration procedure is still one of the major facts of West Coast waterfront employment and has been copied on the East Coast. It works to the employers' advantage on some occasions and to the union's advantage on others.

Part of the proposed contract was an agreement to "freeze" registration —that is, to register no new men until the extent of the changes in work opportunity and the size of the work force required could be appraised. This means merely that no workers will be hired during a period when work opportunity is expected to decline. The implication is more subtle and more important: If jobs prove unnecessary, they will not be maintained and so cannot be offered to new workers who might be brought in to maintain union membership at strength. Hopefully, the elimination of unnecessary jobs will encourage more traffic and thus generate new jobs for more men. But if not, the work force will stabilize with fewer members.

There were pressures on the union to maintain jobs so that sons and other relatives could be brought into the work force, but other union interests prevailed. It was this basic decision of the union membership which made an automation contract meaningful and possible: The union men decided to profit by bringing the work force into balance with a modernized industry. It was a remarkable move for a union to propose that, if necessary, membership should dwindle over a period of time so that there would be better jobs and better opportunities for the future work force. Union leadership does not often curtail the base from which it operates for the benefit of the rank-and-file worker. (As it happens, this risk paid off for the union. The industry has recently added new workers to replace men who have retired.) The decision was made because the union believed in the benefits which could come of bargaining along such lines.

In addition to the fully registered work force (A men), there are men with partial registration (B men) and there are the casuals. The men with partial registration are probational; they will qualify for A registration only if they have shown their ability and willingness to work as longshoremen. They are promoted to the A list in their home port only when the parties have jointly determined that there should be additions to that list, which will be when the port needs men—that is, when there is the prospect of sufficient work to provide a livelihood for the men who will be promoted.

From 5 to 8 per cent of the hours are worked by casual workers, mostly members of other unions who are temporarily unemployed and who often work as longshoremen as little as one day a year and are not likely to work frequently or for any extended period of time. The industry employs almost as many casuals as it does regular workers during the course of a year because there is a widely fluctuating demand for workers, because of irregular ship-arrival patterns. A sudden influx of ships into a particular port will result in a demand for workers far exceeding the available work force. In such cases, casuals are employed, but their number is limited by the number of skilled workers in the basic force. In a subsequent period, there will be few ships in port and not enough work for the regular long-shoremen.

The *B* men and the casuals account for from 10 to 15 per cent of the hours worked and are a major factor in the job security picture. Because *B* men and casuals have second and third preference for the work opportunity and are not established as part of the regular work force, a decline in work opportunity does not fall fully and directly on the *A* workers but partly on the "conditional" work force. This was taken into account when the guarantees for the regular work force were under consideration: If man-hour savings reduce the work opportunity, *A* men can maintain their earnings by performing some of the work which now goes to the *B* and casual men. Though *B* and casual workers bear the first brunt of declining work opportunity, *B* and casual work are not likely to be totally eliminated. The parties did not make the payment of benefits dependent upon a reduction in the proportion of *B* and casual hours. The programs which were instituted sought to induce the older regular worker to retire early. This was done because it was believed that the principal problem relating to man-hour savings and changing work opportunity rested in the regular work force and would have to be dealt with there. It tied automation benefits to the professional longshoreman as a means of cushioning auto-mation impact.

In each port, men are assigned their work by a dispatching hall which is jointly operated by the parties and serves all the employers in the port. A man is given preference for dispatch based on whether he has had more or less work than others who are seeking jobs. Under the dispatching system, he goes from job to job and from employer to employer (sometimes from port to port), working from one to five days at a time. At the conclusion of each job, he returns to the hall for his next dispatch. He may refuse the job he is offered, and he is not required to make himself available for work, though there are some rules on the subject of availability. The practices of the dispatching halls are involved, and they are nearly sacrosanct, for the union considers that the establishment of the halls was a major job security victory. Any guarantees provided by the agreement had to be based on the assumption that there could be no immediate major change in the existing system of job seeking and dispatching.

Such, then, was the work force which would be affected by the changes which management hoped to institute. Unlike a manufacturing or other type of operation where proposed changes usually relate to specific men in specific jobs or skills, changes in this system would not apply to tasks individually assigned but would affect all men equally in some degree. Changes would have to be of considerable consequence before individuals would note any loss of work opportunity or loss of pay. On the other hand, a new operation would affect not just a few men, but a great many men rotating through the new type of job who would individually have to adjust to the change and who would individually be able to evaluate the impact of the change.

When the bargaining began in 1960, the industry had welfare and vacation plans which had been established for a number of years and a pension plan which had been operating for nine years. There was a pension reopener due in the following year. The pension plan provided pensions of $100 per month for workers age 65 or older with 25 years of service. Retirement for eligibles was mandatory at age 68. Service credits could accrue after age 68 if a man did not have the necessary credits and continued to work (as many did). Disability pensions of $100 per month were provided for men with 25 years of service who were permanently and totally disabled. There were no provisions for retirement before age 65 and no pensions for men with less than 25 years of service. However, the requirements for a qualifying year of service were low—as little as 800 hours of work per year.

There were about 15,000 registered men in the work force in 1960, and 800 of these were over age 65. An additional 4,700 were over age 54. Many of this group joined the industry during World War II and could be expected to complete their 25 years of service in years subsequent to 1966, when the anticipated annual retirements would be more than double the annual retirements of the prior period. One major port had a work force generally younger than the Coast average. This was the background when bargaining began.

As has been said above, management anticipated widespread changes of considerable impact but could not determine in detail the amount and kind of work which would be eliminated. Also, it had been the earlier experience of the stevedoring industry that it was one thing to write a contract providing for changes in work practices and another thing to realize the changes on the job. The management discussions of these problems began several years before the actual bargaining and in the earlier phases turned on the idea that payment to the union should be proportional to the savings realized. A "C.O.D." attitude characterized the thinking, and this seemed eminently reasonable in the circumstances since one of the major complaints of the industry during the Fifties was that worker productivity had been declining even more than the industry was accustomed to claim. The complaint could not be substantiated with figures because the work measurement systems of the industry, if they existed at all, were incompatible and of dubious quality. However, such indexes as there were did show declining productivity. Accordingly, the industry set out to "measure the savings," and to do so it established the first of the two work measurements systems which were launched during that period.

While the work measurement systems were being tried out, the situation of the employers vis-à-vis the union and the workers was changing. Two major contract changes were negotiated, and the employers initiated a program to bring about performance of the contract in keeping with the spirit in which it had been negotiated and written. The major contract changes were (1) reduction of the workshift from nine to eight hours and (2) provision of an eight-hour guarantee for men "turned to." There were changes in the work rules to make these contract changes feasible, and they demonstrated the benefits of "flexibility"—escape from the confines of earlier rules.

The employers learned that if they cooperated as a group, output could be improved and changes in the contract could be realized. The changes were accomplished by demanding conformance to the contract. The demand was firm and reasonable and backed up with supervision, control, and whatever action might be necessary. These developments, and distrust of the work measurement systems which were being tried out, brought about changes in the thinking about job security payments. It was no longer desirable to talk about "savings" in the sense that the workers might become entitled to a portion of all improvements made in the future, a concept which is implied when payments are tied to gains. The employers noted that future savings, as distinguished from those immediately anticipated, might be required to keep the industry competitive and preserve jobs. The new thinking was that current savings, if any, should be used to help cushion the changes during the transition period. After the transition period, when the work force and the available work were again in equilibrium, productivity gains could be shared through the normal process of collective bargaining. Gains should not be distributed through any automatic "socialistic" mechanism which might give the workers a special claim on industry earnings with no responsibilities or risks.

The earlier thinking had been born of the industry's mistrust of what could be accomplished, and it was now put aside. The original questions were asked again: "What will it cost to cushion the impact of the changes which will occur?" "Can we afford to pay the union for the changes proposed and still benefit ourselves?" The first answer was: "We do not know the extent of the impact; therefore, we do not know what cushion will be required." And the second answer was: "We don't know the full extent of the impact, but in our best judgment and on the basis of our experience, there is a reasonable price for the improvements which we anticipate. If the contract is amended in respects A, B, and C, the employers will gain and X dollars can be paid for the benefit of the employees."

The industry offered the union an annual lump-sum payment for certain changes in the contract, providing also that the contract would run for at least five years. The principal features of the offer were as follows:

1. The contract was to run for at least five years. It was necessary to have time to put the improvement programs into effect. It was necessary to have time in which to court the confidence of the customers of the industry.

2. The payment was in lump sum. The fixed amount was named for the period of the contract, and there was no commitment beyond the expiration of the contract. The amount was payable regardless of the volume of trade handled. Benefits were limited to the amount available; benefit programs would have to be framed so that benefit costs did not exceed the sums provided. In general, benefits would be paid during the contract period; there would not be any on-going programs. If programs exceeded estimates, benefits would have to be curtailed.

3. The manner of raising the money was left to the employer.

4. The money had to be spent for benefits which related to the impact of automation, and the parties agreed upon the general scope of these before signing the contract. The lump sum could not be used for wage increases or similar items; these were covered separately in the agreement.

5. The sum was subject to abatement in the event of a work stoppage in violation of the contract or if the union, or individual locals

thereof, refused to apply the provisions of the agreement. This issue was subject to arbitration.

Before the union accepted the lump-sum concept, it advanced a proposal to raise a fund by taxing each ton handled. The cost of handling cargo would be lower because of the work improvement program, and, accordingly, every ton would contribute to the fund. This has obvious affinities with the contribution to the Mine Workers' Welfare Fund for each ton of coal produce. The proposal is, of course, a share-the-savings plan without the saving grace of "C.O.D." provisions, and the employers rejected it both for this and for the reasons noted earlier.

After the lump-sum pattern had been agreed upon and the changes in the contract written out, the price was negotiated—$5 million per year for 5 and one-half years (the life of the agreement) plus $1.5 million which had been accumulated in earlier years as a token of good faith in the matter of automation bargaining. The total was $29 million, and it was divided among three different benefit programs.

Approximately $2 million a year was to be spent on a benefit designed to induce early retirement. The plan misleadingly labels this benefit a "vesting benefit." A man who has the necessary 25 years of qualifying service and who attains his sixty-second birthday before June 1, 1966, may leave the work force and receive special payments of $220 per month for three years. The $220 monthly payment is equal to a social security payment of $120 plus a pension of $100. (In 1960 the industry pension was $100 per month; in 1961 it became $115 per month.) Benefits can be paid in a single payment or at an accelerated rate if the trustees approve. Men who accept the benefit retain their rights to an industry pension at age 65. The benefit is not mandatory, and a man may delay his retirement until he is 68. If he retires before July 1, 1966, and has the necessary qualifying years of service, he may claim the special benefit whatever his age when he leaves the work force. If, however, he is eligible for the benefit and dies while he is still an active member of the work force, no part of the benefit accrues to his estate. Men age 62 or older must leave the work force and claim the benefit by July 1, 1966, or lose their rights to benefits, and in this sense, there is pressure on individuals to leave the work force, for they cannot be certain that they will obtain equivalent benefits under another contract. It has been determined that all those eligible for the benefit are covered by the amounts allocated, except as noted below.

A total of $11 million has been allocated to a Supplemental Wage Plan. Roughly, the plan provides for payments such that the combined total of weekly earnings and the sums paid will be $100. The $100 represents 35 hours of straight-time pay at 1960 rates, and the trustees of the plan are authorized to increase the weekly amount to 35 times the current hourly straight-time rate. No adjustment is made for overtime earnings. A man can earn $100 by working 20 hours or less but he would not be entitled to supplemental wage payments by reason of the $100 earnings.

Supplemental wages are payable when work opportunity has declined because of automation, but they are not payable when work opportunity has declined because there is less cargo traffic. When cargo traffic drops, the weekly $100 is reduced proportionately. This is accomplished by multiplying the payment amount by a traffic index figure for the local area in question.

Ordinarily, a number of men will be eligible for supplemental wage payments if any one man is eligible. No man is entitled to a benefit unless he has been regularly available for work; and if a man has been regularly available for work, he will have worked hours approximating the average for his port because of the manner in which the dispatching hall equalizes work opportunity. Therefore, if one man qualifies for a supplemental wage payment, there will probably be a group of individuals who qualify. The first test of whether an individual has been available for work is that he must have worked hours equal to or more than 93 per cent of the "average hours" worked during the four weeks of the base or "benefit" period. Average hours are computed for a port area and for a "representative" group of workers.

The representative group is a device which excludes the nonavailable worker when base "average hours" are computed. If this was not done, the base average hours would be depressed by reason of the registered workers who did not appear for work or who declined work when it was offered. The test of whether a man has appeared for work or accepted the work when offered is whether his hours of work have been equalized with the other workers in his port area. A man who does not have hours of work approximating the average is assumed to have been absent by his own choice. A man who is absent above the "normal" is excluded from the representative group. As a result, the average, which is the test of who is eligible for benefits, is raised so that it reflects the performance of the "regular" worker. If all workers are available for work, the representative group will include 100 per cent of the workers. Sick credits and other allowances are added to a man's hours before the membership of the representative group is determined, and such hours are included when the average is computed.

The Supplemental Wage Plan was designed as a second line of defense. The funds were available if automation changes brought about a major decline in the available hours of work. However, if cargo traffic increased so as to offset the decline in hours due to automation, the Supplemental Wage Plan would not come into play. Also, early retirements under the Vesting Benefit Plan would delay the time when supplemental wage payments might be required. And the "cushion" of B and casual work which has been discussed above would also mitigate any decline in work opportunity. No supplemental wage payments have been made to date, and none seem likely before the contract expires. It seems probable that the parties will have to renegotiate the application of some or all of this money at some future date.

The remaining benefits provided under the plan were not specifically job security benefits. About $1 million a year was allocated for death benefits and severance payments to permanently disabled men who resigned from the industry. The amount of the death benefit was based on years of service: $2,640 if a man had five years of service at death, $5,000 if a man had 20 or more years of service at death. The amount of the severance payments to disabled men was similarly determined: $2,640 if a man had 15 years of service at the date he left the industry, $7,920 if the man had 25 or more years of service at the date he left the industry. (The $2,640 and $7,920 amounts are related to the value of the vesting benefit, but there are no compelling reasons supporting the relationship.)

Vesting benefits, death benefits, and severance for disability benefits are paid from a common pool of funds. The amount of the supplemental wage fund is set apart by the agreement. The allocations for vesting benefits on the one hand and for death and disability benefits on the other are for actuarial convenience only. Benefit claims against the pool are on a first-come, first-serve basis. There now seems to be a tendency for men to claim disability severance payments if they do not have the age qualifications for vesting benefits. (The regular pension plan pays disability pensions equal to regular pensions, if any, if a man has the required qualifying service and is permanently and totally disabled.) This could bring a pressure on the available funds not contemplated when the plan was established. It is not of serious consequence, and the trustees can avoid the difficulty by tightening the qualifications for disability severance payments.

The parties established the vesting benefit trust and the supplemental wage benefit trust to accomplish the plan; and the existing welfare trust was amended so that it could handle death and disability payments. The parties encountered some difficulty in framing the plan so that it would satisfy Internal Revenue Service requirements. The industry's regular pension plan could not be used as a vehicle for the early retirement payments because the pooled employment practices of the industry make it very difficult to identify the past service of individual men in connection with particular employers. The problem was solved by creating a pay-as-you-go pension plan. The vesting benefit trust has absolutely no funds on hand and no reserves. It receives money from the employers on demand to meet current obligations. This arrangement serves to accomplish the intentions of the parties but requires a great deal of sophisticated budgeting.

The most delicate problem is that of assigning (assessing) shares of the fund to the companies concerned. It will be recalled that the agreement provided that the employers would have sole jurisdiction over the manner in which the fund was to be raised. The parties of interest were steamship companies, but the contributors to the fund had to be stevedores because they were the direct employers of the men covered. Contributions to the fund also had to bear a direct relationship to the amount of work performed. Pension and welfare contributions were on a man-hour basis, but the industry thought that man-hours should not be used as a basis for assessing the modernization fund because a company which benefited most by reducing man-hours per ton handled would pay least on the man-hour assessment basis. It was suggested that the cost should be borne solely by those who benefited under the agreement in proportion to the benefit received—the reduction in the man-hours per ton worked. This suggestion was opposed by another group of companies who said that all companies had obtained the *opportunity* to improve operations and, therefore, one group of companies should not be expected to pay the portion of the fund due from another group if the latter group had neglected to take advantage of the agreement or had failed to realize the benefits possible. In the end, the still-present difficulty of measuring improvement and assigning it to the companies made the discussion academic, but the issue is still very much alive.

The funds are presently collected by charging an assessment to each ton of cargo stevedored. The rates differ on several broad classes of cargo, and this difference copies differences observed in an assessment system long used by the industry in another connection. The system also reflects the relationship between work performed and funds collected. The method is similar to the union proposal which was rejected by the industry, but the purpose served is very different. There has been litigation by a shipper who is neither a member of the Association nor an employer of longshoremen, asserting (1) that the application of the assessment is rate making within the purview of regulatory laws and (2) that his operation is unfairly discriminated against.

Subsequent to the establishment of the modernization plan, the parties modified the regular pension plan. The modification was agreed upon during the regular five-year pension reopener and not as a consequence of the modernization agreement. The pension benefit was increased from $100 to $115 per month at age 65 with 25 years of service. The parties established a new class of pensions such that at age 65, men with as little as 13 years of service could retire with reduced pension benefits—one twenty-fifth of the normal monthly pension for each year of service. Retirement on a reduced pension at age 68 was made mandatory. As a result of this amendment to the pension plan, a number of men who were over 65 years of age but who had not been eligible for normal pensions retired. Later, similar pensions were offered to men permanently and totally disabled with no age requirement. These further cuts in the work force helped to maintain work opportunity.

Management has obtained a good portion of what it was looking for when the contract was negotiated. There have been difficulties in changing the work patterns of long-established operations, but it is being accomplished. There have been sufficient man-hour savings in the industry to pay for the plan and to pay a return to the companies concerned. Thanks to a complex of factors, among which the benefit programs are important, the man-hour savings have been accomplished without any reduction of the hours or earnings of the regular workers. The plan was designed for the period of the revised contract, a transition period, and not for an extended future. It has served the needs of that period well. The parties will determine the future of the plan in 1966 when they reconsider the situation and the problems with which they are then faced.

RETRAINING: BACKGROUND, ACTIONS, AND PROSPECTS •

DONALD W. DEVINE

Retraining, both as a concept and as a problem on the American business and industrial scene, is by no means new. Since the inception of our country, we have been confronted with the job of preparing adequate manpower. In earlier times, this preparation consisted primarily of providing learning experiences which would help individuals master skills in crafts and trades. As our society has become more complex, it has been necessary to give deeper thought to the development of an adequate labor force at all levels, including skilled, professional, and managerial levels. Included within these groups are individuals whose present jobs will be eliminated, employees whose present job content is subject to change but who will not be displaced, and young people who have not as yet been gainfully employed but who represent tomorrow's labor supply.

Currently, the problems of retraining have assumed massive proportions, in terms of the numbers and types of people who are involved in the effort either as disseminators or recipients of retraining activities. More specifically, a number of conditions are contributing to the present dilemma in retraining. These conditions have to do with technological developments which are occurring at a rapidly accelerated rate, difficulties in our educa-

---

Donald W. Devine is Personnel Development Coordinator, Xerox Corporation, Rochester, New York.

tional systems, strife in union management relationships, insufficient coordination of planning efforts by those addressing themselves to the task of retraining, archaic Federal and state legislation, and anxieties which workers have developed about the entire process of retraining.[1]

Fortunately, a number of efforts have been made to resolve some of the problems that have been brought about by the conditions mentioned above. As we look at these efforts, we can develop some generalizations which are useful in successfully meeting the challenge which is presented to us in retraining of workers in our society. In some cases, research has been conducted, and in other instances there is evidence of an observational and descriptive nature, which, although not as thoroughly documented as we would like it to be, nevertheless must be taken into account in approaching the problem of a more integrated way than has been apparent to date.

The information presented in the following situations has been gathered from a variety of sources: published articles, unpublished research, personal consultations with those who have been intimately involved in the situations, and the experiences that the writer has had over the past ten years. To simplify the explanations about some of these retraining situations, an attempt has been made to extract from the data, insights about the important and necessary elements for successful retraining. Hopefully, an understanding of these elements will be helpful in achieving desirable results from future ventures.

AN ANALYSIS OF EFFORTS TO DATE

Armour and Company. This company, a short time ago, set aside $500,-000 for retraining. A committee was appointed to handle this fund, and the organization was provided with an early opportunity to initiate retraining efforts when one of their plants closed, idling 433 people. Of these 170 applied for retraining programs. The committee set up a series of tests for these people, and only 58 qualified for any type of retraining program. They were trained in typing, upholstery, blueprint reading, meat cutting, welding, real estate selling, electronics, auto mechanics, and so forth. Of the 13 who completed the course in meat cutting, two found jobs; others became janitors, or warehousemen; and a number remained unemployed.

In March 1962, Armour and Company announced the impending shut-

[1] An excellent overview of these conditions is presented by Mali, Paul, "Retraining for the Unemployed," *Journal of the American Society of Training Directors,* August 1962, pp. 44-51.

down of its main meatpacking plant in Fort Worth, Texas.[2] Ultimately, 1,000 production workers and maintenance workers were displaced by December 1962. To retrain these workers, the Armour Automation Committee appropriated $50,000, and $40,000 had been expended or committed by January 1964. However, 144 people were subsequently employed at an edible oils refinery and a distribution center which Armour continued to operate in the Fort Worth area; 11 workers were employed in a new company plant at San Angelo, Texas; 101 persons retired under different plans included in the labor agreement; and 75 workers had transferable craft skills. Consequently, the committee's work focused on the remaining 650 workers.

Although placement efforts were initiated with the Texas Employment Commission, 600 firms in the Fort Worth area and local union offices, the results (in the words of two committee members) were "modest." Over 400 referrals were made, and 45 placements were made, including the placement of retrainees. Extremely low wage opportunities, lack of qualified persons for skilled occupations, illiteracy, and physical and other types of disabilities severely mitigated against placement. Apparently, direct placement measures met with only modest success for workers with limited or nontransferable skills.

The results of retraining efforts in Fort Worth were severely limited by the practice of racial segregation. School officials indicated a willingness to provide training for Negroes on an integrated basis if 15 people or more wanted a course that was offered only at the white school and not the Negro school, and on a segregated basis where the course was offered at both the Negro and white schools and where 15 people or more were involved.

Training programs were entered into by 164 people: auto repair, welding, retail meat cutting, food service, and warehouse and stock management. For the most part, the courses were conducted in the evening to insure that trainees would not be disqualified from unemployment compensation and to permit regular employment during the day.

In September 1963, 105 had completed retraining and 91 were employed (86.5 percent). Seventy-five had jobs directly or indirectly related to retraining. In general, it was concluded that the relative employment experience was better for the trainees than the nontrainees. Moreover, relative

---

[2]For a detailed report of this retraining experience see "The Fort Worth Project of the Armour Automation Committee." *Monthly Labor Review*, LXXXVII, No. 1 (January, 1964), pp. 53-57.

unemployment tended to increase with the age of the group for both trainees and nontrainees, but not as fast for the former. In addition, it was possible that poorer employment rates were due, in part, to the reluctance of individuals to accept low wages. Finally, there appeared to be value in providing a minimal increment of education such as that offered in the retraining program.

The State of Connecticut. During 1960, the state of Connecticut began an ambitious retraining program. It started with a mail survey by the State Department of Labor to determine the nature of jobs which would be available two months, six months, and two years from the date of the survey. The State Employment Service conducted tests for prospective job applicants so as to outline the training program. Initially, the retraining was aimed at preparing machinists, ranging in age from those in their early twenties to a high of 54. Altogether, 35 people were trained and placed in jobs. From a modest beginning, the Connecticut job retraining program has broadened to include other fields such as pipefitting, sewing machine operators, shipfitters, and outside electricians.[3]

In one program on welding training conducted for General Dynamics/Electric Boat in Groton, representatives of the Connecticut State Department of Labor, Connecticut State Department of Education, and Electric Boat met and agreed to a method by which unemployed citizens in the depressed areas of the state could make themselves employable by Electric Boat by participating and qualifying in a special welding training program. Seventy-two trainees from varied job backgrounds but with mechanical aptitudes and a will to learn completed the five-week program. That all 72 graduates have qualified to Navy Bureau of Ship Standards and are now employed in submarine constructing attests to the success of the program. Through the provisions of the Manpower Retraining Act of 1962, it is anticipated that retraining will be broadened to include more people.[4]

Xerox Corporation. In 1958, Xerox management made a decision to retrain certain employees with ten or more years of service so as to make them eligible for transfer from their paper plant to Machine Manufacturing operations of the company.[5] Fortunately, expansion in the office-copying

---

[3]Mali, *op. cit.,* p. 48.
[4]"State Praised for Job Retraining Program," *The New York Times,* May 6, 1962, Section 11, p. 13.
[5]A comprehensive explanation is presented by Felician F. Foltman in "Xerox Corporation. A Case Study in Retraining," *Management of Personnel Quarterly,* Autumn-Winter 1962, I, No. 5, pp. 8-20.

part of the business provided job opportunities for those to be retrained. Moreover, the anticipated curtailment in the operations of the paper plant was to be accomplished over a period of a year, and this provided enough time to plan for the retraining effort. Finally, cooperative working relationships with union personnel provided a climate within which retraining could be made effective.

Altogether, 192 employees were considered to be eligible for the retraining program, provided they could qualify by passing the tests. Of this total, 101 employees were tested and 68 were enrolled and completed the program. Ninety-one men made the decision not to participate. Of the 68 who completed the program, 63 are still in the Machine Manufacturing Division.

Surveys were administered by staff members of the New York State School of Industrial and Labor Relations at Cornell University prior to the program and recently when the program had been completed. Those who participated in the surveys included members who chose to remain in their positions and those who were interested but did not pass the tests, as well as those who took the course. The results of the first survey indicated that there was some concern with regard to guaranteed job placement subsequent to the training. Furthermore, a number of employees made their decision to participate on the basis of consideration of the immediate economics consequences. Conversely, those who indicated their interest in participating felt that the retraining program would assist them in protecting their jobs and equity in the company. The immediate loss of take-home pay was the most compelling reason cited by those who made the decision not to participate in the program. Another feeling expressed by those who had some doubt or reluctance to participate had to do with honest doubts about abilities as students and concern about the program arrangements made by the company and union for placement in jobs after training. In this situation, employee attitudes about retraining were directly related to the degree of confidence which they had in management. Those employees who had grave doubts about the motivations behind the arrangements were not generally positive in their attitudes about retraining.

In the second survey conducted in 1963, an attempt was made to discover how employees felt about the retraining program before it was initiated, after it had been concluded, and at a point in time when the retrainees had been reassigned. Whereas the morale was high prior to the program, there was a lessening of morale subsequent to the completion of the program; and now morale has returned almost to its original point.

From the evidence of the second survey, it has become apparent that a number of factors were related to program success. These factors included: age, fear of loss of seniority by moving to a new job situation, and lack of formal education. For some, retraining meant a golden opportunity to learn and enhance the possibilities of obtaining more secure positions. For others, there was some fear and anxiety generated by the formalized classroom methods that were applied during and throughout the training sessions. Lectures, homework assignments, and grading were particularly onerous to a number of the retrainees. Despite the efforts to sell the program, it was patently obvious that a variety of approaches could have been applied in stimulating potential program participants to a better and more acceptable recognition of the importance of the activity in meeting individual needs.

Babcock & Wilcox Company. A substantial amount of retraining involves the preparation of individuals whose job content is changing as a result of technological advancements. These are individuals who will not be displaced from their jobs, but who will continue to make contributions as members of organizational work forces. It includes groups of personnel ranging from unskilled to highly technical. Such efforts can do much in helping us to bridge the gap between the present and future work demands without replacing members of the work force on a massive scale. Since a large part of retraining is aimed at this large group, it might be termed "bread and butter" retraining. That this will continue to be with us has been well stated by Dr. Thomas Stelson, the head of the Civil Engineering Department at Carnegie Tech:

> With modern technology advancing so rapidly, the indications are that the experienced man may have to devote about a third of his time to self-education. The decline in value, or obsolescence, of engineering personnel may likely become an increasingly serious problem in modern technology unless professional societies, employers, and educational institutions recognize its importance and develop suitable remedies.[6]

At Babcock & Wilcox, the bulk of retraining efforts are directed toward nondisplaced workers. This is the situation in the Atomic Energy Division in Lynchburg, Virginia, where plans are under way to establish programs leading to a master's degree in the areas of materials science or nuclear engineering. This is being done in collaboration with the University of Virginia. Among the interesting highlights of this collaboration are the following:

[6]*New York Times, op. cit.*

1. Courses taught at the facility.
2. A partial waiving of university residence requirements.
3. Use of division personnel as instructors.
4. The selection of a thesis topic based upon work within the facility.

The problems confronting Babcock & Wilcox are somewhat unique since many of the facilities are not geographically located near vocational schools and post-secondary schools. Therefore, there is a compelling reason to make arrangements which are somewhat unique. Those in similar circumstances can appreciate the necessity for initiating programs which are not run of the mill type of education. The arrangements for the master's degree programs provide only one example of this. In other plants of Babcock & Wilcox, there are programs such as blueprint reading, shop mathematics, and computer programing. Furthermore, there has been intensive retraining in the area of improving reading comprehension of workers since it is a company management belief, based upon analysis of test data, that some workers need such a program as a prerequisite to other types of retraining. In all situations, plant personnel development people relate such training to meeting the "here and now" needs of workers while at the same time providing foundation training for future job demands. One of the most recent examples of this type of retraining occurred in the Milwaukee plant of the Tubular Products Division.

A few years ago, the top management of Babcock & Wilcox decided to install IBM equipment in the Milwaukee operation. They knew that talent would be needed to program the material to be put into the computer. Test data gave an indication as to those individuals who might be considered for such work. Further testing of college and university personnel, along with interviews, helped in the selection of a team of four men who would work well together in the work environment to which programers would be exposed. This group embarked upon a long training program offered under IBM auspices. For those who were to be displaced, efforts were made to search out job opportunities which were anticipated as a result of the reorganization of departments within the plant. Counseling played an important role in determining whether or not an individual's abilities could be utilized. In this sense, retraining of workers was practical because enough lead time was given to do the job. In one case, an individual began work at a local engineering school to prepare himself to be a draftsman, a much-needed skill in the Milwaukee plant. With the aid of individual department heads, manpower planning and retraining was started to meet the demands brought about by advancing technical developments.

The Brentwood Experience. In 1960, a nationally known U.S. Labor Department leader commented that our vocational schools were failing to provide their students with marketable skills in keeping with the needs of industry.[7] Since that time, similar comments have been made in many quarters and in many different ways. And added to this problem is the problem of dropouts at the secondary school level. In 1962, a magazine article exposed the waste of a million young people each year in schools throughout the nation.[8] If the inadequacies of our present offerings in vocational and secondary schools continue and if school dropouts continue to rise, those concerned with retraining will be confronted with a sorry state of affairs. The problems of retraining might be compounded to such a point that the prospects for success would appear very dim indeed.

In Brentwood, New York, an interesting experiment has been under way for the past few years. The objective of the experiment is to prepare youth for fruitful careers in an era of technological change. Its approach focuses on the high school dropout, and counseling plays a major role in accomplishing the resolution of this problem. Since the beginning of the program, the Brentwood solution has become a model of its kind of educational approach.

The school counselors in Brentwood have set as their objective providing guidance for youngsters in the third grade. Thereafter, guidance counselors endeavor to help students to make decisions which will be useful to them in finding work that is truly satisfying and in keeping with their individual abilities, aptitudes, needs, and interest. According to Gerald Smith, guidance director for the Brentwood school system, the most crucial time for counseling is the transition from elementary school to junior high school. Close attention is given to working with individual students who are thinking about dropping out. Talks center on the student's background and his abilities. A concentrated effort is made to determine what areas the student may have a feeling for.

If the student decides to drop out, the counselor usually recommends three or four private vocational schools. As soon as the student enrolls, Brentwood counselors are notified; and when the student completes his course and is placed in a job, his Brentwood counselor writes to him and urges him to complete his high school credits in evening school. But long before all of these things become reality, the educational staff works

[7]"The Hard Realities of Training," *Fortune,* July 1961, p. 246.
[8]"We Waste a Million Kids a Year," *Saturday Evening Post,* March 10, 1962, pp. 15-22.

diligently in locating part-time jobs for seniors, sponsoring career talks by business and industrial people, conducting guidance seminars and occupation courses, and using new classroom techniques which make learning more exciting and meaningful for young people.

THE IMPORTANCE OF RETRAINING

The decision to retrain manpower must be based upon sound program planning, design, implementation, and evaluation. Each of these steps require considerable time and effort of those who have recognized and accepted the fact that retraining is a continuing commitment if our society and way of life is to be perpetuated and improved upon.

Peter Drucker has said: "Even the impact of automation on the totally unskilled worker on the assembly line might have been alleviated had business thought of training and placing people at the time it started designing the new equipment."[9] What Drucker says makes sense. In terms of retraining, it is important that careful consideration be given to the plans initiated by top management personnel. An underlying assumption behind this statement is the belief that top management planning sets the stage for monetary expenditures and technological innovation in our business and industrial society. Unfortunately, in the past many training directors, legislators, and professional educators have not been aware of the pulse of top management thinking. The other side of the coin is that some top management people have not kept themselves well informed of government legislation affecting the employment and training of manpower—for example, the Fair Employment Practices Act and the Manpower Development and Training Act of 1962—and educational discoveries and innovations occurring at various levels of education in private as well as public schools.

Certainly these matters should have a direct effect on personnel development activities from the beginning of an individual's association with an organization and throughout his work career. What is proposed is greater, more intensive planning to answer the question "What must be done to prepare manpower to achieve long-range business and industrial objectives that have been established while at the same time helping individuals to experience personal growth and self-realization?" The highest degree of cooperation and commitment to this task is a prerequisite to the success of retraining. A proper starting point would be establishment of personnel

[9]Peter F. Drucker, "Big Business and the National Purpose," *Harvard Business Review*, March-April 1962, p. 52.

development planning groups within business and industrial organizations. Beyond this, it would be desirable to set up local, regional, and national planning groups which would resolve such problems as geographical movement and job placement of manpower. To some degree, this is already being done. However, much broader and more thorough planning and cooperation is needed.

Once a decision has been made to retrain manpower, effectively designed programs must be developed. Past experience reveals that those associated with this phase of retraining have not given proper attention to the fundamental considerations required to meet the needs of adult learners. There is too much work in retraining program design which smacks of pedagogical theory of a lecture, textbook, homework, and graded-assignment nature. Outmoded theories and concepts must be discarded in view of the research that has been compiled on adult learners. For this reason alone, it is desirable to have industrial and business training directors more intimately involved in program design work. And in the process, educators who represent institutions of learning outside the mainstream of business and industrial work will have to develop a greater degree of flexibility in devising curricula and methods of instruction which are more in keeping with the meeting of adult learner needs.

Although sound planning may take place and adequate retraining programs are designed, workers must be located in vocationally productive work. In the past, serious difficulties have become apparent in the placement of workers, either because of nonexistent work opportunities or because of regional attitudes toward minority groups. Because of these circumstances, those who are involved in the selection and placement of personnel must endeavor to examine and forecast accurately the potential marketability of newly developed skills acquired through retraining. Coupled with this, must be a desire on the part of employers to fulfill their legal and moral obligations in hiring people of diverse backgrounds. In a real sense, this can only serve to establish the democratic principle as a practical, working asset which serves our society.

There is much yet that needs to be known about retraining successes and failures. As we continue to become more enlightened about these matters, our efforts will become less compromised. In contributing to the growing fund of research data, we have taken a forward step. But only if we react to what research tells us. At times, the evidence may not be to our individual likings—but, after all, the good researcher searches not only for what he wants to find but for that which is really there. Research in the area of retraining offers us a golden opportunity to examine some fundamental assumptions on which we operate in relationship to our fellow men. If we use the opportunity wisely and treat new facts with a sense of objectivity, we will have accomplished an important mission.

This mission is based upon the recognition that continuous educational opportunity to learn and to work productively is an inherent right of citizens in an open society, and indeed to men everywhere. And so long as any person is denied these opportunities, we will have failed in our mission. In the final analysis, training is basic to everything that we do. It is perhaps the only field of endeavor without which a civilization cannot endure. True, we will have to amass the best human, technical, and financial resources to cope with it. It will require that each of us become active participants and masters in planning, executing, and evaluating sound training for all levels and for children as well as our adult population. The future strength and survival of our civilization will bear testimony to what we have done.

BROAD-BASED RETRAINING: AN APPROACH TO SKILLS AND KNOWLEDGE OBSOLESCENCE •

A. D. KELLNER
and
H. C. LAPARO

THE TWO WORDS WHICH are most characteristic of today's electronic industry are "growth" and "change." However, the same technological advances which are providing the wherewithal for new markets and products are also causing one of the industry's most perplexing problems—the obsolescence of employee skills and knowledge.

The dimensions of the problem of technological obsolescence in the electronic industry are such that they can readily excite the imagination and ingenuity of anyone involved in manpower planning or industrial education. First and foremost, the impact of technological advancements is being felt by all segments of the work force—from the production worker through the engineering ranks on up to the top executives.

Further, changes in equipment, processes, and products are bringing about corresponding changes in existing job requirements, as well as substantially increasing the demand for personnel qualified to fill the many new positions continually being created through the process of technological change. Another interesting and significant aspect of the overall problem

A. D. KELLNER is Director, Personnel Planning, Development and Training, and H. C. LAPARO is Manager of Training and Education, ITT Federal Laboratories, Nutley, New Jersey.

is the decreasing time span between technological innovations and their actual application and utilization. The human side of the problem involves, in addition to the individual employee's ability and desire to keep abreast of changes in his job, the difficulty of teaching new skills and knowledge to employees whose age or educational background are not equal to them.

In bringing the retraining picture into sharper focus, it is necessary, not only to consider the implications of technological advancements, but to do so in the light of the company's short- and long-range business plans and programs. Our experience indicates that a meaningful and effective retraining effort is essentially the melding of the company's business forecast and manpower forecast to provide a solid and realistic foundation on which long-range educational and developmental programs can be planned. Such an approach avoids the "working in a vacuum" feeling that often plagues manpower planners.

It also is apparent that for most segments of the work force, retraining has to be thought of as a long-range proposition. To date, retraining has been considered mainly within the framework of vocational, apprentice type of training aimed toward reshaping of specialized skills. Up until now, short intensive retraining programs have proved effective primarily with select categories of hourly production employees. In contrast, retraining at ITT Federal Laboratories is set up on a broader basis, covering hourly, technical, professional, and managerial people. In addition to its breadth, the scope of the program is extensive in time, with its basis in the long-range business plans of the organization.

GUIDELINES FOR RETRAINING AT ITTFL

Against this background of long-range company objectives, the retraining effort at ITT Federal Laboratories is based on the following guidelines:
1. Technological change is directly affecting the entire work force.
2. Technological advancements are and will continue to be a way of life in the electronics industry and changes in equipments, processes, and procedures the order of the day.
3. Manpower planning must be an integral part of the business forecast.
4. The individual employee bears a substantial portion of the responsibility for his own career development (retraining in a broader context).
5. The company must maintain training and development programs which will encourage and permit employees to develop to their

capacity in light of the company's current and future manning requirements.

6. The guidance and direction for an employee's career development must come primarily from the employee's immediate supervisor, with staff advice available when necessary.

7. The company must maintain a work force capable of meeting the requirements imposed upon it by the customer, as well as the changing state of the art.

"Retraining," like so many other words, can have a number of different meanings, depending on the general orientation of the person using it. At ITTFL, retraining is basically viewed as "a continuing process of employee development aimed at keeping the work force abreast of current or anticipated changes in the skills or knowledge requirements in their job." Unfortunately, the word "retraining," in and of itself, does not carry with it a feeling of time dimension. We find it more meaningful to use the term "career development," inasmuch as the word seems to express better the idea that training is a continuing process as well as an integral part of the employee's occupational career. Our objective, basically, is to effect guided changes in employees' capabilities over a period of time. This orientation is perhaps influenced by the highly technical nature of the work of our organization.

Our experience to date indicates that in planning and developing broad-gauge retraining or career development programs, it is desirable and necessary to define in concrete terms as many of those factors as possible that directly inhibit or enhance the job performance abilities of employees. Also, in our approach we place emphasis on a limited number of well-defined, long-range, career-development programs with only occasional, highly selective short courses aimed at meeting near-term objectives. In carrying out the longer-range programs, we have tried to keep them sufficiently flexible so that they can be modified to accommodate new or changing conditions. Basically, ITTFL's retraining efforts fall into two somewhat distinct areas of application: (1) on-job training and (2) off-job training.

ON-JOB TRAINING

It is felt that in ITTFL, as well as in other organizations, on-job training has tremendous potential for improving employee capability. Here the supervisor is the key man, since he is in a position to exercise direct control over both the employee's activities and his work environment. It's simply a matter of multiplication of effort. No training department is large enough to direct individual attention to all employees; yet by working through the supervisors—training the trainers in effect—a great deal can be accomplished in the way of employee growth and development.

Unfortunately, however, too many supervisors are unconvinced of the benefits that can be derived through planned on-the-job training of their employees. Even among those supervisors who do recognize on-the-job training as an excellent way of accelerating and enhancing the development of their people, there are many who, for what they feel are good and valid reasons, prefer to steer clear of on-the-job training. When the concept of career development was first being introduced at ITTFL, many people in management expressed the thought that it was more practical and efficient for employees to learn new skills and knowledge in a formal classroom situation than on the job. In essence, they readily recognized and accepted the need for employee training, but they were reluctant to have it become an integral part of the work situation, feeling that it might impinge on work output and efficiency.

To create a more fertile climate for employee development, particularly in regard to on-the-job training, a general orientation program was conducted to acquaint all levels of management with the advantages as well as the techniques and mechanics of career development. In bringing home the need for career development, a concerted effort was made to show tangibly its direct relationship to the continued well-being and success of the organization in a changing technical climate. During the orientation period, continual and intensive use was made of the various in-house communication media, such as management newsletters, feature articles in the company publication, and management meetings.

An important part of career development at ITTFL is the use of employee appraisals. In spite of the recognized inherent limitations in the performance appraisal technique, it has proved useful in this organization, perhaps at least partly because separate forms have been developed for major job categories (technician, engineer, manager, and so on). This characteristic highlights job *results* in relatively concrete terms. Perhaps more important as far as career development is concerned is that in addition to immediate job performance improvement, the appraisals focus attention on long-range developmental needs. Evaluations are made of the employee's long-term potential and the activities and developmental actions needed to help him reach it.

Many of the recommended developmental actions, of course, are off the job in nature. However, numerous job-centered activities are brought into play, including job coaching, committee work and special assignments, and temporary replacement of the superior.

The point has been made to our managers that coaching occurs whenever the supervisor discusses performance with a subordinate. Job coaching is based on close contact between manager and boss. It involves the important factor of feedback—the employee learns which aspects of his behavior are producing good results and which behavior is inappropriate. Also, through careful coaching, the boss can help the manager to expand his knowledge and the scope of his behavior, particularly moving into new areas such as the retraining requirements of the organization.

The basic purpose of committee work and special assignments is to provide some new and enlightening experiences to the manager which will contribute to his total growth. We find that to create a worthwhile developmental situation, the objectives of the committee work or special assignment must be clearly delineated and some sort of control must be set up to measure achievement. The primary concern is with the method the man employs to perform the activity which will help him contribute to his total growth.

Assignment to a superior's position during vacation periods, illness, or absence for other reasons gives the incumbent an opportunity to "spread his wings" on a relatively protected basis. He gains some insights into the activities and problems at the next higher echelon and can look beyond his own job into some of his collateral functions.

These, just briefly, are a few of the many specific actions which can be taken in the immediate work situation and which are encouraged within ITTFL. Basically, job-oriented activities such as these broaden the scope of the man's experience, stress his capabilities in new areas, and give him a chance to "learn by doing" under guided circumstances. On-job retraining allows the supervisor to "test the man's limits" and to provide him with new experiences which will develop his self-concept along desirable lines.

It's a good deal easier to cite the values of on-job training than it is to get line supervision to accept and use it. This is largely due to the fact that the criterion used in evaluating the supervisor's performance (immediate production—short-range goal) and the objective of on-job training (employee development—long-range goal) are completely out of phase with one another. Further, on-job training frequently means adding even more to an already heavy workload. Therefore, the major roadblock in setting up a climate conducive to carrying out on-job training is overcoming this natural resistance on the part of line supervision. Our experience indicates that this can be done by convincing supervisors that on-job training is a necessary long-term investment with a corresponding long-range payoff.

OFF-JOB TRAINING

The other half of the career development or retraining coin consists of off-job training and education programs. As might be expected, this type of training takes up where on-job development activities leave off. Within reason, all off-job training programs are designed with the idea in mind that the employee should have as much interest as the company has in his own self-development.

Again, as with on-job developmental experiences, off-job training programs lack meaning and direction unless the immediate supervisor is directly involved in determining the purpose of the employee's participation. In recognition of this, the administrative procedures are such that an employee can participate only after his immediate supervisor has approved his participation and has indicated in writing specifically how participation will improve the employee's current or future job performance.

Among the more productive and successful off-job training efforts at ITTFL are (1) an evening education program; (2) intensive daytime skills training; (3) tuition reimbursement and school leave programs; (4) a doctoral study program; and (5) off-premise courses, seminars, and conferences.

The evening education program. This program comes closest to incorporating the intent and objectives of ITTFL's retraining philosophy. This program operates much like a college evening extension program. Courses are given on a semester basis, meeting one or two evenings per week for two hours. Instructors are both company employees as well as faculty members from local universities and vocational schools. This program, which is composed almost entirely of job-oriented courses, has enjoyed by far the most spectacular growth of any of the off-job training efforts. In the fall of 1960, the evening education program had an offering of only six courses with an enrollment of just 87 employees. By the fall of 1963, it had grown to 57 courses and over 1,000 students.

The following are some of the inherent advantages in the evening education program that accrue to both the company and the employee:

1. The courses can be selected and structured to meet ITTFL's specific and immediate training needs.
2. Self-development opportunities are made available to all segments of the work force.
3. The employee has a vested interest in that he attends classes on his own time and pays for his own texts.
4. The sequence of courses can be developed to accommodate the long-range career goals of the employees (see Exhibit 1).
5. Adults can attend classes with other adults with similar backgrounds.
6. The need is minimized for the company to conduct costly on-hours training programs.
7. Attention is focused on those employees (instructors and students) who have a definite interest in their own self-development.

Employees from all levels of the organization are enrolled in the evening program. Clerical workers and building maintenance personnel can be found taking courses in the fundamentals of electricity, mechanics, and electronic circuits; engineers can be found attending classes on digital computer methods; and assembly-line supervisors can be found studying supervisory techniques. Several assembly-line wiremen, after completing electronics and mathematics courses at the evening school, applied for and passed company exams advancing them to technicians. A listing of courses from a recent catalog illustrates this scope of the evening education program (see Exhibit 2).

Intensive daytime skills training. These sessions are arranged for individual groups. In the fall of 1961, for example, we invited 11 middle-aged women whose rather simple assembly-line duties at our Clifton plant had been outmoded to attend a special electrical wiring course to prepare them for new, more skilled duties at the same plant. After three weeks of retraining, which included the reading of schematic diagrams, as well as proper soldering and wiring techniques, these "displaced" ladies were reassigned to assembly jobs, wiring components for the United States defense effort.

The doctoral study program. This program was instituted to enable those employees who had completed their course work in the evening to get time off during the day to complete their doctoral dissertations. After taking into consideration the many variables involved in meeting the doctoral degree requirements at local colleges and universities, it was decided to give employees the option of taking a leave of absence or taking time off.

PLANNING GUIDE FOR EVENING EDUCATION PROGRAM

How to use this guide:

1. Select the course in which you are interested.

2. Retrace all the flow lines coming up from other courses into the course you have selected. All courses connected to these flow lines are your prerequisites.

3. To know what courses are open to you, find the courses you have completed, then follow the flow lines leading up from those courses. The next courses connected by those lines may be taken next.

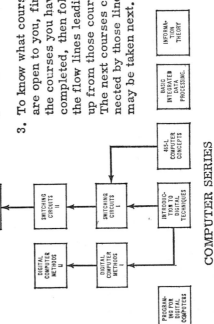

SUPPORT TECHNICAL SERIES

COMPUTER SERIES

EXHIBIT 1

COURSES IN EVENING EDUCATION PROGRAM

ENGINEERING AND ADMINISTRATIVE PROGRAM	SUPPORT-TECHNICAL PROGRAM

ENGINEERING AND ADMINISTRATIVE PROGRAM

COURSE INDEX

A — Supervision and Administration
B — Engineers
C — Secretaries

	Available To
Transistor and Vacuum-Tube Circuit Analysis	B
Electronic Circuit Micro-Miniaturization	B
Space-Age Astronomy	B
Classical Mechanics	B
Astrodynamics I	B
Astrodynamics II	B
Information Theory	B
Statistical Theory of Communication	B
Analog to Digital Conversion Systems II	B
Modulation Theory and Communication Systems Design II	B
Microwave Circuits	B
Parametric Amplifiers	B
Introduction to Digital Techniques	B
Switching Circuits I	B
Switching Circuits II	B
Computer Design	B
Numerical Analysis II	B
Differential & Integral Calculus II	B
Matrix Algebra	B
Engineering Statistics	B
Introduction to Transistor Electronics	B
Value Engineering and Analysis	B
Reliability and Maintainability I	B
Reliability and Maintainability II	B
Algol-Fortram Programing	B
Cobol Programing	A&B
Basic Integrated Data Processing	A&B
Basic Computer Programing	A&B
Department of Defense Specification Requirements	A&B
Government Contracts	A&B
Planning and Scheduling Techniques (CPM, PERT, LOB)	A&B
Business Application of Computers	A&B
Basic Electronics for Non-Technical Managerial Personnel	A&B
Scientific Russian Translation	A&B
Effective Writing	A&B
Speed Reading	A&B
Management Techniques	A&B
Basics of Supervision	A&B
Techniques of Interviewing	A&B
Advanced Secretarial Techniques	C

SUPPORT-TECHNICAL PROGRAM

Conducted in Cooperation with Essex County Vocational Schools

COURSE INDEX

D — Technicians, Testers
E — Clerical
F — Drafting
G — Shop
H — Inspectors
I — Maintenance

	Available To
Mathematics (Programed Learning)	D E F G H I
Basic Mechanics	D F
D-C Fundamentals	D E F G H I
A-C Fundamentals	D E F G H I
Electronic Fundamentals	D E F G H I
Transistors	D F H
Data Processing Concepts for Design Applications	F
Basics for Digital Computers	D F
Pulse Circuits and Wave Shaping	D
Schematic Diagram Reading	D E F G H I
Sheet Metal Fabrication	G
Quality Control	D E F G H I
Manufacturing Under A Government Surveillance System (MIL-Q-9858)	D G H
Foundry Practice	F G H
Soldering, Wiring, and Assembly	D E F G H I

"An investment in knowledge pays the best dividends."

—Franklin

EXHIBIT 2

Under the leave-of-absence plan, educational leaves of absence are granted for one academic year. During this period, the employee receives three-fourths of his base salary up to a maximum of $10,000. Under the time-off plan, time off is granted up to a maximum of 16 hours per week for four academic semesters, with the employee receiving full pay for the first eight hours of each week. Under both plans, the employee is reimbursed for all tuition costs.

The growing importance of the doctoral study program as a means of developing high-caliber technical personnel within the organization is dramatically pointed up by the fact that there are now approximately 25 employees working toward their doctoral degrees. In addition, it enables the 60 employees who earned master's degrees under the company tuition-reimbursement program during the last two years to realign their self-development sights to include a doctoral degree.

These off-job training programs have one characteristic in common—they involve a heavy time and effort commitment on the part of the individual employee in his own self-development. The high rate of participation in these programs would indicate a correspondingly high degree of interest among employees in their self-development. These programs represent a pool of development resources which can be drawn upon by each employee according to his own individual career development requirements and aspirations.

RETRAINING IN A CHANGING BUSINESS WORLD

It is evident that our economy is currently going through a manpower revolution. Senate hearings on this topic conducted in 1963 developed a wealth of material relating to the changing economic patterns and the resultant manpower problems we are facing. In the defense industry, particularly, many changes lie ahead. Reduction in defense spending will undoubtedly mean that many firms currently involved in military-based work will have to realign their manpower capabilities to meet the requirements of the commercial market.

An important question on retraining which is continually being raised is "Retraining for what?" Industrial organizations are often in a better position than public agencies to answer this question. In essence, the problem is a matter of careful study of future trends in company objectives and the accompanying manpower needs. It has been possible in our operation to state with reasonable clarity the terminal objectives of our retraining programs. In short, it is easier to train persons already employed for specific company job assignments than to ascertain the receptivity of a broad labor market to a graduating group of community-trained workers. This being the case, it would be beneficial and feasible to develop a close relationship between those in government and industry who are directly involved in planning and implementing retraining programs. It seems that this purpose will be achieved as the implementation of the Manpower Development and Training Act is further extended to include selected, on-going retraining efforts in industry.

In conclusion, our experience to date at ITTFL would indicate that short-range crash programs are not the real answer to the retraining problem. Instead, long-range programs aimed toward broad upgrading of the work force in keeping with shifting patterns of manpower requirements appear more feasible.

SECTION II

Changes in Collective Bargaining

There have been a number of significant developments in collective bargaining. Many feel the pendulum in labor relations, having swung at one time toward management and at another toward organized labor, is now more evenly balanced between the two. Attempts at greater cooperation between the two are illustrated by year-round bargaining, progress-sharing plans, and other efforts to work together rather than pull in opposite directions.

THE OUTLOOK FOR UNIONS •

ROBERT J. DOOLAN

$\mathbf{F}$OR MANY YEARS NOW, management has been bewailing the power of labor unions. In the swelling ranks of organized labor, many have seen a very real danger of encroachment on management's right to manage and a threat to the effective operation of the free enterprise system, based as it is on the ability to produce goods and provide services at a reasonable profit.

On the surface, cold figures would seem to justify management's concern. From the time of the passage of the Wagner Act in 1935 up until 1950, union membership increased from roughly 3.5 million to 14 million people. From 1950 to the present time, it has increased to a total of not more than 17.5 million, or in summary there has been an increase in a period of 29 years of approximately 14 million members. At the same time, the nation's total nonfarm work force increased by more than 30 million to a current figure in excess of 61 million. Total work force doubled—union membership went up fourfold.

What these figures do not show, however, is an actual decline in the percentage of union membership to total nonagricultural employment since 1945; a necessary shift of organizing activity in the past two decades to industries and types of workers more difficult to unionize; a very substantial decline in the average number of employees eligible to vote in government-conducted union-representation elections; a significant decrease in the percentage of elections won by unions; and many organizing cam-

---

ROBERT J. DOOLAN is Vice President and Counsel, Stern's, New York, New York.

paigns in which the union has failed to obtain even enough employee support to warrant petitioning the proper government agency to conduct an election. The cold facts in these areas and the particularly unfavorable current trends are causing furrowed brows in informed labor circles.

In 1940, the National Labor Relations Board conducted 1,192 representation elections; the average number of employees eligible to vote in each of these elections was 495, and a union was victorious in 75 per cent of the cases. In 1950, there were 5,731 such elections, but there was only a comparatively modest increase in the total number of eligible voters and a decrease in the number of eligible voters per election to an average of 157; still, a union was victorious in 74 per cent of the cases. In fiscal 1960, there were 6,617 elections; yet despite the tremendous increase in the organizing potential, the total number of eligible voters was less than in 1940, the average number of eligible voters had declined to 76, and the percentage of elections won by a union had dropped to 58 per cent. Statistically, this 20-year story indicates a practical standstill in union growth; in terms of capitalizing on potential, it is a record that would dismay any large corporation.

Union membership as a percentage of the total nonfarm work force increased from 13.4 per cent in 1935 to a high point of 35.8 in 1945. By 1958, the percentage had declined to 33.7 per cent. The extent of union membership is now not more than 25 per cent of all nonfarm workers. Of course, some of this is attributable to automation and improved technology; some to the shrinking number of production workers, who represent about one-half of all union members; some to recessions; and some to high unemployment levels. Nevertheless, the trend is hardly an encouraging one for the union movement, and there are few indications of any marked reversal.

Unions have turned their attention to the organization of the workers engaged in pursuits other than "manual" or "blue collar"—that is, the sales clerks, office workers, engineers, technicians, and similar employees. There is good reason for this. According to data compiled by the U.S. Departments of Labor and Commerce, white-collar workers now represent about 45 per cent of a total work force estimated at 70 million people. Manual workers make up another 35 per cent; service workers, including those working in households, another 13 per cent; and farm workers, the remaining 7 per cent. Of the white-collar workers, approximately 25 per cent are professional and technical workers, another 25 per cent are in the ranks of management (whether as proprietors or as employees), about one-third are essentially in office clerical positions, and the remainder are engaged in one type of selling or another.

Taking this one step further, approximately 2.8 million of the nation's 31.5 million white-collar employees are unionized, but the rate of growth of unionization has been exceedingly slow. Of this 2.8 million, an estimated 370,000 are in the most prominent and the largest of the blue-collar unions: the Teamsters, the Steelworkers, the Automobile Workers, the Machinists, and the Electrical Workers (IBEW). These unions have a total membership of roughly 5.5 million, and of them the Steelworkers has the highest percentage of white-collar membership to total membership —11 per cent.

The largest white-collar unions are the Retail Clerks International Association, the American Federation of Musicians, the Brotherhood of Railway and Steamship Clerks, the Communications Workers of America, the United Federation of Postal Clerks, and the National Association of Letter Carriers. The largest and fastest growing of the unions which are fundamentally white collar is the Retail Clerks International Association, with an estimated total membership of 400,000; yet even here generalizations can be dangerous because much of this membership is in the food-chain industry, and many would dispute that this union is essentially white collar in nature.

These are just some of the facts and figures that point to the inescapable conclusion that unions have tough sledding ahead in their attempts to organize a larger portion of the work force. Now let us look at the major "why's" of the situation.

Department of Labor manpower projections show a "much faster" or "faster" increase of employment for the next decade in many areas of the economy: construction, finance, insurance, real estate, wholesale and retail trade, government services, and "other services." Manufacturing employment is projected as stabilized; and the mining, transportation, and public utilities industries are projected as subject to a "much slower" increase in employment. Of all these, construction, manufacturing, mining, transportation, and public utilities have a high incidence of unionization. This means that the service industries, largely white collar and the least unionized as well as the most resistant to unionization, are by and large in for the highest rate of growth in employment. Moreover, the total work force will have a higher percentage of women workers and part-time workers, both of which have been more difficult to unionize primarily because they are often working for reasons other than individual or family support.

Already employment in service industries well exceeds employment in production industries. This is especially noteworthy because white-collar unionization has grown at a snail's pace. Not more than 10 per cent of white-collar employees are unionized, and experience shows that given reasonably good personnel practices, reasonably good supervision, and a reasonably good working environment, they prefer to remain nonunion.

Moreover, unions have, on the whole, failed to change from the organizing appeals of the 1930's. These appeals dealt almost entirely with bread-and-butter matters and the protection of job security through seniority, grievance procedures, and so on. They found fertile soil in a general climate of unusual zeal for social reform, widespread distrust of employers, and management abuses of power. Today, however, such appeals will no longer do. Workers want something more, and unions must demonstrate that they can provide it or they are not likely to meet with any significant degree of success. (Of course, the passage of avowedly prolabor legislation might enable unions to gain successes through force, but this would require a change in the prevailing political climate.)

What is the "something more" that workers want? Unions must be able to show that (1) the collective bargaining process is not inconsistent with the preservation of individual rights and the recognition of individual worth, (2) there need be no loss of status because of being unionized (highly important to the white-collar worker), (3) the risk of violence or strikes is minimal, and (4) unionization will not endanger the health of the business. The still large number of nonunion production workers and the essentially blue-collar employees of low-wage service industries may not be too difficult to convince, but satisfying the doubts of professional, technical, clerical, and sales workers will be a huge order. This is clear from the fact that successful major organizational campaigns directed at insurance companies, banks, brokerage houses, central offices of large corporations, department stores, technical laboratories, and the like are such a rarity that they warrant headline treatment.

But let us suppose that labor is able to deliver on this monumental challenge. Let us assume that the total organizing appeal has been broadened to include this "something more" and that it can be supported by sound and persuasive reasoning; let us assume, too, that there has been brought into the fray on labor's side a large and dedicated corps of organizers of a markedly different type—men and women whom white-collar employees can consider "like one of us"; yet who can appeal to the nonunion production and blue-collar service industry workers.

Even with all this, would labor have a good enough package? It seems doubtful. For there still remain two vitally important considerations. In the first place, from the employees' point of view, even a union that can meet all these conditions has only removed some of the barriers to union membership. It must still answer the basic question, "What's in it for me?" And the answer, in a great many and probably the majority of cases, will be, "Little or nothing." Especially in the case of white-collar and technical employees, there is little in the way of financial gains or increased security that a union can offer to offset the identification with the company that such employees feel—and most managements have made it a point to see that they offer their employees as much as or more than unionized employees in similar organizations are receiving.

Moreover, from the union point of view, there are administrative and public relations considerations to weigh in the balance. A vast number of white-collar employees work in comparatively small offices, which are notoriously expensive and difficult to organize. Add to that the fact that unions must carefully assess, in terms of their overall objectives, the reaction of the public to strikes that cause serious inconvenience, and it becomes clear that the financial and public relations costs of any vigorous effort to organize white-collar and technical workers will frequently be greater than the gains that might be realized.

The union appeals of the 1930's and early 1940's were often angry and radical appeals. The union leader or organizer of that time worked in an atmosphere in which "employer" was a suspect word—the atmosphere of the labor spy, the sit-down strike, and recognition through violence. The "inevitability" of some marked degree of socialism was a subject of sobering concern to believers in the free enterprise system.

Today, the union organizer is talking to a far different audience. Management is fully as respected as labor, and to most of the audience, genuine economic hardship and the searing experiences of the great depression are matters of vicarious knowledge. But the labor excesses of the immediate postwar period, which did so much to assist the passage of the Taft-Hartley Law, and the labor abuses disclosed primarily by the McClellan Committee, which did so much to assist the passage of the Landrum-Griffin Law, are not vicarious matters to the bulk of workers. They are real, and even apart from specific provisions that are helpful to management, what they symbolize has hurt the cause of the labor organizer.

Moreover, few employers agree to the unionization of their workers without putting up a fight. This is in distinct contrast to the late 1930's and early 1940's, when a great many employers voluntarily recognized unions because they believed that unionization was inevitable and it would be better to secure mutually good relationships.

Why is the nonunion employer of today so different? Because through contacts with other employers, he hears again and again the same theme song: Avoid unionization, be as interested in the legitimate welfare of your employees as the unions presumably are, and spare yourself the interferences with operating freedom, the drain on executive time, and other onerous burdens that unionization imposes. Unfortunately for labor, there is much wisdom in this line of reasoning. All too often, union recognition has meant not "the securing of mutually good relationships" but undue militancy, being "grievanced to death," restrictions on output, "make-work," and strikes, sometimes in total disregard of the public interest or even of the interests of the employees involved. A quarter of a century has elapsed since the Wagner Act went on the books; yet labor has still to prove that it can really establish and enforce clear-cut jurisdictional lines, that it can make fully effective the code of ethical practices forced upon it by public opinion, and that it has matured sufficiently to realize that in many bargaining situations the demanding of "more, more, more" is no sound answer at all.

The Taft-Hartley Act is "equalizing" legislation. Under the Wagner Act, it was the declared public policy of the United States to foster unionization. In pursuance of this objective, the law gave workers protection against unfair or illegal employer conduct, but unions and their representatives could do little wrong. The Taft-Hartley Law changed this basic policy to the extent of letting employees decide, of their own free will, whether or not they want unionization. It established union as well as employer unfair labor practices; through what is known as the "extent of organization" doctrine, it prevented the National Labor Relations Board from decreeing voting units (classifications of employees eligible to vote in elections) that had little logic to support them; and it specifically provided for complete freedom for management to address employees, as long as what is said does not tend to coerce or to promise benefits for rejecting unionization.

The Landrum-Griffin Act of 1959 added one especially significant provision: It placed severe limitations on the extent to which a union can use the tactic of "organizational" or "recognitional" picketing to force recognition regardless of what the employees may think of the proposition.

These changes are based on the fundamental principle that unionization is to be decided by peaceful persuasion, not compulsion. Although they are designed to correct previous inequities, they are changes that, on balance, are proving beneficial to management.

Historically, unions whose jurisdictional interest has been primarily in white-collar workers—for example, the Offices Employees International Union and the Retail Clerks International Association—have believed their most solid organizing appeal to be the superior wage gains of blue-collar employees. This was true during the late thirties and the forties, but during the fifties, the picture changed sharply.

According to Census Bureau data, from 1939 to 1950, clerical and related workers improved their income by 111 per cent. Professional, technical, and related workers did only a trifle better. In the same period blue-collar workers improved their income by over 170 per cent. In contrast, between 1950 and 1958 both white-collar groups mentioned did better than the blue-collar employees. The white-collar percentages are 53.7 per cent and 46.5 per cent respectively, whereas blue-collar "operatives and kindred workers" went ahead 42.9 per cent and blue-collar "laborers" went ahead 34.4 per cent.

The implications of this development are clear. As AFL-CIO economist Everett Kassalow put it, "Conceivably labor market changes might reverse the trend of the past decade or so, but official forecasts of the demand for labor in the next decade and more do not support this possibility. From a purely tactical viewpoint, so far as relative economic conditions are concerned, it is probable that large numbers of white-collar workers were more ripe for unionism in the decade of the forties."

Probably the most meaningful development of all is the increased importance of the personnel function, through which more and more employers are demonstrating their view that there are better ways of serving the employees' interest than through collectively bargaining with a union.

With perfect honesty, a vast number of employers today can say to their employees: "Our personnel practices, including wages, hours, and employee benefits, are equal or superior to those of other employers, including unionized employers, offering similar kinds of work. We have a grievance procedure that assures every employee a fair and considerate hearing whenever he has a job problem or complaint or even a problem of a personal nature that affects his job. We never lay off or discharge a person without good cause; so you have as much job security as any union contract could give you. Under these circumstances, why should you assume the costs and other obligations of union membership? Why should you run the risks involved in unionization—risks of poor leadership or of picketing and strike duty?"

These are potent arguments, and in an increasing number of companies, a majority of the employees are reaching the conclusion that the continuance of their present relationship with management is preferable to placing their welfare in the hands of an organizing union.

The personnel or industrial relations function in industry has witnessed a vast growth during the past 45 years. World War I gave the function its first tremendous impetus; the growth of unionization and the social legislation of the thirties provided another push; and World War II provided still another. Then, too, there has been a growing sophistication in the science and art of management itself—a sophistication evidenced in many of our companies by more and better training, executive development programs, carefully conceived employee benefit programs, well-developed job classification plans, and so forth. These facts of our times are truly ominous for the union movement, because in direct contrast to earlier days, unionism is being counteracted on the ground that it represents for the employees themselves a needless and risky appendage.

No one can argue, of course, that union strength today is anything but great. There are many who believe that further legislation is needed to curb the "monopoly power" of some unions, which they consider the prime mover in our long-term inflationary spiral, and to outlaw union security clauses that require some form of compulsory union membership as a condition of employment. And there are many who are alarmed at the sheer might of some unions—the Teamsters and the AFL craft unions in particular—whose power derives from their control over absolutely essential work.

But labor has its problems, too, and they are far from small ones. On balance, when one considers the declining growth rate of unions and the organizing problems that they face, it seems clear that organized labor will be fighting an uphill battle just to hold on to its present degree of power, much less to expand it in the years ahead.

YEAR-ROUND BARGAINING •

I. The U.S. Steel Experience

R. HEATH LARRY

WHAT IS A HUMAN RELATIONS COMMITTEE? Essentially it's a name, people, a procedure, and an atmosphere. It's an effort to convert bargaining from what you might call "trial by combat" into an endless succession of public and private maneuvers. It is a private approach to problem solving in which there is an opportunity to apply reason and fact in continuous discussion away from the pressure of deadlines and without the continuous barrage of public propaganda which usually surrounds approaches to bargaining.

Its origin was in the disastrous experience which we shared with the Steel Workers in 1959 and 1960. I don't know if anybody ever learns much out of a strike except the simple fact that a strike doesn't settle much, but that's a great deal of learning. We did learn that much in 1959 and 1960. We also learned that we were going to have to find a different way, and we began to try to find it. We set up a human relations committee co-chaired by R. Conrad Cooper, executive vice president of personnel services for U.S. Steel, and David MacDonald, president of the Steel Workers.

Two coordinators were appointed representing both sides: Marvin Miller for the Steel Workers and myself for the companies. It was our task to try and organize and deal with the various problems which had been listed for attention by the committee plus any other problems which might come up from time to time. Small subcommittees made up of four or five people from each side were established. We did our best to pick from the companies and from the various areas in the union those men who had some

---

R. HEATH LARRY is Administrative Vice President—Personnel Services, United States Steel Corporation, Pittsburgh, Pennsylvania.

particular knowledge and competence in the field to be studied. Then we had the problem of getting together.

At the outset we did not, in setting ourselves up, involve ourselves with a third party. That decision wasn't reached out of a belief on either side that the public had no interest in the outcome of our endeavors but out of a belief that if we progressed in our relationship as we hoped we could, we would come as near to a fair accommodation of public interest as any third party actions or recommendations would. The decision not to have a third party was made not out of any disrespect for many of the well-known third parties, so-called neutrals who could be brought to mind, but out of a respect for our obligation to ourselves and to the institution of collective bargaining. We felt that if we could establish the necessary degree of understanding, mutual confidence, and respect on our own, it was clearly our responsibility to try.

We have now had two successful negotiations without a strike or even a threat of one. The first one, in 1962, was concluded before the date on which a reopening notice could have been served. The second and more recent one was not concluded until substantially after a notice could have been served. Both settlements contained provisions much more tolerable than the settlements of the previous 25 years, and this gives considerable hope to our decision not to include third parties.

There are essentially four ingredients necessary to the successful accomplishment of continuous discussion like this. The first two are almost inseparable. The first is a will, an attitude, a desire. The second is a mechanism or a procedure. The third is a competent staff, and the fourth is some flexibility in points of time. You can have the best mechanism in the world, and without the proper desire to make it work the mechanism is useless. By the same token, you can have the best attitude and the best will in the world, and if you don't have a mechanism through which to funnel the desire and the effort, the will is useless. We have them both.

The will. The first ingredient came from various sources. It couldn't help but come in some measure from the cataclysmic experiences of 1959 and 1960. It could not be entirely disassociated from some of the potential results in external areas which came about as a result of that experience.

There was also increasing evidence that unless something were done somewhere, the Government was going to do something, although it wasn't very clear what. It could have been in the direction of compulsory arbitration, it could have been in the direction of restructuring the parties involved, or it could have been something else. But there was a concern as to future

Government involvement, and while perhaps at one time the unions were less concerned over Government involvement than they are now, more and more they have come to the belief that the proper avenue is not that one because they may be gobbled up in the process. Their desire to preserve free collective bargaining is of itself a motivating desire to make collective bargaining operate more effectively than before.

The third possible source of the desire to cooperate this way is just simply a growing maturity. People do grow older and wiser from their experiences, and they begin to appreciate the necessity of giving due regard to the economic necessities of life. In an earlier time they might not have felt the necessity to do this. There grows an increasing belief that conflict is of itself not essential to progress and in fact may preclude it.

But whatever the basis for the origin of a real, sincere desire on the part of both the top management of the steel industry and the officers of the steel union, the will and the desire are the ultimate foundation for progress. If they die, disappear, or diminish at some point, the whole mechanism will serve very little purpose. I was much disturbed by a speech which suggested that we ought to require by law continuous year-round discussions. I can think of nothing more fruitless than telling two people who are mad at each other to get in a room to try to kiss and make up. It just won't happen that way. The motivation has got to come from within and not from law.

The procedure. This was the most difficult area of all as we began to work. After all, we had had 25 years of really slugging it out with each other; we had 25 years of experience in which every time somebody split an infinitive or dropped a hint he was forever bound to whatever he had said, and there was no retraction from position. It was publicized and there you stayed. When these subcommittees were organized, it wasn't easy to get what you would call "objective discussion" going. Tradition is pretty hard to overcome quickly.

But little by little we have evolved a few ground rules, one of which is that we aren't going to do anything in the way of researching, reaching conclusions, putting out reports, making minutes, or anything else unless we do it by mutual agreement. That doesn't mean we agree on everything. I wouldn't want anybody to conclude that because we engage in this kind of thing, the institutional robes of both parties have been chucked off and the origins of differences of view, different conceptions of fact, different philosophies have gone. However, if you take a couple of rough objects and rub them together long enough, their edges will tend to smooth down. That's what's going on in our upper tier.

We decided that no matter what it was, whether it was research into fact or a determination to use a particular approach in studying the circumstances relating to a problem, we would do it by agreement. This kept both parties from having a free hunting license. It was frustrating to both of us from time to time, but a little experience proved that we weren't going to make real progress unless we worked that way.

The second thing we concluded was that there could be no record and no publication. Whatever we said could have no relevance either to future formal bargaining or to the grievance and arbitration settlements between the parties which had to go on because if it did we would be back in the old framework again, with everybody afraid to open his mouth for fear that he would prejudice some future position. This was the hardest thing to do because tradition had taught us that we would be tripped up by our mistakes or misstatements.

But we moved along with that concept, found its utility, and added another procedural understanding: that anybody can say today that his firm conviction of the right answer or the fact is thus and so and ten minutes, a half hour, a day, or a month later deny that he ever said it, if that is his desire, without being accused of bad faith.

Often in the course of some of our efforts to evolve recommendations concerning changes in our seniority program, our supplementary unemployment benefits programs, or our extended vacation programs, the union was on this side, the company on the other, and a month later it was just the opposite. It happened time and time again that both of us found out that the things we absolutely knew to be true had no foundation. We would finally decide on something which was often quite different from what either of us thought to be the right and the only sure answer to start with.

A competent staff. The third requisite is staff, staff for the union as well as staff for the company. In this respect the Steel Workers are quite fortunate because they have, probably not as many as they wish they had, but a sizable group of very sophisticated, very well-educated, very sound people. That doesn't mean I always find myself in total agreement with them or they with me, but it does mean that when we are attempting to engage in a disposition of something in the process of reasoning and in the process of understanding the surrounding circumstances and the facts, we're talking to somebody that can respond on the same basis; and all of us have had occasional instances where experience has not justified that kind of observation.

Flexibility of time. We originally had fallen into the pattern of a three-year agreement with a fixed termination date. When the date came, you were through. If you didn't have the job done, that was all, at least so it seemed, because the tradition was that way. We began to move away from that toward a flexible reopening date. Someone described it as an "Ivory Soap" termination: it floats. It doesn't have to be observed on the dates that the notice can be given. That's all to the good. In 1963 we knew we were making progress. We also knew we would be totally unable to make the progress which we needed to make by the time the notice could first be served. But in an atmosphere in which we were both conscious of some progress being made, it became wholly unnecessary to serve the notice.

It is essential when someone attempts to engage in an off-the-record, slow-moving way with complex problems, bringing some intelligence and experience to them, that they untether themselves from absolute deadlines in terms of an agreement.

II. The U.S. Rubber Experience

CHARLES H. PARCELLS

Y EAR-ROUND BARGAINING IS not the answer to all the problems that exist between labor and management. There is a basic diversity of interests which prevents this. This type of bargaining can, however, permit solutions to many problems that normally cannot be resolved during the heat of contract negotiations. There is a certain rigidness that surrounds contract negotiations that does not permit free discussion. The wrong word at the wrong time may lead people to believe that there is something to

CHARLES H. PARCELLS is Assistant Director of Industrial Relations, United States Rubber Company, New York, New York.

come that is not going to come at all. For this reason we must carefully phrase each statement we make. The free discussion of any problem under these circumstances is considerably hampered.

For the last 25 years, U.S. Rubber has indulged in a practice which, while it does not resemble in magnitude of activity the Human Relations Committee of U.S. Steel, is akin in some respects to it. We have conducted meetings with the United Rubber Workers. Since we are made up of a number of divisions—tires, footwear, mechanical goods, and chemicals— we arrange a meeting of presidents of the local unions for each of the plants in that division, one or two other representatives, international union representatives, people from our corporate staff, personnel people in the plant, sometimes a production manager of the division, and sometimes even the vice president in charge of the division. And we discuss the problems facing that particular division.

These meetings generally last for three days, and the subjects discussed are of varying nature. The first day the company presents to the union the problems that it seeks to solve. Part of the second day is devoted to the same subjects, but perhaps then the union has a complaint about employee policy or practice of the company. The third day we try and reach some solution of both union and company problems. We never lose anything in one of these meetings, and frequently we accomplish things.

People who normally do not attend contract negotiations with union people are often amazed at the quiet, reasonable approach that union people take to problems under these circumstances. It is a little alarming because some of the vice presidents go away wondering why we can't get along with such reasonable people.

It is this experience and an appraisal of the U.S. Steel Company's efforts that led U.S. Rubber to agree to a joint study committee in our last contract negotiations. This joint study committee will be comprised of not more than four members from the company and four from the union. There may be fewer. We anticipate that we will appoint three.

Under the agreement the committee is to study *only problems referred to it by the parties*. The committee has no authority to bargain, and any recommendations that it makes to the parties are to be considered confidential.

We believe that unless something is done to prevent the major conflicts that have occurred in the past, we will face Government intervention. Many unions share this fear and agree that we should try to avoid such intervention if we can.

III. The Alan Wood Experience

ROBERT F. GROVES

Alan wood steel company is an integrated steel producer with two iron ore mines located in New Jersey and primary production facilities and rolling mills located in Conshohocken, Pennsylvania.

Our primary production facilities consist of a coke plant, a sintering plant, two blast furnaces, and nine open hearth furnaces. Our product is flat-rolled carbon steel, and we produce to various specifications on our blooming mill, 110-inch plate mill, hot strip mill, and cold strip mill.

We also have these three subsidiary operations:

1. An iron powder plant (molding powder for pressure castings).
2. A small fabricating unit producing steel lockers, cabinets, adjustable shelving, and allied items.
3. The Upper Merion and Plymouth Railroad serving the steel works and neighboring industries with 17 miles of main line track—and a rapidly growing piggyback terminal service.

The production and maintenance employees of the steel operations in Conshohocken are represented by the United Steel Workers of America. This bargaining unit has existed since the company voluntarily recognized the union in 1937. It averages about 2,000 employees, but we have rather wide fluctuations which ride with the business volume. Our production and maintenance employees at the mines and iron powder plant are also represented by the United Steel Workers. We do not have any clerical or technical units among our 750 salaried personnel.

Robert F. Groves is Personnel Director, Alan Wood Steel Company, Conshohocken, Pennsylvania.

Essentially, the company has enjoyed good labor relations over the years. This was clearly reflected in our labor contracts, which we considered economically competitive and not excessively restrictive. The last time the bargaining-unit employees struck the operation was in 1946. This strike coincided with a general industry strike. However, there has not been a work stoppage connected with labor contract negotiations since that time, and we seldom have unauthorized or wildcat interruptions.

This record, which is favorable compared with the industry in general, is explained by the following:

1. Alan Wood represents less than 1 per cent of the steel producing capacity in this country. Therefore, economic action on the part of the international union brings absolutely no pressure on the industry and very little pressure on the consuming industries or general public.

2. We have been able to settle our local issues prior to contract termination dates, leaving only the economic issues which the local union and the international would not want to settle prior to agreement with the major companies in the industry. In other words, in most instances a strike against Alan Wood would produce no effective result for the international union or local employees unless we were not willing to follow the basic steel patterns.

3. For many years the company had contract termination dates which lagged several months behind the contract dates of the major companies. Over the years, however, this was gradually whittled down, and in 1959 this date was brought into line with most of the agreements in the industry.

Our contract contains most of the provisions found in the basic steel agreements although we do not have the "2-B Clause," and we have some major variations in our incentive plan administration, pensions, and seniority provisions.

You might logically conclude that we had no apparent need for a human relations committee since our policy was generally to follow patterns developed in the industry. However, in 1962 we went into negotiations on local issues with several very serious problems. Among these were incentive plan practices, seniority units, scheduling, and a serious backlog of grievances.

The union proposal on incentives was in effect a demand for incentive plan administration paralleling that of the major companies, and we felt these provisions were not practical for our operations. The proposal on seniority units involved a demand to consolidate some separate maintenance units which had only one year previously been split off from our central maintenance unit to provide specialized coverage for our new mills. The matter of scheduling was also a serious problem because the effort was to restrict our freedom to change schedules once they were established. Such restrictions would have adversely affected our ability to maintain delivery promises to customers. The problem on the grievance procedure was perhaps generated by company actions in our effort to streamline the procedure and eliminate the backlog of grievances that had been allowed to accumulate over the years and yet had not been moved to arbitration.

All of these issues required careful study, and the officers of the company were prepared to take strong positions on all of them. We were also influenced to a great extent by the fact that we were in the midst of our second consecutive year of red-ink operations, and the cost of a strike would not have hurt us appreciably.

At this point, however, the major steel companies reached a contract settlement well in advance of the 1962 contract termination dates, admittedly putting heavy pressure on the Alan Wood bargaining situation from a competitive standpoint. It was with this situation facing us that we decided to discuss the activities of the Human Relations Committee that had been organized by the union and the major steel producers in 1960. It was with great doubt and many misgivings that our local union finally agreed to organize a local human relations committee at Alan Wood and set forth the approach as part of our 1962 contract settlement.

The critical issues previously mentioned were placed on the agenda as the initial assignment for the committee. It was to be the task to study these issues and come up with solutions within a one-year period. Although it took both parties off the hook temporarily, we knew we would be facing the same problems the following year if our committee was not successful.

The philosophy and ground rules behind our Human Relations Committee were spelled out in broad terms in a separate section of our 1962 agreement. It was our intent to keep the committee organization as informal as possible but provide clear objectives. Some of the general provisions of this section of the contract include the following:

1. The objective of the committee is to further the good relationship between the parties and to avoid to the extent possible the critical situations which may otherwise develop if major problems are held in abeyance and handled through normal contract negotiations.

2. The function of the committee is to study specific problems which

are assigned as a result of mutual agreement between the parties and to make joint recommendations for the solution of such problems.

3. Only matters of substantial importance are referred to the committee, and this group is not to be involved in handling routine grievance matters.

4. The committee may call upon specialists and technicians to assist on projects assigned.

5. Only those reports fully supported by all members of the committee and signed as a joint report are to be considered by the parties for further action.

6. The chairmanship of the committee is rotated with each regular member serving as chairman for a three-month period.

7. The committee has two regular meeting days each month, and special meetings may be called by the chairman as necessary. The committee may not meet unless all members or their alternates are present.

During the first critical year our committee came up with solutions to three of the four problems assigned. These solutions in the form of recommendations by the committee were incorporated into our contract in the course of our 1963 negotiations. Specifically, our studies brought to light that the industrial engineers and operating personnel had not been satisfied with our practices with regard to incentive compensation. We had always had considerable difficulty and loss of productivity when incentive plans were revised or when new units were placed into operation, and as a result we completely reversed the strong position we had originally taken on the union proposal and accepted the incentive provisions which generally prevail in the industry. These revised provisions may very well prove to be an advantage to the company, and we admit we were dead wrong in our original position.

We reached an effective compromise on the establishment of maintenance seniority units which met the objectives of both parties. The seniority-unit problem was for the most part worked out by our operating superintendents, who met with the committee on this particular subject. The other solution obtained was with regard to streamlining the grievance procedure. A task force was organized by the committee to review all pending grievances, and as a result the backlog of some 450 grievances was reduced to approximately 100, all of which were reasonably current. Today we have approximately 50 grievances in process.

The one issue involving scheduling turned out to be much more difficult than we anticipated. After one year of study both parties have a good understanding of the problems and are not quite as rigid in their position. This subject was again referred to the committee for continued study.

Another subject before the committee at this time is profit sharing. During the past six months we have devoted a major part of our time to this study. Our studies with regard to profit sharing have brought our president and controller into the committee meetings on this subject, and we have also involved representatives of the international union who had specific experience in developing the Kaiser Sharing Program. It is difficult to predict the outcome of our studies with regard to a sharing program, but our progress so far clearly indicates a definite interest, and we have high hopes that the sharing concept will be developed at Alan Wood within the next year.

The term "year-round bargaining" is perhaps misleading. Our experience shows that we have spent much more time discussing these problems in committee sessions, but the same time would have been consumed in considering these problems if we had not had a human relations committee. We would simply have referred to it as "preparation for negotiations," and both parties would have prepared in their own way. The committee approach merely involves joint study and preparation. And even if it is true that we are spending more time, we are also doing a better job. Most important, we have an effective communication vehicle through the committee which is well worth the time spent.

These advance studies of problems or proposals have a tendency to limit the issues brought forth in contract negotiations. This is an advantage to both the company and the union and makes for smoother bargaining sessions and a more businesslike approach with both parties working toward more or less predetermined results.

One concern we do have with the future comes from the fact that committee activities, although not necessarily secret, are not generally discussed until the committee members have reached specific conclusions and have made their formal recommendations.

It has been the practice of our local union representatives to give a report to the membership each month on the activities of the committee, but these reports are so general and perhaps somewhat vague in nature that there exists among the membership some suspicion with regard to the committee activities at this point.

This could develop into a very serious problem. It might conceivably be an important contributing factor to the failure of this approach in the years ahead. We are working on this, but any regular reporting of committee activities which involved setting forth details of progress would be even more discouraging to the bargaining-unit employees. Many times we change our approach completely after spending considerable time. Without full knowledge of the facts or reasons behind such changes of position or opinion, it could very well appear that the committee is wasting time or is even incompetent.

At this point we are satisfied with the results, and we have developed confidence in our human relations committee. But it is far from a proven technique, and it will have to stand the test of time.

PROGRESS SHARING AT AMERICAN MOTORS •

I. The Background and the Planning

GEORGE E. GULLEN, JR.

THE AMERICAN MOTORS Profit Sharing Plan has gotten a great deal of publicity. Many people are curious to know the reason for it. It came about not as an accident of collective bargaining but as a direct result of a policy decision. We wanted it, we went after it, and we got it. This is not so strange because the profit sharing principle is not a new one. When we adopted it, we joined about 40,000 other American firms who have found it to be an important and valuable measure to take.

American Motors was the result of a merger between the Hudson Motor Car Company and the Nash Motor Car Company, a couple of struggling, independent automobile companies in an industry that's highly competitive. When these two companies came together in 1954, they found that though they were one of the smaller companies, their wages were higher than those of the big three, their working agreements were noncompetitive, their seniority provisions were almost ridiculous, their relief-time situation was

---

GEORGE E. GULLEN, JR. is Vice President—Industrial Relations, American Motors Corporation, Detroit, Michigan.

bad, and they were subject to what has been called "pattern plus"—that is, once a pattern is set in negotiations with the big companies, the little companies were expected by the international union to adopt it and add something to it. This resulted in more expensive benefit programs, higher wages, and noncompetitive agreements.

American Motors is also involved in the appliance business where prices are down and costs are up. Because we were also automobile producers, however, our appliance contracts were caught up in the automobile whirl: We were giving automobile benefits and increases in an appliance industry that couldn't stand it.

In 1954, when the merger took place, we came to the conclusion that there had to be some basic policy decisions if the company was going to be effective in these two highly competitive industries. These policy decisions had to be based upon objectives and not upon expediency. They had to be carried out from day to day, because it is in the day-to-day operations of the plant that we tend to give the plant away and change the contract we have negotiated. And we had to begin to interpret the objectives and policies for our employees. We found ourselves in a position where the union had taken over all but direct communication with the employees. It had become almost wrong for management to talk with its own people.

We had to make supervisors better personnel directors and to do a better job of keeping top management informed about the policies and the objectives that they had helped form and carry out. And we had to translate all this into a basic policy statement that could be communicated.

The president of the corporation wrote to Walter Reuther at that time, suggesting that the union had to wake up to the fact that American Motors was a different corporation in a big industry. We were not unwilling to be competitive with anybody else in the industry, he wrote, but we were unwilling to pay more for less.

All of these things were done in the light of some convictions about collective bargaining. One of them is that collective bargaining has been and is on trial. It is still viewed with suspicion by most of the parties to it. We believe, however, and want to make sure the union understands that collective bargaining has made a contribution and can continue to make a contribution. We have accepted it as part of the industrial relations process. We recognize the fact that there are some unlearned lessons. The company and the union can learn together and help each other. We feel that an adequate job is not being done. We recognize the fact that public tolerance of strikes is very low because it doesn't understand the strike situation.

We have to find a way to head off the kind of third-party intervention that we think is harmful to collective bargaining and find a way to come to conclusions ourselves.

We wanted to explain our motives and method of operation to the union and to sell it on the need for greater productivity. Employees had to begin to understand that costs could not continue to rise unless some consideration was given to productivity in our company. We wanted to find a way of recognizing that we had mutual goals. We weren't talking about the automobile industry: we were bargaining for American Motors.

Along with all this, we had some basic convictions about the collective bargaining process. We felt that there were stages that had to be recognized. The first stage is one of conflict and competition, where we are constantly competing with one another for the loyalty of the workers. The second stage is one of mutual accommodation where, while there are still power plays, we begin to understand that we have to live with the situation, and we do all we can to make it really work.

The last stage should be characterized by voluntary cooperation. People laugh at this sometimes, but it is based on the simple fact that we think there ought to be mutual respect for the rights of both parties and that these rights ought to be spelled out clearly. We ought to exercise our responsibilities in the most enlightened way that we can, and both parties should contribute to the total enterprise.

At American Motors, we like to think that our profit sharing program is a step toward this voluntary cooperation. We don't think we do everything better, but we think our basic policy considerations ought to help us.

In 1955, in the automobile negotiations, we broke out of the pattern-plus situation. We got away from all of the increases in the automobile industry. The unions were unwilling to roll back the gains of 30 years, but they did make it possible for us to cut our expenses by millions of dollars at a time when we needed to so desperately. In 1954, 1955, and 1956, we were in the unhealthy process of losing about $90 million. In 1958, we went at this thing on the same policy basis, and we managed to find a break in the appliance situation. We got the story across that something had to be done.

Our president had been talking about profit sharing since 1955. He called it "progress sharing," because he wanted to make sure the employee, the dealers, the stockholders, and the customers understood that we wanted to grow and that we wanted to grow by sharing our progress with everybody in some equitable manner.

The union wasn't interested in asking us for profit sharing in 1958 because we had just broken into the black for the first time. But in 1961 we pointed out that we were still not competitive in our seniority agreements or in our relief time, that our standard procedures were not good, and that our wages and benefits were about the same as those of the big three. We told them that we were willing to share our progress with them, but we wanted to be sure first that our managerial rights were clearly identified in our contracts. We wanted to cut down our relief time so as to get competitive with the automotive industry and to see that any increases in our benefit program were paid for out of profits. We wanted to set up what we called an American Motors-United Automobile Workers conference, so we could have continuing conversations away from the bargaining table. We wanted to meet not periodically, but regularly, to talk about matters that ought to be of mutual concern. And then, we wanted competitive working agreements in every way that we could get them.

Thus for the first time management was asking for something instead of waiting for the union to tell it what it was going to bargain about. We assured the union that we had no intent to break it with a progress or profit sharing program. This program was not designed to weaken the effectiveness of the union but, rather, to increase our mutual effectiveness by making our corporation a healthy one.

We have gone a long way toward our goal. We weren't completely successful, but we corrected our seniority provisions to make them competitive. We significantly improved our relief situation. We wrote a training concept into the contract to help relieve the seniority situation. People who are laid off now because they don't have the ability to do the job are given the opportunity to get training without paying extra money for it. The benefit concept of improving benefits only out of profits was accepted. The conference idea was put to work. The management's rights' clause was written, and we think it is a strong clause. Finally, our profit sharing program with the intangible motivational values that we attribute to it was adopted.

II. How the Plan Operates

ROBERT McCOY

THERE ONCE WAS A MAN named Wolfstrum who created a machine called "Wolfstrum's Wonder" that outdid all computers. It had wheels, belts, lights, and bells that all worked at the right signal. It was a beautiful thing to behold, but what did it do? There was the rub: It did nothing; it was just wheels, lights, belts, and bells.

This is *not* a description of our Progress Sharing Plan. It is *not* complicated, it doesn't have all those fancy wheels, lights, belts, and bells, and it's not fancy. But it *does do* something.

"Progress Sharing" is our own term. It describes our philosophy of distributing the rewards of superior teamwork among all the members of the American Motors family: customers, employees, suppliers, dealers, and owners. American Motors pioneered in our industries by producing the compact car and the "constant basic improvement" idea in appliances, and we feel that we have benefited from this pioneering. We are now pioneering in our industries by our plan for progress sharing, and we feel that we can benefit from this pioneering too.

Our plan provides basically that at the end of each fiscal year, depending on that year's profits, each employee receives two things: (1) more liberal employee benefits and (2) shares of American Motors stock, which are credited to his account and held in trust.

The basis for the growth of the Progress Sharing Fund is the profit from United States manufacturing operations before taxes and before any deductions for Progress Sharing. This does not include the earnings of Redisco, our finance subsidiary; profits or losses from the sale of real estate or from securities and investments; or earnings from foreign operations. These are things upon which employees have no impact.

For example, suppose that the base profit (as defined above) is $75

ROBERT McCOY is Manager of Personnel Services, American Motors Corporation, Detroit, Michigan.

million. Ten per cent of the adjusted net worth, which is the total net worth at the beginning of the fiscal year less the amount attributable to the company's stockholdings in Redisco and foreign companies, is deducted. Let us say that this net worth is $200 million; so we deduct $20 million. That leaves us with a balance of $55 million, which is the "Progress Sharing Fund Base." The company's independent certified public accountants determine all of these adjustments.

The company's contribution to the Progress Sharing Fund is an amount equal to 15 per cent of the Progress Sharing Fund Base or, in our example, about $8.25 million. This total amount is divided into two parts. Two-thirds of the total, or $5.5 million in our example, is designated for employee benefits, and one-third of the total, or about $2.75 million, is used for American Motors stock.

As regards the distribution of these funds, basically, there are two parts, *A* and *B*. Part *A* is two-thirds of each year's contribution by the company. This is available for maintaining present employee benefits; setting up reserves for the future payment of such benefits; and providing new or higher benefits. Part *B,* the other one-third of each year's contribution by the company is in the form of American Motors stock, which is credited to the employees' accounts and held in trust.

There are definite priorities on the use of the employee benefits. These priorities are specified in the plan as negotiated by the company and the union. They are as follows:

1. To meet the cost of pension plan improvements arising from the 1961 negotiations.
2. To meet certain costs of the group insurance plan.
3. To build up a reserve equal to twice the annual amounts needed for these pension and insurance costs.
4. To finance a "special account" reserve in the supplementary unemployment benefits trust fund.
5. To build up general reserves from which may flow new or increased employee benefits.

In case there are insufficient Part-*A* funds to meet the above pension and insurance costs, a portion of the annual improvement factor wage increase which is due in September of each year may be diverted, or the effective date of the annual improvement factor may be delayed, in order to pay such costs. Sufficient profits will make it unnecessary to divert or delay any part of the annual improvement factor wage increase.

Part *B* is credited to employees in terms of shares of American Motors stock and held in trust. The total shares of stock to be credited to all members of the plan is determined by dividing the company's contribution by the average daily selling price on the New York Stock Exchange during the period November 1 through 15. The fiscal year ends on September 30, which means we have a "high-low mean," a high quotation and a low quotation each day for those 15 days. The average of that becomes the average figure to be used in the computation. Each employee's part is figured this way: The total shares of the stock contributed are divided in half. One-half is credited to each person in proportion to his Progress Sharing Fund hours compared with the total Progress Sharing Fund hours of all participating employees for the fiscal year. In other words, this is his share of the total. The other half is credited to each employee in proportion to his Progress Sharing Fund compensation compared with the total Progress Sharing Fund compensation of all participating employees for the fiscal year.

This is basically a deferred security type of plan. Therefore, employees are encouraged to keep the American Motors stock credited to their accounts in the Part *B* fund as personal savings funds for themselves and their families. It is not a "get rich quick" or a "dart in and get your benefits and get out" kind of thing. It is, rather, a *security plan*. However, stock may be drawn out and cashed under the following conditions:

1. If a man retires, he collects all of his stock.
2. If he is laid off for one year and exhausts his unemployment compensation, he can collect his stock benefits.
3. If he dies, his beneficiary collects them.
4. If a man leaves for military service, he can collect them if he wants to.
5. If there is illness or disability in the family which is not covered by insurance, he can withdraw them.
6. If he quits or is discharged, he gets what he has built up in the fund.
7. If there are other reasons, he can request withdrawal through the committee. He then can withdraw upon that request that part of his account that has been credited more than two years before the request.

Basic decisions regarding the administration of the plan are made by the Joint Administrative Committee. This committee is made up of three American Motors Company representatives and three United Automobile Workers representatives. A Progress Sharing Plan Administration Department has been established by the company to place these decisions in effect.

Perhaps it would be meaningful to show the actual application of the provisions which have been discussed to the specific 1963 fiscal year at American Motors. In 1963 we started with a profit of $82,479,802 before taxes and Progress Sharing. We set aside 10 per cent of stockholders' investment, which was $20,827,411, leaving us a Progress Sharing Fund Base of $61,652,391. Fifteen per cent of that is $9,247,859, which was the Progress Sharing Fund. Two-thirds of that, or more than $6 million, went for benefits; and one-third, or a little more than $3 million, went for stock. This is the best demonstration of how Progress Sharing works at American Motors.

OPPORTUNITIES FOR GREATER COOPERATION BETWEEN LABOR AND MANAGEMENT •

ROBERT A. NEIMAN

L ABOR–MANAGEMENT BATTLES ARE more civilized these days than they were in the 1930's, and there are, of course, periods of truce and even a certain amount of cooperation; but, essentially, organized labor and management still think of themselves as opposing power blocs. This view is rooted in the history and tradition of a continuing struggle, with each side maneuvering for more and more leverage to pry its demands from the other. Both sides gather allies; both contend for the support of government at all levels; both put up a stiff fight for public sympathy. They are formidable opponents, drawn up on area and industry lines.

To keep pace with this struggle, an elaborate system of labor relations has been developed. The paraphernalia of labor relations—collective bargaining, grievance procedures, National Labor Relations Board regulations and practices, and an array of legislation—are all designed not only as means for labor and management to deal with each other, but as means of regulating and controlling their practices.

In theory, these mechanisms should insure peace on the industrial scene, but in reality recurring eruptions demonstrate their inadequacy. For example, they could not avert the crippling New York newspaper strike nor recent East and Gulf Coast port strikes. More important, they couldn't provide a real resolution of the issues at stake even when the strikes were settled at long last.

Efforts to refine and extend the means for conflict resolution are inherently limited in effectiveness. They are, first of all, founded on the

---

ROBERT A. NEIMAN is associated with Robert H. Schaffer & Associates, Stamford, Connecticut.

basic assumption that one side is trying to put something over on the other. Both parties are forced to defend their positions, to try to get as much as possible from each other. Within this framework, a solution of conflicts can be achieved only through give and take; and even though a "fair compromise" may be achieved, neither side is ever really satisfied. In other words, mechanisms for conflict resolution commit the parties to remain basically opponents. Such mechanisms offer no way out: Either one side or both sides must lose something if agreement is to be reached; or, if agreement is easily reached, both sides wonder if they shouldn't have demanded more.

Second, such mechanisms bring labor and management people together for the wrong reasons. Traditionally, unions and managements confront each other only on matters of differences between them: higher wages and benefits versus higher profits; promotion by seniority versus promotion by merit; more labor-saving machinery versus less; and so forth. The entire relationship is centered on problems, conflicts, one-sided demands.

MUTUALITY OF INTERESTS

Are there better ways to approach labor-management relations? Can progress for both sides be accelerated? Can less costly solutions be devised?

If we are to answer these questions affirmatively, I believe that we are going to have to rethink the fundamental labor-management relationship.

Fundamentally better solutions can be arrived at if the parties take as their point of departure the elements of shared common interest. Surely there can be no quarrel about the desirability of upgrading the productivity and economic value of human effort, serving and protecting consumer interests, improving communities, and developing new business and new jobs. In fact, labor and management have far more such shared purposes than is generally recognized. But because it is customary to concentrate on the narrow range of problems and difficulties, they have failed to see and explore opportunities for collaboration in pursuit of these aims. For the most part, such matters are simply excluded from the labor-management arena.

As these areas of shared interest are given more attention, problems and differences can become less thorny. We might well take as an example the interaction between citizen and government, which is characterized chiefly by collaborative effort, with the citizen contributing funds and the government, services. In the husband-wife relationship, too, differences and problems are usually handled within the wider context of mutual help.

If labor and management see each other only as opponents, it is natural enough that each side should come to regard the other as narrow-minded, combative, unrealistic, and selfish. In the setting of such hostile and suspicious feelings, the difficulty of solving tough economic and technical problems is going to be all the greater.

These obstacles are not only negative, but niggling. Broader interaction in situations where each side is called upon for constructive contributions might be an eye opener to them both. Working together in these broader kinds of relationships might breed better understanding of the particular problems and viewpoints of each faction and lead to more positive solutions of their differences.

New kinds of relationships between managements and unions are already emerging; and though only a few of them involve collaborative efforts, those few have been successful enough to warrant study and suggest further possibilities. For example, joint union-management committees have been set up in factories such as in those of the Firestone Tire & Rubber Company to deal with problems of safety. Other plants have formed joint union-management job evaluation committees. The creation of new jobs and the setting of rates and standards are plainly matters of dual interest and are being treated as such in still other companies. Joint committees, charged with the responsibility of defining jobs, have also been tried successfully.

A notable success story of this sort is told by a store manager who was facing mounting losses and saw that drastic changes in manning were needed. He anticipated union resistance; so rather than negotiate the changes, he turned the tables and asked the union people to help him find better ways to run the shop. They came up with several sound ideas—combining jobs, changing shift assignments, and the like. These changes put the store in the black; and at the same time the union members gained more job security, better pay, and a greater sense of their own value.

This was, of course, a small operation, but similar cooperation is possible on a much larger scale. Howard Coughlin, president of the

Office Employees International Union, illustrates the possibilities in this description* of the labor-management conferences in the Tennessee Valley Authority:

> The management of the Tennessee Valley Authority adopted a policy of close liaison with workers' representatives many years ago. These meetings of TVA management and members of the Office Employees International Union resulted in substantial savings, particularly by the elimination of wasteful operations. These changes were proposed by representatives of the workers, and, in addition, numerous ideas were presented by shop stewards which improved the efficiency of the day-to-day work of TVA.
>
> The TVA management is doing everything possible to expand this contact with its workers' representatives. In addition to annual valleywide labor-management conferences, there were 67 cooperative conferences in 1961 in Alabama, Kentucky, and Tennessee. Some meet monthly, some bimonthly, and a few quarterly. The size of the groups represented by these conferences ranges from 10 to 600 employees.
>
> All of the conferences have problem solving as a major item on the agenda. They cover ideas for making the plants more efficient, more attractive, and more comfortable places in which to work. In addition, improvements in communications, a review of accounting procedures, the possibility of lowering retail electric rates, and numerous other subjects of special interest to TVA are discussed.

United Mine Workers district presidents serve on the National Coal Policy Conference, working with representatives of the coal operators, railroads, mining-equipment manufacturers, and electric utilities to promote coal consumption. Similarly, the Amalgamated Clothing Workers of America's Southern California Joint Board has met with manufacturers to discuss mutual problems such as obsolescent machinery, training skilled workers, and promoting Southern California as a men's clothing market.

Unions can play an important role in facilitating, rather than resisting, major changes that management undertakes. An impressive example of this was the help the Chicago Typographical Union gave the Lerner Newspapers in carrying out a million-dollar improvement program. The change involved a major shift in technology, and the union, determined to protect its jurisdiction over all the innovations, arranged for training its members and supplying local instructors for in-plant training. This

---

* From Coughlin, Howard, "Labor Management Cooperation in the Automotive Age," in *"Manufacturing and the Challenge of Change,"* Management Bulletin 18, American Management Association, New York, 1962.

was certainly more than cooperation on the part of the union; it was a show of initiative that suggests the untapped potential of broader relationships.

An unusual labor agreement concluded some years back included the following provisions:

1. Increase gross output by 3 per cent over the previous year.
2. Increase output per worker by 4.8 per cent over that of the previous year.
3. Carry out the plan for increasing the guarantee on machine tools made in the plant from one year to one and a half years.
4. Put into production 13 new machines.
5. Complete plan for collection and shipment of scrap metal by the end of the year.

This agreement also covered plans for the development of competition, the introduction of progressive technology, and new training programs. It was broad in scope, setting out tasks and responsibilities for both management and workers in the areas of production, welfare, and even community activities.

An agreement like this is a far cry from the elaborate truce that the typical American labor contract amounts to. And for good reason: it was an agreement drawn up in 1958 at the Kiev Tool Works in the Ukraine. This does not mean that we should model American labor relations after Russian practice, but the agreement is, nevertheless, a significant document.

First, like American contracts, it suggests that the parties recognize mutual obligations and outlines steps each must take to carry out its responsibility under the agreement, but there is also a commitment to move in some direction. Compare this with a narrow settlement or truce with each side acceding to the other's demands only in return for a price. Second, the areas considered appropriate for discussion are far broader than in typical American contracts—including plant operation, which in this country is seen as the concern solely of management. The fundamental and most important difference though is that it is not a truce; it is a plan. It sets forth goals for accomplishment; it does not represent compromise and settlement of differences alone. It represents commitment for action, and the nature of that action is spelled out. This implies that labor and management should work together in planning and carrying out their shared aims.

BROADENING THE OBJECTIVES

While the processes of free interchange which we believe should attend joint goal setting don't exist in Russia, they are certainly present in the United States. So there is no reason, except for tradition, why many of the long hours of hard work devoted to bargaining cannot be more fruitfully used for planning the progress both sides want. And bargaining aside, there is no reason why joint planning for progress can't be an everyday activity.

Let's examine a hypothetical factory production department. How can the manager go about broadening the role of union men working in his shop? Must the worker be harnessed to his machine or, so far as extra effort goes, at most serve on grievance committees? I think not.

The manager might begin a serious effort to make broader demands on workers by interviewing them to get an idea of their willingness and ability to assume more responsibility for the performance of the department. He might ask, "What do you think is needed to make this place run better? What would you do to improve the quality of our products? How can we reduce waste?" More than likely, these questions will draw a surprising number of ideas and reveal a willingness to act that management is all too prone to overlook in the union ranks.

After surveying the ideas of his workers, the manager might next assemble people for action. Discussion will stimulate ideas, and group support will encourage individuals to act. The manager should have no trouble in making assignments to tackle improvements the workers believe they can and should make.

Managers who make more challenging demands of their employees boost morale in the process. The worker now has a useful role to play in conferences; he takes on responsibility for improving procedures, not just for following instructions. He now has a role to play in planning improvements in productivity, not just his old one of demanding more pay.

This does not mean that managers should hand all management responsibility over to workers. But most managers are convinced that workers should take far more responsibility for the work of the enterprise than they now do and hesitate to ask them only because tradition says that unionized people are just not interested. Managers *can,* more often than they seem to realize, make greater demands on workers. Enough of them will welcome the added responsibility to make the move rewarding all around.

There are opportunities for increased collaborative effort at many levels and in many functions. Engineers planning to install new machinery can let it be known that they expect union representatives to help plan the reassignments of operators. Training directors with the job of providing skilled workers for present and future operations can ask union help in selecting and training them. Personnel directors might go beyond haggling over provisions of benefit plans and set up long-range benefit and retirement planning groups, tapping both union and management people for help.

Just as fruitfully, unions might work with management in the area of consumer needs: Market research, trial of new products, and control and regulation of substandard products are all areas where the resources of unions might be combined productively with those of manufacturers. Unions and managements might work together in industrial development, too. Cooperating with state agencies, they can make a joint project of developing industrial parks to attract new kinds of industry into low-employment areas.

The burgeoning of year-round bargaining and problem-solving committees is another sign of hope. These committees have already gone a long way toward reducing tensions and have provided realistic machinery for dealing with the vast complexities of current contracts. The real test of these committees will come when the members begin to sense that they might go beyond just solving one problem after another and someone in a reflective mood sits back and says, "If we really put our minds to it, I wonder how far we could go toward . . ." Those who have the wit and courage to grasp the wisps of ideas that will inevitably come up in these sessions and coalesce them into concrete programs of action will make the real breakthroughs in labor-management relations.

The process of improving the relationship between unions and managements can be started at any point, from the top management level to the production floor. New ways of working together—ways designed to help each side make more rapid progress toward its goals—can be devised by anyone who sees the opportunity and elects to take the initiative in his own area of responsibility.

Step-by-step extension of these activities will gradually create the climate needed for expeditious as well as judicious settlement of differences. The mechanisms of conflict resolution can come into perspective, not as the sole meeting ground for unions and managements, but as essential elements in a much broader and more mature relationship.

SECTION III

The Special Problems of the Skilled Worker

The technological and office revolutions of the past few years have created a number of special problems in personnel. The scientist, the engineer, and the technician occupy an increasingly important position in many companies. The office is requiring a greater number of highly skilled employees. The growing importance of these workers is placing new demands on traditional personnel methods.

THE CHANGING WORK FORCE •

JOHN R. HINRICHS

ONE OF THE MOST COMPELLING FACTS of our time is that we are living in an era of rapid change. And in this fast-moving and complex world of technology, an uprooting and modification of traditional institutions has been going on almost unnoticed. Within the past few decades, entire industries and functions have been displaced to make room for such vast new fields as computer technology, aerospace, and television. Along with changes in the traditional institutions of our society, we have scarcely noticed the rapid changes in the kinds of skills which are being demanded for our new industries.

However, a glance through the classified advertisements of a Sunday newspaper will reveal a demand in large numbers for scientific disciplines which did not even exist ten years ago—for example, solid state physics, cryogenics, and astro-dynamics. Statistics from the census vividly summarize the drastic changes that have taken place in the past 20 years in the kinds of skills employed in the labor force. Highlights of some of these changes are shown in Table 1. These trends are clear from the following statistics:

1. There has been an especially rapid growth of professional and technical occupations in industry.
2. The number of white-collar workers has increased to the point where they now outnumber blue-collar workers.
3. Service workers have grown in numbers over the last few decades.

JOHN R. HINRICHS is Personnel Research Associate, Data Processing Division, International Business Machines Corporation, White Plains, New York.

EMPLOYED CIVILIAN WORKERS IN SELECTED OCCUPATIONAL GROUPS

Occupational Groups	Number (in thousands)			Per cent increase	
	1960	1950	1940	1940-50	1950-60
All employed persons	64,639	56,435	45,070	25.2	14.5
Prof., tech., & kindred	7,232	4,921	3,580	37.5	47.0
Engineers	854	520	276	88.6	64.3
Natural scientists	149	117	*	*	27.7
Technicians, elect. & electronic	91	12	*	*	679.2
Technicians, other	184	91	*	*	101.8
Other prof., tech., & kindred	5,954	4,181	*	*	42.4
Managers, officials, and proprietors	5,410	5,037	3,634	*	7.4
Salaried	3,388	2,509	*	*	35.0
Self-employed	2,022	2,528	*	*	—20.0
Clerical & kindred	9,307	6,954	4,382	58.7	33.8
Sales workers	4,639	3,907	3,081	26.8	18.7
Manual workers	23,746	22,437	16,394	36.9	5.8
Craftsmen, foremen & kindred	8,741	7,821	5,171	51.2	11.8
Operatives & kindred	11,898	11,180	8,080	38.4	6.4
Laborers (ex. farm & mine)	3,108	3,436	3,143	9.3	—9.6
Service workers	7,171	5,708	5,292	7.9	25.6
Agricultural workers	3,950	6,728	8,290	—18.8	—41.3

*Data not available. (The source of this table is Rutzich, Max, and Swerdloff, Sol, "The Occupational Structure of U.S. Employment, 1940-1960," *Monthly Labor Review*, November 1962.)

TABLE 1

Around 1950 for the first time, employment in service industries surpassed that in production. This trend undoubtedly reflects our rising standard of living and increasing pursuit of leisure.

4. There has been a moderate growth of skilled and semiskilled operatives over the last decade.

5. There has been a decline of entrepreneurs or "self-employed managers."

6. There has also been a decline of laborers and agricultural workers.

Although our society is going through a period of rapid change, one point with regard to manpower is unequivocally clear: There is a firm trend to higher skill requirements throughout all American industry.

THE PROBLEM OF PROFESSIONAL AND TECHNICAL MANPOWER

The most serious future shortages are expected in the ranks of professional and technical manpower—engineers, scientists, and technicians—which are essential to the development, operation, and maintenance of our increasingly complex economy.

The demand for and supply of engineers. The nation's resources of engineering manpower represent one of the few areas where there have been concerted efforts at quantitative studies of the demand side of the supply-demand equation. These efforts undoubtedly reflect the anticipated importance of engineers in the nation's future; they also illustrate how much more difficult it is to forecast future manpower demand than it is to project potential supply.

In a study conducted in 1961 by the National Science Foundation, an analytical approach to forecasting future demand for engineers was used. The study evaluated the ratios of scientific and engineering employment to total employment for the period 1954-59. These ratios were evaluated separately for various significant sectors of the economy. They were then applied to independent estimates of the probable total labor force in 1970, which had previously been projected by the Bureau of Labor Statistics. The result was a forecast of the anticipated 1970 demand for scientists and engineers.

The study forecast a net growth of 936,000 scientists and engineers over the period from 1959 to 1970; but because of deaths and retirements, a total average requirement of 106,000 scientists and engineers was forecast (81,000 engineers and 25,000 scientists). Thus the data predicted a staggering 90 per cent net increase in the employment of engineers over the 11-year period (as compared to a 64 per cent increase in the number of men working as professional engineers between 1950 and 1960, which was nine times the total growth of male employment during the 1950's).

To meet this demand, the study estimated that 72,000 new engineering graduates per year and 83,000 in the sciences would be required during the 1960's. These estimates take into account engineering graduates who will not enter the profession as well as the considerable numbers of nondegree holders expected to enter engineering. The study concluded that there would be enough science graduates but an insufficient number of engineering graduates (58,000 average annual engineering degrees versus an average demand for 72,000 engineers per year).

In 1962 the Engineering Manpower Commission made a survey of the demand for engineers. This was one of a series of surveys which had been made since 1951. The 1962 survey was based upon projections made by 517 companies and Government agencies employing 287,630 engineers, engineering technicians, and physical scientists.

The companies and agencies surveyed anticipated a 45 per cent overall rise in their employment of engineers between 1961 and 1971. When this anticipated increase was projected against the nation's total of about 900,000 engineers, an expected increase of about 402,000 during the ten-year period was presumed. After accounting for losses due to death and retirement (anticipated to be 1.1 per cent), for nondegree entrants to the profession (17.5 per cent), and for graduates who do not enter the engineering profession (estimated at 10 per cent), the study concluded that an annual average of 48,000 new bachelor of science graduates in engineering will be needed each year between 1961 and 1971.

A comparison of the projections made by these two independent studies is shown in Table 2. The different results obtained are striking; the net demand forecast by the National Science Foundation is over 50 per cent

COMPARISON OF PROJECTIONS OF THE DEMAND FOR ENGINEERS

	Engineering Manpower Commission 1961-71 (10 years)	National Science Foundation 1959-70 (11 years)
Average anticipated yearly net increase	40,200	64,000
Anticipated average annual attrition due to death and retirement	11,890	17,000
Anticipated total average yearly demand	52,090	81,000
Anticipated yearly input of nondegree holding engineers	17.5%	23%
Average annual new graduates entering profession required to meet demand	43,000	62,000
Percent of new graduates not expected to enter the profession	10%	14%
Total new graduates required per year to meet demand	48,000	72,000

TABLE 2

greater than that forecast by the Engineering Manpower Commission. The extreme importance of accurate basic assumptions in the forecasting process is evident from this comparison. For example, differing estimates of the number of nondegree entrants to the profession, the fraction of new graduates not entering the engineering profession, rates of attrition due to death and retirement, and so on—when applied to very different basic forecasts of net demand—lead to quite different projections of the overall manpower supply problem. In any event, that there are very real problems in getting reliable predictions in the demand side of the equation is obvious.

As for the supply of engineers, the Engineering Manpower Commission study revealed that there were 53,000 graduates with degrees in engineering in 1950. This was the first wave of veterans in the postwar college rush. In that year there were dire predictions of unemployment and of a surplus of engineers. Partly as a result of these predictions, freshmen engineering enrollments in 1950 dropped to 34,000; and this group produced only 22,000 graduates in 1954. In the meantime, the demand for engineers shot up sharply with the advent of the Korean War, and enrollments in freshmen engineering programs gradually rose along with this increased demand.

Again in 1957, a recession year, widespread talk of an oversupply of engineering graduates resulted in reduced freshmen engineering enrollments, and they have declined steadily since then. This decline has been not only in absolute numbers of freshmen enrolling in engineering programs but also in the percentage which engineering enrollments represent of total college enrollments. In 1957 they represented 11 per cent; in 1961 they represented only 6.5 per cent.

Most recent indications are that the five-year decline may be reversing. Between 1961 and 1962, freshman engineering enrollments dropped by 2.3 per cent. In the fall of 1963, freshman enrollments were up 1.6 per cent over 1962 levels—approximately the same percentage increase as in freshman enrollments in all curricula.

The Engineering Manpower Commission pointed out that the decline in freshmen enrollments which started in 1957 is just beginning to be felt as these freshmen get their degrees. Although the decline in freshman engineering enrollments may now be reversing, it will be four years before the resultant decline in the number of first-degree graduates can be reversed.

The Commission also pointed out that during the period following 1957, retention rates dropped—that is, a smaller percentage of entering freshmen followed through to complete their degree requirements in engineering. Retention rates have been running about 50 per cent in recent years. The

Commission estimated that if, luckily, retention rates stay at this level, there may be about 34,000 first-degree graduates in 1965; if they drop much below 50 per cent, there may be as few as 31,000 graduates. These estimates are probably fairly accurate, since they are based on students *already enrolled* in university engineering programs. When they are compared to the estimated demand as forecast in the two studies discussed (from 48,000 to 72,000 new graduates per year), they point to some significant near-term shortages of engineering talent.

The demand for and supply of scientists. As in the case of engineers, employment of natural scientists increased markedly between 1950 and 1960—from 117,000 to 149,000, or an increase of 27.7 per cent. This may be compared to a 14.5 per cent overall increase in employed persons and a 64.3 per cent increase in engineers for the same period. Among natural scientists, mathematicians and physicists showed the greatest growth in the past decade.

The National Science Foundation study predicted that there would be a 75 per cent increase in the employment of natural scientists over the 11-year period from 1959 to 1970, with the biggest growth shown by mathematicians and physicists. The study projected an average annual demand for 25,000 new scientists between 1959 and 1970 and also forecast that approximately 83,000 graduates in science each year will be needed to meet this demand. The study indicated that the demand could be met, though there may be some problems in regard to advanced-degree graduates in science.

The Engineering Manpower Commission survey also evaluated anticipated demand for physical scientists and projected a 57 per cent growth between 1961 and 1971 in employment of physical scientists, based on estimates by 486 companies and government organizations. The Manpower Commission pointed out that enrollments in university science programs have been growing in recent years—about in line with overall college enrollments—and concurred with the National Science Foundation estimate that there should not be serious shortages of physical scientists in the future. Problems in this area may be anticipated in terms of quality rather than sheer numbers of people as is the case with engineering graduates.

The demand for and supply of technicians. Technicians, or semiprofessional technical manpower, represented one of the fastest growing manpower groups in the decade between 1950 and 1960. This was particularly true of the electrical and electronics occupations, which experienced a 679.2 per cent increase—from 12,000 to 91,000—over the decade.

Employment of other engineering and physical science technicians doubled during the decade to 184,000. During 1961, the number of employed engineering technicians rose by 5 per cent. We may project these trends into the future to predict an increasing demand for engineering and physical science technicians.

On the supply side, it has been determined that the number of engineering technicians enrolled in technical institutes has been at a virtual standstill for the last five years. Graduates have dropped from about 17,600 in 1959-60 to 15,900 in 1961-62. We are not producing enough technicians per graduating engineer. There is an evident need for increased efforts in the development of qualified technicians, both as a supplement to strained engineering manpower and as an outlet for manpower not able to complete a full four-year program.

The demand for and supply of office and clerical employees. As the statistics in Table 1 indicate, the number of civilian workers in clerical jobs more than doubled during the two decades between 1940 and 1960— from 4.4 to 9.3 million persons. The biggest growth occurred in the war and recovery decade of the 1940's in which workers in clerical and kindred jobs increased by 58 per cent. This was followed by an additional 33 per cent growth during the 1950's. In large measure this growth was a reflection of the growing size and complexity of American industry with the attendant burgeoning requirements for record keeping, reporting, communications, and other clerical functions. Our age of bureaucracy has spawned a growing army of clerical workers in the labor force.

Forecasts for the decade of the 1960's are that the rate of growth of the past decade will continue. A 31 per cent growth to 12.8 million clerical workers between 1960 and 1970 is anticipated. By 1975 it is expected that there will be 14.2 million clerical and kindred workers in the labor force.

To be sure, some reduction in the requirements for personnel is anticipated through the growing introduction of data-processing equipment in office functions. However, such reductions should be largely confined to the more repetitive and routine accounting and record-keeping functions and should be more than offset by the overall increasing requirements for clerical personnel in our growing economy.

The effects of automation on employment levels are currently the subject of heated debate in many circles. When they get down to the nub of the issue, however, most experts admit that we really have only a very shaky and incomplete knowledge of the true impact of automation on employment levels. This is especially true in the area of office or white-collar automation. Forecasts range from dire predictions of wholesale displacement to estimates of a greatly increased demand for clerical personnel. The most reasoned view—reflected in the statistics quoted above from forecasts by the U.S. Department of Labor—is that clerical personnel displaced by automation will be more than counterbalanced by increased requirements due to overall growth in the economy and by demands for personnel with new skills, such as programers and business machine operators.

The question of adequate manpower supply in clerical fields has never been as critical as it has been for technical and professional personnel. Specific, relatively short-term training—as opposed to years of university study or technical training—can usually develop the required skills when demand exceeds supply. With the flood of new entrants into the labor market, the majority of whom have at least completed high school, there are few anticipated problems in the basic supply of clerical personnel to meet growing future demands.

The demand for and supply of service workers. The service occupations represent a rather amorphous group which has in the past received very little attention or study on the part of labor economists. In most labor force tabulations and manpower studies, the service-worker classification has more the flavor of an "other" or "miscellaneous" category than of a distinct and conceptually clear occupational grouping. The jobs of policeman, charwoman, cook, hospital attendant, and fireman have little occupational content in common which can be used as a base for extensive analysis of manpower supply and demand.

However, based on trends in prior years (a 7.9 per cent increase in service workers from 1940 to 1950 and a 25.6 per cent increase between 1950 and 1960) on population growth, on anticipated increases in the standard of living in our country, and on a growing emphasis on recreational and leisure time activities, the Department of Labor anticipates that service workers will increase by 51 per cent from 1960 to 1975—to 12.5 million workers representing 14.3 per cent of the labor force. Among the major occupational groups tallied by the Department of Labor, this forecasted growth rate for service workers is second only to the growth anticipated for professional and technical workers.

Few problems are anticipated on the supply side of the manpower equation. Rather than being viewed apprehensively, the growing demand for service workers is usually looked on as a major—though still inadequate—relief valve for the pressures of unemployment and for the sharply increasing numbers of new entrants to the labor force.

CONCLUSIONS AND IMPLICATIONS

At the end of World War II, it was anticipated that the flood of returning veterans and the end of war production would result in widespread unemployment and economic depression. The Full Employment Act of 1946, which founded the President's Council of Economic Advisors, was an effort to deal with these anticipated problems. However, widespread unemployment never materialized as a result of the postwar economic boom.

Our nation experienced a booming birth rate, which accompanied the economic boom of the late 1940's and 1950's. In the 1960's this bulge in our population is being felt as a sharp increase in the number of young people entering the labor force. Ironically, this influx is taking place at the same time that our economy is in the midst of serious realignment from the patterns of the postwar economic boom. Pervasive technological changes in the process of production have forced quantitative and qualitative changes in the structure of the labor force. Increasing competition, both domestic and overseas, has forced belt tightening and cost-consciousness, particularly with regard to labor costs. As a result of these economic changes, and the continuing entry into the labor force of large numbers of young and inexperienced workers, persistent unemployment has now become one of the most pressing concerns of the Council of Economic Advisors.

However, the United States economy is growing, and there are good prospects that it will remain vigorous in the years ahead. The paradox of persistent unemployment in a period of economic growth highlights the changes which are taking place and also highlights the changes which are being forced onto the nation's manpower resource: at the same time that there is a surplus of unskilled and untrained manpower, there are marked shortages of specialized and high-talent personnel.

Today, we no longer tend to view the manpower resource problem primarily with an economic focus on the demand and supply of units of labor. Instead, the emphasis is on the modification and development of skills among major segments of the population, as illustrated by the Manpower Development and Training Act and the training provisions of the Area Redevelopment Act. This growing emphasis on manpower development and training—or retraining—is evident in other areas besides that of Federal legislation. It also appears in public policy at the state and local levels. It is reflected in union agreements, in management-sponsored programs, and in the efforts of a variety of educational institutions. We may anticipate this changing emphasis to be expressed in a number of ways:

1. Manpower planning and forecasting will begin to receive the same attention and care as present planning of market strategy or of products. Of necessity, companies will provide more support for efforts to develop the tools and techniques of manpower analysis and planning. Company-sponsored manpower research will receive new impetus.

2. The emphasis will be expressed in new and expanded employee development and training programs within industry. The scarcity of trained manpower will increasingly lead to programs to develop within the company the skills needed for the future. Unions, motivated by job-security considerations, will also press for programs of in-company retraining and skill upgrading. Government and public opinion will provide additional pressures for such programs.

3. As a corollary to expanded in-company development programs, there will be increased emphasis on potential rather than immediately useful skills in hiring new employees. Capable people will tend to be advanced rapidly to positions of responsibility.

4. Industry will continue to provide extensive support, both financial and other, to the nation's schools, colleges, and universities. Direct dollar aid to education will increase, in recognition of formal education's vital contribution to the success of industry. Companies will increasingly support education at the community level, primarily through contributions of money, equipment, and faculty to community colleges. Cooperative work programs, scholarships, and public relations efforts will attempt to maintain the flow of candidates to engineering and other specialized curricula. Company programs for educational tuition refund for employees or for educational leaves of absence will become more extensive.

5. Companies will pay more careful attention to the full utilization of manpower skills, particularly at the higher skill levels. Technicians, draftsmen, and other assistants will be used more extensively.

Increased efforts in the field of manpower development cannot be viewed as a cure-all for our country's manpower problems. Imbalances and dislocations are inevitable, and there will always be a significant segment of the labor force for which skill development will be impossible. But nationwide emphasis on human resource development will undoubtedly be the most fruitful primary direction for thrust in dealing with present and anticipated manpower resource problems.

RECRUITING ADVANCED-DEGREE PERSONNEL •

JOHN K. WOLFE

WITH THE RECENT EMPHASIS on research and development, increased numbers of advanced-degree personnel have been required in industry. This trend has been particularly evident in those industries maintaining leadership at the forefront of technology. Changes in the make-up of the technological work force place a distinct premium on the man who can make original technological contributions in the fields of interest to the company. Military and space problems have added new dimensions and have required large numbers of doctoral personnel. Personnel directors must make periodic assessments of the level of employee needed to undertake research and development work.

The university must be considered the primary source for technical competency in industry, and the number of advanced degrees granted has been continuously increasing. Although natural science departments in most universities have had a large proportion of masters' and doctors' degrees, engineering departments have only recently gathered momentum toward this end. The degrees awarded in American universities in 1964 show a pronounced increase in engineering advanced degrees, and this trend will continue. The number of engineering advanced degrees will probably surpass the total number in science before 1970. The trend toward attainment of advanced degrees carries with it a selection which must be carefully noted. With 25 to 30 per cent of the bachelor-degree class going on for graduate study, a relatively small number of students from the upper 25 per cent will be available for direct hire at the bachelor level. Correspondingly,

---

JOHN K. WOLFE is Manager—Advanced Degree Personnel, Engineering Services Division, General Electric Company, Schenectady, New York.

many of the master of engineering or science graduates in the upper 25 per cent will be proceeding toward further study to ultimately obtain the doctorate. If a company expects to traditionally hire the upper 25 per cent student in overall capability, it must move in the direction of hiring him at the masters' and doctoral levels.

The recruiting process for Ph.D. personnel differs from that used in many companies for other technical levels. The company image on the college campus and, more particularly, rapport with the individual professor become important factors. The interview is often conducted with a person at the same technical level rather than an individual with a purely personnel background. Evaluation and plant visit are much more complex and individual matters. The offer of employment must in many cases define more carefully the man's duties and obligations, often with mention of peripheral technical benefits such as publication policies and attendance at professional meetings. Offer follow-up becomes an important part of the recruiting process since many of these candidates will go on for post-doctoral study in the United States or abroad and may be available for employment at a later date.

Before beginning advanced-degree recruiting, the manpower planning process must be evaluated in a most critical fashion. First, the need for advanced-degree people must be clearly established. The company should be in a favorable position to attract these people, and it must provide the atmosphere in which they can be retained over a two- to three-year period (as a minimum). Since the cost of advanced-degree people, both from a continuing salary and a recruiting standpoint, is high, the company must be sure it can afford such talent.

The sources of doctoral personnel may be divided into two major categories: the university and the open-market sources. Of course, students at graduate levels in the university are the prime available group, but many peripheral areas warrant careful consideration. There are postdoctoral students, faculty members who will not be retained on a permanent basis, research personnel in institutes, and research organizations often directly affiliated with the university. Open-market sources include advertising, recruiting at technical society meetings, assistance from executive search organizations, and referrals from company employees.

University coverage for new students is a more concentrated matter for masters' and doctoral students. There are approximately 200 schools in the United States available for bachelor of science coverage, with only 100 for master of science, narrowing down to 50 schools for Ph.D. students.

When interviewing is conducted at the university, the company is often faced with a decision as to the interview breakdown. The decision will often be based on the number of candidates needed and the interviewers who will be on campus to undertake this work. We at General Electric interview bachelors' and masters' students together, placing Ph.D. and post-doctoral students in a group to be seen by technical specialists with competence in a particular field.

A further breakdown is advantageous when the needs are great enough to recruit by discipline. Engineering, science, and mathematics students can be interviewed by one team, but advanced-degree students in the arts, social sciences, and business require specialists in those fields. Most universities schedule these two groups at different times and at different areas on campus.

The measurement of recruiting effectiveness becomes a most difficult matter in the case of advanced-degree students. One is often inclined to measure effectiveness on a statistical basis. In reality, a single highly capable individual in one field may be much more important than several of mediocre ability in the same component. One can, however, get a measure of the effectiveness at various stages by calculating numbers at several phases of the recruiting process. We prefer to measure the following: number considered, number interviewed, number referred to company components, candidates making plant visit, number of offers, and number of hires. Comparing these numbers with the overall figures for General Electric for the past few years allows us to assess recruiting effectiveness at various stages in the process.

Employment decision factors for advanced-degree candidates often differ from those for bachelor of science candidates. In a recent survey of candidates considered at the doctoral level, important decision factors were found to be company image, plant location, nature of technical work, company publication policy, effectiveness of technical management, presence of similarly trained associates, and salary offered.

Over the years some of the more highly technically oriented companies have sought capable advanced-degree personnel as part of their manpower planning process. It should be pointed out that the future technical capabilities of the particular company are often directly determined by the number of technical innovators hired by the personnel function. These people may determine in a direct way new products and processes for the company. The personnel executive serves then to determine, at least in part, the innovative posture of the company by the selection of persons he interviews

and attracts. A very small number of technical innovators are often responsible for a large segment of the new product and process development.
We can show in General Electric, for example, that about 5 per cent of
our total people generate approximately half of the new technical ideas.
A much higher percentage of these innovators appear at the masters' and
doctoral levels than at the bachelor of science or technician levels. The
personnel director determines the most efficient recruiting procedure for
his company. Can these people be recruited by persons trained in the
personnel function, or can this task be carried out more efficiently by technical specialists? Experience with some selected companies has shown
that, when properly trained, the technical specialist can make a very
effective recruiter for advanced-degree personnel.

KEY FACTORS IN MOTIVATING PROFESSIONALS •

FRANK D. LEAMER

Y ALE J. LAITIN, PRESIDENT OF SURVEY Research Associates, has said, "The last big business frontier for profit improvement may be through employee motivation. It's one of the few flexible aspects of overhead left to management." As I see it, the problem confronting the management of professional and technical people is: What can we do to make relevant innovation rewarding and self-motivating to the individual professional?

Jack Morton, vice president of Bell Laboratories, expresses it this way: "Strategically, top management's role can be likened to that of the system-engineer for a large complex information-processing machine. The manager's components are living, creative people. Each has different capabilities, needs, and motivations. Importantly, this gives the manager the opportunity to create a living dynamic organism, one that not just follows the program, but also can learn, adapt, innovate, and grow."

MOTIVATION OF THE INDIVIDUAL

Psychologists refer to motivation as the process by which an individual is impelled to act or respond in a certain manner. Its significance becomes clear in the contrast between the superior performance of a highly motivated employee and the lower productivity of an individual with equal abilities but lesser motivation.

All motivational stimuli are not equally effective with all people. There

FRANK D. LEAMER is Executive Director, Personnel Division, Bell Telephone Laboratories, Murray Hill, New Jersey.

are some, however, that are generally effective, and we shall concentrate on these. Moreover, people of a common culture and background are more likely to respond uniformly to a given set of stimuli than are people of widely differing experience. This fact is important in considering the key factors in motivating professional technical people.

Experience has shown that individuals attain outstanding results when they accomplish goals of their own free choice. Conversely, they attain only mediocre results at best if they are directed or driven by external forces rather than motivated from within. Thus the balance between internal or self-generating influences and external or environmental influences which affect motivation is a delicate one and extremely important.

I like to think of motivation as that quality in every individual that is evidenced by his accepted objectives, goals, and ambitions coupled with the energy, drive, self-sacrifice, and effort he is willing to put forward to achieve them. It also involves a sensitivity to interaction between individuals.

As Douglas McGregor states in *The Human Side of Enterprise,* "Man is a wanting animal—as soon as one of his needs is satisfied, another appears in its place. The process is unending. It continues from birth to death. Man continuously puts forth effort—works, if you please—to satisfy his needs." McGregor has pointed out that human needs are organized in a series of levels—a hierarchy of importance—but when a need has been satisfied it is no longer a motivator of behavior: "When the physiological needs are reasonably satisfied, needs at the next higher level begin to dominate man's behavior—to motivate him." Thus we proceed through the hierarchy from *physiological* to *safety* needs (protection against danger, threat, deprivation) to *social* needs (for belonging, for association, for acceptance, for giving and receiving friendship and love) and then on to *egoistic* needs, which are the needs of greatest significance to management and to man himself. These needs are rarely, if ever, completely satisfied. They are of two kinds, McGregor says:

1. "Those that relate to one's self-esteem: needs for self-respect and self-confidence, for autonomy, for achievement, for competence, for knowledge."
2. "Those that relate to one's reputation: needs for status, for recognition, for appreciation, for the deserved respect of one's fellows."

Finally, in the hierarchy of needs, there are the needs for *self-fulfillment* —that is, the needs for realizing one's own potentialities, for continuing self-development, for being creative in reaching objectives. McGregor points out that "conditions of modern industrial life give only limited opportunity for these relatively dormant human needs to find expression."

Professional technical personnel are more likely to seek satisfaction of these higher needs than are production or service workers. The awareness of this fact has been slow in reaching the managers of technical personnel. The application of knowledge about what forces influence the contribution of professionals has also been slow.

It is impossible to catalog and adequately describe all of the factors that influence the motivation of an individual, particularly that of professionals seeking satisfaction of egoistic and self-fulfillment needs. However, the responsibility of management to understand what makes such employees tick, to know something about the stimuli to which they are likely to respond, and to create a proper climate in which they will put forth their best efforts is very great indeed.

Professor Frederick Hertzberg's motivational analysis of scientists and engineers found that the levels of job satisfaction, motivation, and productivity are closely related to two sets of factors which he labels "dissatisfiers" and "motivators."

Dissatisfiers are made up, essentially, of such matters as pay, supplemental benefits, company policy and administration, behavior of supervision, working conditions, and several other factors somewhat peripheral to the task. Although traditionally thought of as motivators, they are actually more potent as dissatisfiers. High motivation does not result from their improvement, but dissatisfaction does result from their deterioration. Negative motivators can be dissatisfiers, too. For example, while achievement is a motivator, failure to achieve can, of course, be a dissatisfier. Motivators, on the other hand, are made up of achievement, recognition, responsibility, growth, advancement, and other matters associated with the self-actualization or self-fulfillment of the individual on the job. Job satisfaction and high production are associated with motivators, while disappointments and ineffectiveness are usually associated with dissatisfiers. The differentiation between those two sets of factors is fundamental in our thinking about motivation.

Their importance is further verified by the results of a survey by Eugene Randsipp, director of psychological research at Deutsch and Shea. In this survey, a thousand engineers and engineering managers were questioned to determine the factors which influence engineers in choosing a place in which to work. The results are shown in the accompanying table.

Dr. Morris I. Stein, professor of psychology at New York University, has pointed out some rather interesting personality variations between the

JOB FACTORS THAT ATTRACT

	Managers	Engineers
	(In percentages)	
Challenging work	60	56
Good salary	36	46
Desirable location	30	36
Opportunity for advancement	30	34
Company's sound reputation	28	25
Stability of company	4	12
Company's growth record	14	11
Fringe benefits offered	8	9
Enlightened personnel policies	4	8
Educational assistance	4	8
Good working conditions and facilities	6	6
Enlarged technical responsibilities	8	6
Progressive management	9	5
Miscellaneous	9	22

JOB FACTORS THAT REPEL

	Managers	Engineers
	(In percentages)	
Uninteresting work	42	32
Undesirable location	26	31
Salary not competitive	34	28
Company too large	2	14
Poor employment department	10	13
Poor working conditions	2	6
Questionable reputation of company	10	6
Vagueness of job description	2	4
Low status of engineers	—	4
Job insecurity	4	4
Poor advancement possibilities	2	—
Lack of offers	4	—
Miscellaneous	10	12

more creative and the less creative research man in industry. He has found, for example, that the more creative man is less submissive to authority and less receptive to tradition. He is more dynamic, more autonomous, and sees himself as differing generally from the less creative workers. He is likely to be oriented more in the direction of nonconformity and tends to cut the bonds of convention and custom. He has a more positive picture of himself but is usually of the restless type. We seldom see the complacent, self-satisfied individual come up with new and revolutionary ideas.

Robert G. Chollar has said, "We must consider both the creative man who is internally motivated and the man who is potentially creative but needs to be extremely motivated. We must consider the man who is self-propelled and is upset when doing nothing, who has more ideas than he can handle. . . . We must be concerned about the man who is beset with emotional problems and the man who is ignorant of the real problems because the communication line has not been adequate. We must give consideration both to the man of fundamental interests who seeks recognition at the professional level and to the integrated individual whose goal may be administrative in nature."

Above all, in my opinion, we must recognize that for most scientists, loyalty to their profession comes ahead of loyalty to the employer. If we provide the setting in which they can attain high professional satisfaction, loyalty to employer will most likely follow.

In trying to categorize broadly the key factors that have a direct influence on the human needs of scientists and engineers, special attention has been directed toward those motivational needs *in the higher hierarchies*—egoistic needs and self-fulfillment needs. Broadly speaking, there are three key factors that we at Bell Laboratories believe are important in motivating professionals:

1. Purpose of the organization of which they are a part.
2. Associates with whom they work.
3. A work environment which provides the climate, facilities, and services conducive to self-fulfillment.

Companies like people have a wide range of objectives—purposes for being in business. Companies differ in the types of roles they expect their professionals to play. Emphasis may be on science for science's sake, design for production and sales, service to the public, or any one of a number of other objectives. It is important that the purpose of the company be clearly stated and that each professional be able and willing to accept the objectives of the organization of which he is a part and identify himself in a favorable light with its purpose. This is the substance of which the company image is made. Nearly everyone, and professionals in particular, want to belong to an organization that is respected and thought well of in the community, the nation, and the world. At Bell Laboratories, for instance, our objective is the providing of better and cheaper communication services. This objective draws on many sciences and technologies yet carries a unity of purpose that provides a sense of mission to those engaged.

This clearly stated purpose of an industry is closely related to quality of professionals attracted to join the work force. The old adage that birds of a feather flock together has a great deal of truth in building a strong team of professional technical personnel. The stimulation and incentive that come from close association with outstanding individuals in one's profession outweigh all other motivational stimuli. Companies like academic institutions build strong teams of scientists and mathematicians around a nucleus of individuals outstanding in their fields. Among engineers the same influence builds strong development teams.

Every year there comes into the Bell Laboratories a group of young engineers fresh from the college environment. Their ability, as yet untried in actual engineering effort, is potentially of the highest order. But no amount of potential ability, enthusiasm, or energy will enable the beginner to solve at once the complex problems constantly confronting the telephone engineer. The speed with which this ability can be made productive is largely a measure of the older engineer's effort to impart to this younger generation something of the experience he has gained through his years of service and association with the engineers who preceded him. This may be done informally on the job or formally through classes in which the experts teach the neophyte. How to maximize individual development and nourish his will to achieve is a challenge each manager must meet.

The need for self-fulfillment cannot be satisfied in a professional career unless the individual continues to learn and grow along with the technology or science of his field. Varieties of opportunities and encouragement for such growth must be supplied by his employer and community as a vital part of his environment.

A discussion of environment is closely related to the quality of associates, and the most important general motivating factor within the environment provided by a company is communication.

Of all the possible forms of communication, we have found that personal contact is more productive in stimulating innovations than other forms of imparting information. Therefore, natural and contrived devices for stimulating personal contact discussion have been used to get individuals to talk about their work.

The environment for scientific professionals must provide certain freedoms—opportunity for original thinking and unhampered satisfaction of curiosity. This is particularly important in research areas where the work is often unprogramed or unscheduled at least as compared with procedures necessary in the development areas. A creative scientist usually has a strong need to assure himself and be independent. He must have freedom to publish creative contributions and thereby gain prestige in the eyes of his scientific colleagues.

Dr. Ralph Bown, formerly a research administrator at Bell Laboratories, in reflecting on the latitudes necessary to a productive organization saw two freedoms as requiring vigorous defense: the freedom to resist pressures from the development departments to work on their specific problems and the freedom occasionally to carry ideas experimentally into the application stage to a point where merit can be demonstrated. The wise researcher will know that these freedoms have to be merited and that they impose obligations.

The environment must provide other freedoms of the kind that stimulate independent and creative thought. It must be tolerant and understanding of nonconformity or even foster it, so long as such behavior does not go beyond the bounds of social, moral, and community acceptance. If they wish to grow beards—let them grow beards. Their value to the organization should be determined by their contribution—not their looks.

However, environment covers a multitude of other things. It must include adequate facilities for stimulating and testing the creative ideas of scientists, mathematicians, and technologists. It must include policies and working practices which permit a great amount of freedom and independent action and which provide adequate recognition and rewards for achievement in the form of salary, rank, and status. Some professionals gauge themselves principally by acquired salary, rank, and status. These forms of recognition have important values as recognition of accomplishment. There are those who believe that true professionalism rests on hard, disciplined employment of our talents, upon men dedicating themselves to service to others. There are many examples in which this is true. Salary, rank, status, and honors are, however, goads or catalysts to higher performance and are, therefore, important. If any one of these factors in the environment is neglected by management, they acquire overriding importance. The laboratory should not be an arena for cutthroat interpersonal competition. Nonetheless, even professionals are spurred by competition, and an individual needs to be able to measure his relative progress toward his goals.

Whole books could and have been devoted to discussion of physical laboratory equipment and facilities; to policies, working practices, salary administration, and performance rating; to devices for recognition of status and rank. Some of the methods used by some managers of professional technical people to bestow rank on outstanding contributors are, in my opinion, unnecessary and undesirable. I refer to the highly controversial, so-called professional or parallel ladders. Such "ladders" for nonsupervisory engineers and scientists imply a climbing contest unbecoming to the efforts of such respected members of our society.

In addition to those motivational environmental factors already mentioned, opportunities must be deliberately provided for satisfying the needs of a professional for realizing his own potential—for continuing self-development. Encouragement to join and participate in professional societies is one effective way of meeting this need. It has been said that one never graduates from a profession. You either keep on growing in one way or another or you fall behind. The pace setter is change. Managers must provide enthusiastic encouragement and the incentive that will stimulate professionals to keep growing throughout their careers.

In Bell Laboratories we have provided the following educational programs and, more important, the encouragement to participate in them:

1. Communications development training programs.
2. College study plans, including an undergraduate study plan and a graduate study plan.
3. A doctoral support plan.
4. Out-of-hours courses.
5. An out-of-hours lecture series.
6. A program design training program.
7. An operating company training program for Bell Laboratories engineers.
8. Special in-hours courses.
9. An administrative staff training program.
10. An operating engineers training program.

The major emphasis here is on opportunities for professionals to continue their growth. We believe that genius results from work and a well-stocked larder of knowledge.

Often the single most important motivational stimulus in the professionals' environment stems from the technical supervisor. Next to the stimuli received from one's associates are the incentives provided by the boss. In some cases the supervisor may have the greatest influence. E. I. Green, while executive vice president of Bell Telephone Laboratories, put it this way: "The supervisor is the one to foster loyalty and pride of organization. He must develop in his people an understanding of the overall undertaking and a sense of participation by each one in the combined accomplishment. He alone can fully portray the challenges that lie ahead." In other words, the supervisor must understand "what makes Sammy run" and provide the conditions and incentive that will make him want to run.

Another factor falling in the environmental category is the role that assistants play in stimulating creative contribution by professionals. During World War II, Bell Laboratories came to the full realization that if you give a really creative engineer or scientist adequate supporting personnel who are capable and skilled, these people can carry out ideas and designs, assemble and test them, and by so doing multiply the effectiveness of your professional staff many times.

The engineering team concept is now generally accepted. Typically, this team is of the three-man pattern—the engineer or scientist plus the technician plus the craftsman. The engineer or scientist, of course, must take some time to do for himself many tasks associated with his work which do not require or justify his time or talents. However, in many instances today, such work would be done even better by competent aides such as our technical aides. The time and effort of the engineer or scientist thus saved would directly enhance his output, his earning power, and above all his personal satisfaction. Just having someone reporting to you in an aide category somehow acts as an incentive to better planning of the job. Bell Laboratories has gone from a ratio of .67 assistant technical personnel to members of the technical staff in 1950 to about 1.25 in 1963. This ratio is continuing to grow, and it is a real motivational factor.

SUMMARY AND CONCLUSIONS

Here then are a few of the environmental factors that foster maximum contribution of professionals:
1. Form, manner, and frequency of communication.
2. Freedom for independent thinking and action.
3. Facilities and equipment for stimulating and testing ideas.

4. Recognition and reward for achievement.
5. Beneficial interpersonal competition.
6. Professional status.
7. Opportunities and encouragement for continuing self-development.
8. Stimulating supervision and inspired leadership.
9. Assistants to expedite bringing creative ideas to fruition.

It is well known that most companies are not getting as much for their research and engineering dollars as they could. Most are not even managing as well as they know how to do. Some of the things they think they know may not be true or practicable in the context of their own particular industry. Management literature is replete with suggestions for better management of scientific talent. The problem lies in implementing the suggestions.

Some of the details discussed under the broad categories of "Key factors" may be means to improve technical effectiveness outside the purview of motivation. Competition and business purpose are the gadfly serving us well as motivators. Too much interpersonal competition such as formal "parallel ladders" can have a negative effect. In achieving our purpose there is no substitute for the high quality of associates in providing incentive to achieve creative results.

A key factor in stimulating scientists, engineers, and mathematicians to the best efforts of which they are capable is helping them build up their ego-satisfactions and then providing them with all the encouragement, facilities, and services they need to stay there. Nothing succeeds like success. Furthermore, no one can contribute in a vacuum—environment must provide and nourish the incentive to want to contribute and the climate and the facilities for bringing innovations into fruition. Challenge of the job and self-generating enthusiasm for the work itself are necessary motivational factors. Rewards and recognition require the special attention of managers.

Freedom, judiciously applied, is another important motivator of professionals. However, it isn't just freedom alone that releases the creative capacities of the human mind. It is the enthusiasm, dedication, and power that come when you give yourself to a cause because your environment makes you want so to do. There seems to be a strange, almost magic, power that emanates from people who have honest enthusiasm.

Above all, there must be an atmosphere of stimulation, something that is sparked by inspired leadership. The climate is best when colleagues and associates, as well as leaders, are dedicated to finding new truths in science or practical solutions to engineering problems.

DEVELOPING MANAGEMENT
KNOW-HOW AMONG SCIENTISTS •

JOSEPH E. MILANO

THERE IS PROBABLY NO AREA of greater controversy in manager education than that of manager know-how among scientists. Because of the tremendously fast growth of all research in the past few years, there has been little time for study, analysis, and definition of the job of the manager-scientist. This is true, at least, in comparison with the great number of investigations of managers in other areas of business. Consequently, much of the published material deals with the differences, environment, and characteristics of scientists. However, the definition of the responsibilities, authority, and accountability of the scientist-manager is still vague and highly controversial. There is no neat outline such as those produced for other types of managers.

Technical competence and creative potential are the main considerations in employing a scientist, and the same considerations are important in his appointment as a manager. Scientists are reluctant, to use a mild term, to report to a scientist whom they consider to be technically inferior or unfit to evaluate their work. And yet, because the emphasis is on technical competence, loading a scientist-manager with administrative details tends to speed up his technical obsolescence. Not only have we then nulli-

---

JOSEPH E. MILANO is Manager—Research Education, Thomas J. Watson Research Center, International Business Machines Corporation, Yorktown Heights New York.

fied the very reason for employing him in the first place, but we have placed him in a position which makes him more susceptible to technological obsolescence.

Entering upon a managerial position creates an ambivalence that some scientists find difficult to control. Many consider those in administration to be second-class citizens. Their entire academic background has led them to this conclusion. Also, once a scientist enters the administrative area, he feels he may be through as a researcher. He must make his choice. However, he also has the feeling that the road to success, prestige, and status lies in the managerial area. Therefore, even if he desires to take the managerial path, he must oppose it outwardly and appear to acquiesce only at management's request.

Scientists pride themselves on their training in logic and analysis. In numerous situations involving personnel or company policy, they may apply the same rules and reasoning so necessary to their particular disciplines. A situation is either logical or illogical—black or white. The nonlogical or emotional conditions may escape them completely. The result may often be conflict, especially with nontechnical administrators and personnel whose positions may carry the responsibilities of adhering to company policy or procedures. Some may categorize this conflict under the heading of human relations.

A scientist requires an environment that enhances his ability to do research on significant problems and earn recognition for achievement within his chosen field. His major loyalty is to his discipline. Having that status, he has a feeling of independence and the security in his own competence which leads him to question or even protest that which is contrary to his expectations or his felt rights. It is more than his training in logic which makes him a nonconformist to certain requirements of policy or procedure.

He also has the advantage that if the environment does not suit him, he can get immediate employment elsewhere. In other areas of business, a manager may owe his position, prestige, and status to long years of struggle. If he were to leave the company, it would be most difficult for him to find an immediate position elsewhere at the same level with the same status and prestige. Therefore, his loyalty, security, and aspirations are tied to his job, and he tends to be more compliant than the scientist.

At the Thomas J. Watson Research Center, more than 50 per cent of the professionals are Ph.D.'s, less than 30 per cent have an M.S., and less than 20 per cent have a B.S. Most of those with an M.S. or B.S. are actively enrolled for advanced degrees in nearby universities under our Graduate Study Program. The nature of the work involves a broad spectrum of science, background, goals, expectations, and environment within projects. The important concept here is the services provided the professionals in the Center. The technical departments are organized along functional lines but also have an interdisciplinary mix in project areas.

The director of administration heads all of the service groups. Each of the functions attempts to relieve the technical areas of as much "administrivia" as possible. For example, under our controller—in budgets, accounting, payroll, and so on—an intense effort is made to handle details so that the professionals can concentrate on science endeavors.

Similarly, the personnel department is organized so as to assist, provide guidance, and handle administrative matters in a manner that does not cause the technical personnel to absolve themselves of their responsibilities for decisions. This can be and often is a mighty tight rope to walk.

There is another important aid to the scientific manager—this is the staff or administrative assistant. He is responsible for handling the administrative details for his department and coordinates, in many instances, the work of the department and that of the service groups. In a sense, he is the business manager for his department.

The technical manager devotes perhaps 85 to 90 per cent of his time to scientific work while the administrative manager spends his time in an inverse proportion. The latter not only is required to attend to his own broad responsibilities as manager but must also share a portion of the technical manager's load.

IBM puts great emphasis on fair treatment of employees. In this program we weighted it with "need to know" information in those areas to which managers are most exposed in their jobs. We attempted to provide them with know-how which would assist them in avoiding "bear traps" in dealing with personnel. We also wanted them to get better aquainted with those persons who could give them assistance. The changes of pace were provided by members of the IBM Corporate staff.

We conducted a successful management development program in 1963. Many hours were spent in refining and preparing each of the presentations. We did not have total agreement on all of the items in the program. However, we conducted it and learned a lot from the experience. The accompanying exhibit shows the breakdown and schedule of this program.

After receiving approval on the entire program, we identified the more recently appointed managers. The department directors notified their man-

IBM MANAGEMENT DEVELOPMENT PROGRAM

Time	Monday	Tuesday	Wednesday	Thursday	Friday
8:30 A.M.	Material distribution assignments Research manager responsibilities	Role of personnel in IBM policy	Appraisal and counseling	Communications	Developing competence in subordinates Manager's dual role
10:15 A.M.	Break	—	—	—	—
10:30 A.M.	Changing viewpoint	Managerial grid	Handling personnel cases	Interpersonal communication	Medical function mental health Program evaluation
12:30 P.M.	Lunch	—	—	—	—
1:30 P.M.	IBM personnel case	Employee relations in IBM	Salary administration Guides in personnel administration	Technological planning	Business ethics
3:15 P.M.	IBM organization	Employment practices Patent operations	Long-range planning	Organizing, planning, decision making	Closing address, critique
5:30 P.M.	Free time	—	—	—	—
6:15 P.M.	Dinner	—	—	—	—

agers, and it was my job to follow up with each one. No one was ordered into the program. The decision was left entirely to the manager. There were nearly a dozen who declined the invitation. No pressures were exerted by upper management.

Every participant had an evaluation sheet so that every session was rated as to its value to managerial know-how. The results were surprising. We found, overall, much more interest and desire for information than we had dared hope. Every session ran over the allotted time. In nearly all of the presentations by personnel, there was a request for additional sessions.

The session on mental health was most impressive to the participants. We feel that all managers should be aware of mental problems, be observant of danger signals, and seek counsel with our doctor in suspicious cases. The managers shared the feeling, apparently, because they could have kept the doctor answering questions for days. They also exhibited great interest in learning how to handle personnel problems. We presented actual cases which were disguised to prevent identification of persons. They also were most anxious to discuss policy interpretation and application, especially as regards salary administration, appraisals, and business ethics. The presentation on long-range planning by the corporate director of that function ended only because the dinner bell rang.

In view of our experience, we have arrived at the following conclusions:

1. While technical managers resent taking time from their work, once they are involved in a program they exhibit tremendous interest and desire for information which will reduce the anxieties and strains of their jobs.

2. Our own fears, misgivings, and apprehensions concerning the technical managers' interests and desires were mostly unfounded. They showed deep interest in learning about the functions and problems and about the assistance to which they have access in their managerial capacity.

3. A one-week program held off company premises has advantages over a program consisting of one or two scheduled sessions per week spread over a period of four or eight weeks. The uninterrupted one-week program has 100 per cent attendance at all sessions, a concentration on the content, less interference with the technical work, and—most important—greater acceptance by the technical managers.

4. One week is about the limit of tolerance. A number of the managers thought that continuing sessions should be scheduled every three or

four months but certainly not every month. Most were doubtful even about every two months.

5. In checking with managers at the upper levels on the content, there was a wide discrepancy between what they thought the managers should know and the actual interest of the participants. The positive reactions of the participants were surprising to upper management.

6. Our program was too rich in content and ran too long each day. We shall eliminate the speakers at lunch and dinner in future programs. Everyone was emotionally and physically tired by the closing session.

7. New managers should have about six months of experience prior to participating in such a program. Some experience is necessary for full appreciation of the program content. We are scheduling new managers for briefing sessions as soon after their appointment as possible. This will be done individually or in groups, whatever the situation may demand.

8. Upper management actively participated in the program. This was one of the reasons it was well received. Unless one has top management support, endorsement, and involvement, the likelihood of any measure of acceptance and success is very small indeed—especially in a research environment.

OFFICE AUTOMATION AND ITS EFFECTS •

LEON C. MEGGINSON

In ANY SITUATION OF LIFE, it seems to be normal that the first emotion associated with accelerated velocity is a sense of exhilaration and a desire for still further speed. However, as the acceleration continues there comes another feeling, particularly if this change is a radical departure from the normal pace of operations or activities. This feeling is one of apprehension, a sense of misgiving concerning whether this speed can properly be controlled and whether it can be effectively lived with. A related question is whether it is altogether good to have so much power and speed at our finger tips.

We have gone through these stages of exhilaration, desire for more speed, and apprehension and misgiving with most of the inventions of the past—for example, steamboats, trains, the telephone, automobiles, boats, airplanes, radios, television, and now rockets and missiles. However, it may safely be said that in not one of these cases has a unanimous opinion been reached which adequately answers every question raised as to the value of these inventions. Although there is usually a correlation between mechanization and a high standard of living, often the advantages and disadvantages are so intermingled that we arrive, finally, at a sense of frustration.

Nevertheless, the business system functions in a dynamic environment; so mechanization and automation are accepted willingly, or reluctantly, by management and labor. For example, Brendon Sexton, director of educa-

LEON C. MEGGINSON is Professor of Management, College of Business Administration, Louisiana State University, Baton Rouge, Louisiana. The research for this study was conducted under a research grant from the Louisiana State University, College of Business Administration, Division of Research. Peter Drexler, a graduate assistant, aided in its preparation.

tion for the United Auto Workers, said, "We are persuaded that increasing productivity and increasing production may result in the creation of new and more complex human and community problems, but on the whole tend to make life less burdensome for mankind; and therefore, ought to be welcomed. Whether we welcome them or not, however, probably will have no significant effect upon the tempo at which they will be introduced."[1]

The feelings of exhilaration, speed, apprehension, and misgivings have been compounded by the added emotion of frustration in the case of electronic computers. This sense of frustration has resulted largely from some of the optimistic, exaggerated, and often unwarranted claims made for them. One of the more conservative of the optimistic claims is that made by A. Danjon, director of the Paris Observatory and president of the French Computing Association, who said, "The invention of electronic mathematical computers, going back only fifteen years, deserves to be considered a landmark in the history of science in the same way as the invention of lenses or the microscope."[2]

When the electronic computers designed for business applications made their first appearances in 1948, many businessmen who would ordinarily have been cool-headed, critical, and analytical found it almost impossible to resist the promised Utopia offered by the pitched publicity of the more rabid proponents of the new mathematical media. The computers became management's "fair-haired" problem-solving wonder boys. However, the expectations of savings in time, money, and labor were—and still are— often unrealistic and unachieved; and many companies are missing many of the savings offered by technological developments. As a result, disappointments, frustration, and cynicism developed in some areas, and the computer became instead management's (and labor's) whipping boy.

However, if business firms try to stand still or rest on their laurels, they will actually move backward. This principle is true because nothing involving human beings can remain dormant—it must either grow or die, progress or regress, advance or recede, improve or decline—there is no remaining still. Change is the law that governs all living things and all human institutions. Therefore, the more progressive companies, which were philosophically so inclined and financially able, entered the computer field either as producers or users.

---

[1]Sexton, B., "Labor Looks at Automation," *Proceedings Third Annual High-Speed Computer Conference,* Louisiana State University, Baton Rouge, 1956.
[2]"International Conference on Information Processing—The Opening," *Computers and Automation,* July 1959.

THE IMPORTANCE OF THE HUMAN ELEMENT

Some of the less conservative statements of the early writers and speakers indicated that there would be an elimination, or at best a downgrading, of the human element in mental activities in the business world. Experience has shown the results to be quite different. "If there is a competition between man and machines, man is winning it—not for at least two centuries has his position been so important as compared with that of the apparatus with which he works."[3] This means there has been a more effective utilization of manpower by letting the machines do more of the work. As machines have taken over more of the boring and tedious paperwork, office employees have become free to do more interesting and creative work—and this results in an upgrading of their jobs. For example, in one company the industrial engineers were spending 50 per cent of their time gathering data and evaluating results and 50 per cent doing routine mathematical computations. With an electronic computer, their time is now 80 per cent creative and 20 per cent routine calculations.

Generally speaking, the heaviest area of effective application of computers has been in the field of volume iterative work. There is much more to solving a mathematically complex problem than just applying the correct mathematical formulas. Someone must conceive it, determine how it is to be solved, program the machine, and then interpret the results. The average individual business, scientific, or technical problem usually presents such a programing burden that the solution of the problem is much easier than its application to the machine. This programing, or the instructions that the machine must follow, must all be originally written by human beings. It is not important where the formulas originated but merely what the system of equations is and in what sequence they are to be solved.

In relation to the effects of electronic computers on personnel problems, not all work groups have been affected equally. The problem of original data handling has not yet been satisfactorily resolved on a large scale; yet this is the field in which a large percentage of today's clerical labor is employed and one in which the greatest personnel problems probably will be encountered for quite some time. There must still be a vast amount of original recording of sales orders, purchase orders, requisitions, time cards, invoices, and other documents of original entry despite the fringe penetrations that have been made into this area by the machines. As the equipment

[3]Galbraith, John Kenneth, "Men and Capital," *The Saturday Evening Post,* March 5, 1960.

is not better than the human thinking that controls the input of the data or the decisions based upon the results of the machine's manipulation of the data, it is very essential that both the original entry and the egress of the data from the machine be highly accurate. The accuracy of the transmittal of these data into the electronic dragon becomes enormously more important than before, since once they disappear into this monster, errors which are not subject to automatic checking can travel their polylateral ways and produce a correction problem that tends to vitiate the economies of the machine.

This brings into focus another of the personnel problems that has arisen and at least implies the answer to it—that is, a greater premium needs to be placed on the fastest and most accurate workers in the field of initial entry of information. "About one-third of the time of many high speed, digital computers is used to eliminate errors from new programs. De-bugging is a necessary consequence of the fallibility of people and the literalness of computers. For the machine can only do precisely what it has been instructed to do. . . ."[4] Second, an excellent system of control clerks to police the data must be set up because, reduced to their barest essentials, most management problems come down to the one simple frustrating element of the unpredictability of people. Nearly everywhere, particularly in the key decisions in business or industrial operations, wherever an intricate step must be performed or a vital decision made and acted upon, some member of the human race is still found.

It can therefore be seen that machines are not supplanting human thinking and judgment. The machines are merely adjuncts to persons, and the center of personality lies in the environmental life. Therefore, thinking and creativity are still means to an end rather than ends in themselves.

Human inertia is a given factor in any social situation and must be considered in either forecasting future possibilities or evaluating past events; this has been particularly true with the computers.

The machines have had their greatest impact when applied to routine business functions, and this application has provided a background for the education of everyone concerned. Management has looked upon the initial period of the computer's installation as a period of testing and trying and has considered it as experimentation and education that has been subsidized by the savings realized through mechanization of the more routine office operations. Strangely enough, the *greatest savings have been accomplished*

4Blair, C. R., "On Economical Debugging," *Computers and Automation*, May 1959.

through the improvement of regular operations rather than through the use of the machines themselves. Thus the computers have been more effective for companies that are already extremely well organized and managed. Their greatest help to the less well organized companies has been in helping to put their affairs in better order. Also, a survey of many large computer installations revealed that the more successful ones were being supervised actively by top management.[5] The successful systems participated in major functions of the company operations, ranging from production, marketing, distribution, and decision making to accounting. The lesser successes were limited to routine record-keeping activities.

Attention repeatedly has been drawn to the historically paradoxical behavior of high-speed machines in that they first appeared to cause unemployment but then created a far greater number of employment opportunities than was available under the regime of the slower, preceding methods. Of all the new industries that have sprung up during the past 70 years, just 14 (and these are among the most highly automated) give employment, either directly or indirectly, to over 13 million people.[6] It has been estimated that the field of electronics itself will become the largest single industry within the next few years.[7] The history of mechanization shows that an increase in the number and percentage of employees is caused by the new devices. However, a restatement of this historical pattern as a prognosis for computer operations is not generally satisfying or convincing.

COMPUTERS AND UNEMPLOYMENT

Peter F. Drucker has concluded that "automation may bring about more large-scale labor displacement in office jobs than in any other field of employment." A clear delineation needs to be made between *displacement* and *unemployment.*

In a survey among the executives from the 500 largest industrial organizations, it was found that the immediate impact of automation is displacement of labor, but the extent of it depends on how rapidly automation is implemented throughout the industry.[8] The executives did assert that

[5]McKinsey and Company, Inc., "Getting the Most Out of Your Computer," *Data Processing Yearbook,* American Data Processing, Inc., Detroit, 1963.
[6]*The Miracle of America* (Fourth Edition), The Advertising Council, Inc., 1950.
[7]Smith, Robert M., "Automation Opens New Horizons Through New Developments in the First Half of 1959," *Office Management,* July 1959.
[8]Lipstren, Otis, "Personnel Management in the Automated Firm," *Personnel,* March-April 1962.

the new technology would eventually provide more stability in employment than presently exists. Increased responsibility on the part of management will help ease the problems created.

Therefore, the only apparent connection between computers and unemployment is the problem of labor displacement, where employees must adapt themselves to new jobs and new opportunities. Actual unemployment as a result of computer installation is relatively uncommon, for despite the rapid movement to office automation there is relatively little prospect that any substantial number of workers will be thrown out of jobs. In fact, up until recently, the trend has been in the opposite direction.[9] In 1950, clerical workers accounted for 12.3 per cent of the total work force. In 1960, this figure had increased to 14.5 per cent. It appears that the volume of paperwork continues to grow more rapidly than the decrease in jobs caused by the computer revolution, for each year there are usually around 100,000 more workers in the offices than the previous year. According to one source, "White collarites were 31 per cent of the labor force (in any industry) 20 years ago; it's figured they will be 42.5 per cent in 1965."[10] (These figures may be misleading, for the reduction in the labor force through efficiency and mechanization is far greater than the relative increase in the clerical force.)

As in all other radical modifications and changes in work patterns, many employees have suffered and will continue to suffer unfavorable *displacements* as a result of changed skill requirements caused by the computers. The abilities needed and the manual and mental requirements of jobs have increased as a result of the new devices. Numerous and violent job dislocations almost invariably follow a shift to automation in offices. In this respect, it isn't a case of unemployment but of movement, or transfer, within the same company. In nearly every case where a computer has been introduced into the business, the existing workers have been provided for through transfers, upgrading, or normal attrition. A National Office Management Association survey indicated that less than 3 per cent of the employees whose jobs were eliminated or integrated had been laid off.[11] When asked what happened to office employees whose jobs were replaced by electronic data processing, 42 per cent of the companies said no jobs had been replaced, 54 per cent said the employees had been integrated

[9]"Office Automation: How Much Staff Dislocation?" *Personnel,* January-February 1960.
[10]"New Drive for White Collarites," *Business Week,* February 20, 1960.
[11]"Office Automation: How Much Staff Dislocation?" *loc. cit.*

into other jobs, 2.7 per cent had to lay off employees, and less than 1 per cent had been transferred to other locations.

In this connection, Seymour Wolfbein, Deputy Assistant Secretary of Labor and Director of Automation and Manpower, has said population will increase 15 per cent between 1960 and 1970 but the labor force will jump from 73.5 million to 87 million.[12]

In 1957 there were more white-collar than blue-collar workers due to extraordinary changes in productivity. In the last half century gross national product has increased threefold per capita, but the proportion of people working is approximately the same as it was. There is a decline among the young and an increase among women. People are working fewer hours.

Dropouts from schools cause high unemployment figures. The majority drop out because of a lack of meaningful courses of instruction. There will be a need for more and more skilled craftsmen (more than the supply after 1960-1961). More people have been hired in service-producing activities, such as trade, service, finance, state and local government, and teaching. Education and training are a solution to the problem, coupled with increased productivity. More flexible education is needed for possible changes in jobs.

It can thus be seen that the twin factors of shortage of clerical personnel caused by the rapidly increasing volume of paperwork and rapid labor turnover in the clerical work force have eased the transition from noncomputer to computer operations.

NEED FOR SOCIAL SHOCK ABSORBERS

However, it is equally true that many employees who could otherwise be utilized in performing activities associated with computers or related jobs have not been mentally, emotionally, or temperamentally capable of fitting into the mold of these new arrangements of duties and responsibilities. The most troublesome personnel relocation problems have been with the experienced people performing routine jobs not in the value-judgment, decision-making areas. The former, who are usually the older or less educated employees, tend to be relatively inflexible so that there are fewer adjustments that can be made with them. In a period of expanding job opportunities as was true from 1940 to 1957, this problem was not insurmountable. However, in a period of declining or decelerating employment opportunities

[12]Wolfbein, Seymour, "Automation and Manpower in the 1960's" *The Electrical Aftermath of Automation,* Newman Press, Westminister, Md., 1962.

—as occurred from 1957 to 1960—there were, and probably will continue to be, rather loud outbursts against these alterations in the conventional office work patterns. One researcher has concluded that even where there are serious manpower shortages, it is not accurate to state that there has been no labor displacement.

Experience has shown that this problem is not so much attributable to the addition of the new machines as it is to the improvement in systems, the elimination of unnecessary reports, and other work simplification activities. Most companies have trained their operators, key punchers, and similar types of employees to fill other jobs.

Consideration of these displaced persons has led management—both from its own inherent sense of social conscience and from external pressure —to provide all sorts of social shock absorbers, such as severance pay, dislocation pay, pensions (including earlier retirement), unemployment insurance, guaranteed employment or wages (including supplemental unemployment compensation payments), and so forth.

The unions have attempted to obtain interoffice transfers based solely upon seniority, a stronger "guaranteed annual wage," a shorter work week, new job classifications, and other provisions to share the gains from computers with the workers. In addition, the unions have increased their efforts to unionize this increasingly important segment of the labor force. If they cannot, they will be unable to maintain their present power.[13]

CHANGING SKILL REQUIREMENTS AND JOB CONTENT

There is one change which has been repeatedly evident in computer operations—that is, a modification in work patterns. This has manifested itself in changing skill requirements and job content. There is no unanimity of agreement about the direction in which these have gone.

The industrial revolution, with its development of machines to eliminate physical drudgery, led to specialization of effort on the part of the workers. This was based upon the principle of transfer of skill, which holds that the attention and skill required of a worker to use a tool or operate a machine is inversely related to the thought and skill transferred into its mechanism. Therefore, the worker becomes an adjunct to the machine, and the transfer of skill from the expert workman to the machine makes the quality and quantity of work produced dependent upon the machine,

[13]Shaw, Reid L., "The Answer to White Collar Unions," *Personnel,* January-February 1960.

not upon the machine operator. There are degrees in the transfer of thought, skill, and intelligence to the machine. It becomes evident then that the greater the skill transferred to the tool or machine, the less is required of the operator. However, there is a countervailing principle, the principle of individual effectiveness. This principle says that through improved training and working conditions, a person's effectiveness will become greater.

These two principles have worked in opposite directions. The former had led to an extension of specialization as a result of the introduction of computers. The increased demands made on organizations through the use of complex computer machinery and equipment and the related statistical and mathematical techniques have led to the use of more staff specialists; management has had to place greater reliance on them than formerly.

Another group of researchers feels there is a danger in specialization and that demands for computers will lead to less specialization.[14] It seems inevitable that the demand for both computers and an economy based on automation will result in an immensely increased degree of diversification and adaptability on the part of individual employees.

Narrow and rigid job classifications have had to be broadened and possibly will be eliminated in the future. This seems paradoxical in view of the history of the industrial revolution, but it is based upon two rather diverse truths.

First, there is currently a trend in management thinking and philosophy away from minute specialization and toward generalization. Management has begun to think in terms of the whole organization rather than in terms of specific parts of the group. It is thinking more of the little universe that it runs and is attempting to pin down relationships more on the basis of firm analytical reasoning than on an indefinite "feel" for a given situation. This trend is a revolution, or protest, against the history of the last 35 years, which has been characterized by a shortage of managerial personnel with the overall view.[15]

[14]Witty, M. D., "Obsolete—at Age 29," *Computers and Automation,* December 1958.
[15]This is the basic assumption underlying two penetrating reports on higher education for business. See Gordon, Robert A., and Howell, James E., *Higher Education for Business,* Columbia University Press, New York, 1959, particularly, ". . . there is growing agreement on the need for greater breadth and higher standards in collegiate business education" and Pierson, Frank C., *The Education of American Businessmen,* McGraw-Hill, New York, 1959, particularly, "If widening the scale and variety of a company's internal activities were simply to require a different kind of top management, the problem would be difficult enough, but the need for balancing and coordinating a diversity of functions reaches down to many lower level activities."

Second, the very nature of computer operations has led to a generalization of effort rather than specialization. The computer performs operations for the entire organization, not just the office. Formerly, these activities were performed in the production, sales, finance, or other departments by their personnel. Now the data are sent to the computer center, where they are manipulated by the computer personnel, who must have a greater breadth of knowledge and training than was formerly true. Although this tendency to centralize these processing activities exists, there need not be an end to decentralized management responsibilities.

CHANGING COMPOSITION OF THE WORK FORCE

What will the office work force of the future look like? Probably there will be key-punch operators, machine tenders, programers, analysts, research personnel, and decision makers. It will be immediately recognized that the work of the first of these will be relatively routine and require little skill; whereas the higher one rises in the echelon, the greater will be the degree of skill and diversification needed. However, there is the distinct possibility of stratification of workers in this pattern, which is to be avoided if possible.

It seems inevitable that electronic computers ultimately will create a new kind of organizational world, whose impact will be felt not only by management but also by workers. Management is having to face new problems, such as increased capital investment and operating risks, the increased precision reliability required of the total clerical and productive system, and the increased inflexibility and complexity of operations. Intensifying this inflexibility is the fact that the computers have led to a higher ratio of maintenance people to production people and of management to non-management personnel. Therefore, the ratio of indirect labor to direct labor as it is now defined will continue to increase markedly. Even today, many of those people who are considered overhead workers are in reality production personnel just as vital to the continued operation of the business as the machine operators. These factors have caused employment to be less responsive to a business cycle than it was in the past.

SCHEDULING OF WORK

Another personnel policy that has been affected by computers is the scheduling of work. Two factors have led to this problem. First, there must be both preventive and curative maintenance. The former has generally proved to be more economical of time than the latter. Second, as fast as computers are, they are limited in the amount of work they can do simultaneously. Something has to go first, something has to follow, and something has to go last. This truism, as simple as it is, has usually been at the heart of more dissatisfaction than any other single factor associated with computer operations. The cost of the computer is in terms of time, and as this time is so expensive it cannot be permitted to remain idle. As the volume of work to be assigned to it increases relative to its capacity, work must be performed outside the regular eight to five shift. This factor has led to multiple-shift operations, which has been a new and frustrating experience for most clerical workers.

INCREASING IMPORTANCE OF "GOOD" HUMAN RELATIONS

The human relations aspects of electronic computers cannot be overlooked. In addition to changing the work materially, the new equipment has created new job opportunities to use new skills, has raised standards of living, and has resulted in many employees earning a living in a more rewarding and interesting way. Paradoxically, the trend toward the disappearance of the human contributions to product creation, including clerical operations, has been accompanied by an increased need for management to recognize the bipolar nature of employees who must be treated as individuals *and* as members of the group. It has also led to more tolerance for the constructive nonconformist.

There have been two corollary results of the human relations factors in computer activities. First, the process of upgrading has resulted not only in higher pay for the employees but also in an opportunity for them to transcend the clerical status and achieve a measure of professional standing. Second, many employees have found the computers to be a steppingstone to higher positions and also to better positions within their own companies and within other companies.

INCREASING IMPORTANCE OF SUPERVISION

The direction of personnel has assumed an even greater importance than in the past, for the economical and effective operation of computers depends very much upon the efficiency of the staff that operates them. Not only does the computer need a new kind of worker with different vocational qualifications and skills, but its technical and organizational characteristics also call for a new type of supervision. This is true because the managers now have the problem of fitting the changing types of technical personalities and employees into the organization and yet maintaining the morale of all the workers in a situation where their individual contributions to product creation are becoming more and more difficult for them to perceive or assess clearly.

What are these managerial characteristics required by computer operation? Roddy Osborn, in describing the director needed for General Electric's Computer Center at Appliance Park, Kentucky, said, "We were looking for high intelligence and ability to think logically and reason abstractly. In particular, for the leadership of such a group, we wanted someone with enthusiasm, vision, foresight, energy, and optimistic point of view; he should be willing to take risks and devote his entire energies and thoughts to the task at hand."[16] The reason for these characteristics is that the installation of these devices has called for a re-evaluation of the existing clerical system and the designing of a system to coincide with the new advanced thinking in the field.

The development of criteria for selecting the more promising of available manpower to fill these managerial and supervisory positions has presented problems which have varied in their solution. The questions of whether emphasis should be placed on elaborate mathematical background, whether mastery in statistical reasoning should be developed, or whether a combination of logical processes as evidenced by measurable examinations would give the most satisfactory results are still unresolved. However, this much has been proved: These people must have an exploratory approach. Men with the ability and the initiative to bring about a reduction of records and reports to a useful level are desperately needed. In their exploratory approach, these new supervisors should emphasize both internal and external research.

Fortunately or unfortunately, there is no "right" way to program one of these computers. Almost any problem can be solved in a multiplicity of ways and often with the same answer, but not all of these ways are equally good in terms of computer efficiency, and some can be very wasteful of time and effort. This factor often decreases computer efficiency, and since computer time is a very high-priced commodity, this is an important aspect of the overall problem.

[16]Osborn, Roddy F., "G. E. and Univac: Harnessing the High-Speed Computer," *Harvard Business Review,* July-August 1954.

DEMAND AND SUPPLY OF QUALIFIED PERSONNEL

Another key consideration that has limited progress toward installation of computer facilities has been the tremendous demand these facilities create for skilled manpower. Not only was this true during the early years of computer operations, but professional positions in the field have been continually increasing vis-à-vis the supply of trained personnel even during recent years. This disparity has led to a severe shortage of persons professionally trained in the area, and the good ones command premium salaries. During conversion to computer operations, frequent adjustments have had to be made in job evaluations and wage structures as well as organizational plans. This has often led to the dilemma of paying as much or more in many cases, to these "bright young men" as to personnel who have been with the organization for longer periods of time. Needless to say, this has caused strained personnel relations. However, as the law of supply and demand still has validity today, the solution of this problem of scarcity exists. One wise personnel manager said, "Seek (and pay ye well enough) and ye shall ultimately find."[17]

NEED FOR EDUCATION, TRAINING, AND RETRAINING

This shortage of personnel has caused management to scramble to find sufficient men with the necessary education and training. Essentially, there are two sources from which the people can be obtained: from within or from outside the organization, the former being more desirable. However, this forces the company into training its own personnel, and therefore retraining assumes a much greater importance than ever before. This training may be furnished to clerical personnel or others. One way of achieving the training is for the organization to have its own people do as much of the survey work as possible so they can gain experience. The training provided by the companies to their own work force has consisted of on-the-job training. This has been supplemented by short courses provided by the equipment manufacturers and colleges and universities.

The use of outside sources of employees has resulted in two things. First, there has been a pirating of personnel from the manufacturers of the equipment, other users, and university facilities. This, in turn, has led to the emphasis upon training and education for computer operations at the college and even high school level. The bulk of the training job in the

[17]Stoter, Lloyd E., "Instrumentation," *Office Executive*, October 1959.

future will be in regularly scheduled graduate and undergraduate courses and programs in universities. Originally there was much foundering at the college level, with education being provided on a piecemeal basis. However, according to Gardner M. Jones, the piecemeal education ". . . is giving way gradually to better organized, systematic instruction at the college level; at least present developments and announced plans in many schools point in that direction."[18] For the colleges and universities to do an effective job, however, it is possible that the solution will require going back to the level of the secondary schools and altering their educational pattern, particularly as it pertains to their mathematical requirements.

SUMMING IT UP

The short history of office automation has borne out the conclusions of Professor Norbert Wiener that "any use of a human being in which less is demanded of him and less is attributed to him than his full status is a degradation and a waste."[19] The role played by human beings has become more distinctly important as a result of the introduction of electronic computers in the field of business. Since the purpose for which machines are to be used is the most important consideration and since that purpose is still the most effective use of the human mind and since nobody who is now using computers even suggests that they will ever displace thinking in decision making, the only conclusion is that man is more important.

The greatest shifting of personnel that has occurred as a result of the introduction of electronic computers has been in the areas of elimination of drudgery from clerical work and the conversion of office work along more interesting and challenging lines.

Little unemployment has occurred as a result of the introduction of these machines. What unemployment has resulted has been in the form of employees *who have not been hired.* In other words, the companies have used attrition to eliminate any unnecessary employees and the growing need for clerical employees to provide for the dislocation of personnel whose jobs have been discontinued. The dislocation has largely been satisfactorily handled through transfers, which have resulted in more pleasant and often more profitable positions.

[18]Jones, Gardner M., "Computer Education: Dilemma of the Colleges," *Proceedings of the High Speed Computer Conference,* March 5-8, 1957.
[19]Wiener, Norbert, *The Human Use of Human Beings,* Houghton Mifflin Company, Boston, 1950.

Although the conclusion is not quite as clear concerning the effects on job descriptions and classifications, rigid job classifications have in general been relaxed, or at least broadened, to result in an upgrading of present personnel. In some instances, this has resulted in higher job ratings and salaries but has given management greater flexibility.

Managerial and supervisory responsibilities have become greater and assumed a much more important position. This has been true because managerial duties and obligations have been more readily capable of evaluation through the pinpointing of action areas, the reduction in the mass of unimportant details, and the concentration upon more relevant reports.

As the rapidly increasing demand for qualified personnel to utilize this new equipment has outstripped the supply of qualified people available, there has been a drastic change in the relative salaries paid to such personnel. Some of the older employees have had to realize that the new workers were engaged primarily in the decision-making process and that this process affected their lives; consequently the newer employees were paid commensurate with their abilities. This has led to a modification of the wage and organizational structures of many organizations.

The proportion of maintenance types of jobs has increased relative to production types of jobs; the proportion of managerial and supervisory jobs has increased relative to nonmanagerial jobs. These trends have led to a widening of the concept of seniority units so that the conventional thinking regarding job seniority has had to be broadened to include plantwide or even companywide seniority, where unions are involved.

The changing concepts of seniority and the displacement occasioned by the computers (and other forms of automation) have led to pressures being exerted on management, both internally and externally, for social shock absorbers such as the "guaranteed annual wage," severance pay, dislocation pay, pensions (including earlier retirement), unemployment insurance, and others.

The shortage of qualified workers has led to an emphasis upon training and, more important, retraining of employees. As management realized that there was a shortage of people outside the organization, it has had to retrain and upgrade its own personnel. The training programs vary from in-service training within the company to computer manufacturers' schools, colleges and universities (including both undergraduate and graduate programs), and even secondary schools. Concurrent with this, if not because of it, has been the re-emphasis upon mathematical training, both at the college and at the high school level.

Finally, there has been a re-emphasis upon the elimination of unnecessary work, the most effective scheduling of work, and the management-exception principle.

Many of the hopes for savings in time, effort, and money have not been achieved. There are two apparent reasons for this: (1) the computers are called upon to do many jobs they were not originally designed or purchased for and (2) many of the production problems and activities have been shifted to the office and the computers rather than being performed by the production employees as in the past.

These pressures, as well as the changing content of the jobs, the layout of the work, the lack of creativity, the disassociation from management, and the factory-like atmosphere that the emphasis on mass production of data has caused have led rank-and-file office workers to view themselves as related to factory workers. There is a tendency for the computers to deglamorize and dehumanize office work.

SECTION IV

The Plight of the Unskilled Worker

One of the most serious problems facing society and, therefore, industry is how to make productive workers of the vast numbers of those without specific skills. The situation is particularly acute with regard to the younger members of the population with little education and training and older workers whose skills have become obsolete.

UNSKILLED WORKERS: THE DIMENSIONS OF THE PROBLEM •

FELICIAN F. FOLTMAN

IF A PERSONNEL MANAGER ELECTED to view unskilled workers today from a coldly analytical or rational standpoint, he could justify the premise that they did not represent any sort of challenge or problem but were instead, the least of his worries. Indeed, he could argue that there were many unskilled and also unemployed in the work force and, therefore, as a personnel manager he could raise his hiring standards to be very selective about whom he hired. He could not, of course, be completely rational and lower the wage paid to these unskilled workers because this decision would involve forces and factors over which he would have no control. True, when he had to lay off unskilled people or, even worse, when their jobs were wiped out as a result of the introduction of more efficient machines or processes, he would be forced to struggle with complicated questions of equity and costs. But the narrow and short-term perspective that is implied in the outlook just described is, obviously, undesirable even if it were attainable. By now it should be apparent to all managers that it is the unskilled who are untrained and therefore unwanted and unemployed. And this equation affects us all. In the remarks that follow, the dimensions of the unskilled "problem" will be delineated in order to be able to question more thoughtfully the phenomenon and thus be in a position to suggest more intelligent solutions.

PROBLEMS OF DEFINITION

The signs on the statistical road maps that emanate from the U.S. Bureau of the Census or the U.S. Department of Labor are understandable only to those who bother with definitions. To understand the problems of the

---

FELICIAN F. FOLTMAN is Associate Professor, New York State School of Industrial and Labor Relations, Cornell University, Ithaca, New York.

unskilled workers we must first agree as to who or what are unskilled workers. But almost immediately we find that to reach this agreement is not easy because the very concept of skill is illusive. Neither the psychologist nor the economist has come forth with precise definitions.

Unskilled occupations, as defined in what is probably the best collection of occupational data in the world, the *Dictionary of Occupational Titles,* are: "manual occupations that involve the performance of simple duties that may be learned within a short period of time and that require the exercise of little or no independent judgment. Characteristically, such occupations do not require previous experience in the specific occupation in question, although a familiarity with the occupational environment may be necessary and desirable."[1]

In this DOT classification scheme, which is used in our public employment service operations, all of the thousands of jobs are classified as Professional and Managerial; Clerical and Sales; Service; Agriculture, Fishing, Forestry, and Kindred; Skilled; Semi-skilled; and Unskilled. Both theoretical and practical problems arise when using this or other classification schemes. Not so incidentally, the U.S. Census classifies occupations into groups that are slightly different from those used by the Bureau of Employment Security in its dictionary. By and large, occupational data in the *Dictionary of Occupational Titles* is much more detailed than that found in the census. In both schemes, however, there is the problem of deciding whether occupations listed under operatives, service workers, or clerical and kindred are unskilled or not. Is a waiter skilled or unskilled? Is a tape librarian in a computerized data-processing office unskilled or not? Is a chauffeur skilled? When we refer to skill do we mean motor skills exclusively, or should we include social skills as well? Clearly, answers to these and similar questions are important for more than academic reasons. How we define and classify jobs is very consequential to individuals who are employed in particular job categories, to the employer, to the union, and to the public planner. Who or what is unskilled becomes of paramount importance when we attempt to reduce our unemployment by a program of retraining.

On the more positive side, does anyone agree as to who or what is unskilled? From an operational view the one characteristic that helps to delineate skill is the learning time required to acquire an acceptable standard of performance. This definition, too, can be disputed but it will suffice

[1]Shartle, C., *Occupational Information its Development and Application,* Prentice Hall, New York, 1946, p. 118.

for purposes of these remarks. One final point of definition is that these remarks arbitrarily exclude farm occupations on the grounds that they are peripheral to our interests in this report.

THE DEMOGRAPHY OF UNSKILLED WORKERS

Our total manpower situation today can be described by a series of quite paradoxical propositions. The principal findings of the 1960 Census as summarized by Philip Hauser highlight these paradoxes. He notes:

The population stood at a new high (179,323,175 on the day of the census: April 1, 1960); yet more than half the counties in the U.S. had smaller populations than they had at the time of the 1950 census.

The population was more than ever concentrated in urban regions. Nonetheless, 73 cities, including 11 of the 12 largest, lost population.

Americans were younger on the average than in 1950; the median age of the population had declined for the first time in 170 years. But the population was also older, as measured by the proportion of men and women 65 years old or more.[2]

In a similar vein the second annual presidential report on manpower pointed up some of the contrasts in the manpower situation as follows:

More people are now employed in the United States than ever before in our history. But unemployment remains much too high—far above any frictional minimum.

With average earnings and personal income at the highest levels yet achieved in this or any other country, many millions of Americans still live in poverty.

Professional personnel and other highly qualified workers are generally in great demand. Greater numbers of professional and specialized personnel are needed in many fields to speed economic and social progress, while millions of less-skilled workers are unemployed.

Though Negro workers have made substantial gains in education, employment, and income, the gap in employment and earnings between white and non-white people has been wider in recent years than in the immediate postwar period—because the white population has moved ahead even faster than the non-white.

American workers have a higher average level of education than ever before, and college enrollments have reached unprecedented figures. Yet millions of workers lack the basic education required for effective participation in

[2]Hauser, Philip M., "The Census of 1960", *Scientific American*, July 1961, p. 40.

present-day economic life, and nearly a third of our young people continue to drop out of school before completing high school.

And with a tremendous rise in the number of teenage workers immediately ahead, an increase in teenage unemployment is inevitable unless strenuous measures are taken to prevent it.[3]

	1910	1950	1960
		(percentages)	
All Workers	100	100	100
White Collar	22	37	43
Professional and technical	5	9	11
Proprietary and managerial	7	9	11
Clerical and sales	10	19	21
Blue Collar	37	41	36
Skilled	12	14	13
Semiskilled	14	21	18
Unskilled	11	6	5
Service	10	10	13
Farm	31	12	8

How many in our work force are unskilled? As already indicated, answers to the question can be obtained, but care must be used in deciding who does and who does not get counted. If the answer to the above question is comparative rather than absolute, there is remarkable unanimity among our demographers that a shift has occurred and is still occurring in the work force away from unskilled labor and towards higher and more intellectual skills and pursuits. This important trend is dramatized in the accompanying summary table.[4]

As the data in the table and similar data indicate, upward of a quarter of the people who worked at the turn of the century were employed as laborers or in some unskilled capacity. Some 60 years later less than ten per cent of us worked in unskilled occupations. Furthermore, all the indicators point to a declining importance in our work force for unskilled workers. Most of the occupational and industrial shifts that have been cited recently make the same point—namely, unskilled workers are less important to our economy. For example, there has been a shift from goods to services, but

[3]*Manpower Report of the President,* March 1964, Government Printing Office, 1964, pp. 1-2.

[4]Wolfbein, Seymour L., "Automation and Skill," *The Annals,* March 1962, p. 54.

the growth in services has been in local and state government at white-collar and usually professional levels. Another significant trend that is relevant here is the fact that in the last four or five years employment in manufacturing has been declining, signifying that there are fewer job opportunities for unskilled workers. And we know, of course, of the continued expansion in our white-collar and skilled occupations.

But these are relatively esoteric data—abstract, academic sometimes, and cold. They do not really emphasize any of the individual and social problems of the unskilled, nor do they point up the magnitude of the problem for all of us. For insight into the characteristics of the unskilled, it is necessary to turn to unemployment data. Why, one may ask, turn to unemployment data? The answer is that the great majority of our unemployed are unskilled; or, from another perspective, it is the unskilled who becomes unemployed.

No matter from where the evidence comes, the truth of the above noted logic is becoming clearer day by day; the unskilled of the nation are the unemployed, the disfranchised, the disadvantaged (a euphemism currently much in vogue), the poverty stricken, and, by any standards, a problem for an affluent society. The groups which have a high incidence of unemployment have, in each case, a large proportion of unskilled in their ranks. Thus we find high unemployment and few salable skills among persons in the following groups:

Youth. Details of the inordinately high unemployment among youth should be familiar by now even to those who are casual observers of the social scene. Unemployment among youths 14 to 19 years of age was 15.6 per cent in 1963.[5] But this high unemployment rate, unfortunate as it is, must be viewed from the perspective of a population bulge and the disappointing lack of growth of traditional entry jobs which require little or no skill. And also sad is the fact that unemployment among youth persists for ever longer periods. Most vulnerable in the labor market is the youth who happens to be a dropout. The dropout problem is summarized in the *President's Manpower Report* as follows:

> The inadequately educated and ill-trained school dropouts are likely to form the nucleus of the future hard-core unemployed. In the fall of 1962, 9.1 million youths between the ages of 16 and 24 were in the labor force and out of school; some 2.2 million were in the 18- to 19 year-old group and 0.5 million were 16 or 17. One-third of these young persons had not graduated from high school. Those with more education had less unemployment;

[5]*President's Manpower Report, op. cit.,* p. 26.

only 8 per cent of the graduates but over 14 per cent of the dropouts were unemployed.[6]

Any attempt to understand the complicated matrix in which unemployed youth, especially dropouts, find themselves, leads inevitably to an examination of schools and of educational policy. It is encouraging to note that more and more of our youth are staying in school longer, but in the forseeable future we will continue to have unfortunately high dropout rates. Manifestly we must, to paraphrase Lewis Carroll's Red Queen, run twice as fast if we are to find acceptable answers for this particular social problem.

Older workers. Older workers, per se, are not our concern here. But older workers (by definition, 45 years of age or older) who become unemployed tend to remain unemployed longer than younger men. And despite many years of experience, the relatively low educational attainments of the displaced or unemployed older worker becomes a serious handicap. The problem is not skill alone for the unskilled, older worker; his re-employment is complicated by the fact that employers are very interested, and properly so, in realizing a gain on their investment over many years and prefer younger persons for this reason. Nevertheless, the significant point is that older workers who have had many years of service in unskilled or semiskilled capacities do not have too much to offer in today's labor markets.

Negro and other minority workers. The plight of the American Negro is succinctly summarized in the following statistics. In 1963 there were "more than 22 million nonwhites in the U.S. most of whom were Negroes. Nonwhites comprised 11.7 per cent of the population, 11 per cent of the labor force, and 21 per cent of the unemployed."[7] Among Negro youth, unemployment rates are intolerably high. It is certainly beyond the scope of this report, but it is not irrelevant to point out that raising skill will not lower unemployment in this group unless and until discriminatory practices are eliminated.

Public-assistance recipients. There are approximately 7 million persons in the country who share $5 billion a year in various programs of public assistance.[8] But very few of these are potentially employable, as the events

[6]*Ibid.,* p. 128.

[7]*Ibid.,* p. 95.

[8]U.S. Senate Subcommittee on Employment and Manpower, *Toward Full Employment: Proposals for a Comprehensive Employment and Manpower Policy in the United States,* Government Printing Office, 1964, p. 73.

in Newburgh, New York, attest. Too often, however, those who are potentially employable are unskilled in addition to being indigent. Most tragic is the fact that an increasing percentage of welfare recipients are second- or third-generation cases. A welfare subculture seems to be developing in which the recipients of public assistance have little education and no skill to offer; the ramifications of this are only dimly perceived at this time.

The pertinent demographic data about the unskilled are summarized in the following:

1. Blue-collar occupations relative to white-collar occupations are decreasing.
2. The number of unskilled in the work force is declining both relatively and absolutely.
3. Unemployment rates are higher among the unskilled than they are in any other occupational group.
4. Unemployment can be equated with lack of skill.
5. Millions of persons are currently employed in jobs that are unskilled, but there is little future for the individual who is unskilled.

HOW DO UNSKILLED WORKERS FARE IN THE LABOR MARKET?

Unskilled workers have for many years played an interesting and often controversial role in the labor market. The presence of millions of immigrants, most of whom were unskilled, persuaded many employers that their work processes could be rationalized and thereby adapted to the available manpower. And for the first half of this century, unskilled workers found relatively abundant opportunities in the labor market except on those occasions when the economic system was proceeding at something less than full throttle. Today, however, we have noted that the unskilled do not fare too well in our job markets. Not all theorists or men of affairs agree completely as to why unskilled workers fare so poorly in the world of work, but a consensus is being reached. A look at some of the evidence is in order.

Perhaps the most basic problem for the unskilled worker is that he or she does not adapt too well to today's technology. A measure of the challenge that is posed to unskilled workers in a rapidly changing technology can be gained from the following headline that appeared recently: "Obsolescence Brings Worries About Jobs to Some Engineers." The article stated that a new one-year program was being inaugurated at a famous engineering school to help competent, mature engineers stave off obsolescence. That obsolescence is a problem for college-trained engineers would appear to be true. It is even more poignantly true for unskilled workers.

By whatever definition it is known, technological change causes occupational obsolescence. The most obvious example of obsolescence is, of course, in the field of agriculture; for half a century there has been a steady exodus from American farms. In recent years the exodus has accelerated to a very rapid pace. Between 1950 and 1962, farm employment fell from 7.5 million to 4.8 million.[9]

Does automation upgrade skill requirements? Does automation eliminate or produce jobs? Often heatedly debated, these questions can now be answered in the light of impressive evidence, statistical and other, that has been accumulating since the early 1950's. As already noted, there is an expansion in the white-collar part of our work force. At the same time there is less need for the unskilled worker. Two other facts are becoming increasingly clear: employers are raising their educational requirements to be able to deal competitively with the new technology, and employers frequently have unfilled job openings at the professional levels—thus the so-called skill gap or the educational gap. The public debate has shifted to this imbalance in the labor market. Obviously, some say, all that is necessary is to retrain the unskilled to match supply with demand, but like many obvious solutions, the imbalance paradox is not that easily resolved.

Concern with the skill gap has produced at least one positive benefit to the nation: growth of concern with educational attainment and with all aspects of our educational and training system. For this analysis, the significant fact is that ever higher educational attainments are required of workers, which means that improvements in our educational system must continue to have a high priority among our national goals.

Finally, unskilled workers don't fare too well in labor markets because they have little to offer to employers; and, in too many cases, when they do have something to offer, their job hunting is unsystematic and inefficient. Many studies have substantiated the fact that displaced workers often look for new employment on a very random or hit-and-miss basis. But although the unskilled worker's perception of a labor market, of occupations for which he may qualify, or of job opportunities elsewhere may be quite limited, it is also true that part of the problem is insufficient job opportunities.

---

[9]Haber, William, *et al., The Impact of Technological Change*, The Upjohn Institute, Kalamazoo, Michigan, 1963, p. 10.

PUBLIC AND PRIVATE POLICIES

Two general approaches to unemployment and the related problems of skill are being tested today. On the one hand there is the Keynesian approach of the tax cut, and on the other hand there are those policies relating to retraining, educating, and providing for mobility of our manpower so as to make supply relate more closely to demand. Thus far it is hard to determine which of the two policies has produced the best results. There is little question, however, that in the longer run, our education and training policies will be very closely related to the question of whether or not we can use our entire work force in appropriate job responsibilities.

Beginning with the cold-war-induced National Defense Education Act in 1958, continuing with the Area Redevelopment Act of 1961, the Manpower Development and Training Act of 1962, the Vocational Education Act of 1963, and culminating for the moment in the Economic Opportunity Act proposal, there has been increasing interest in and support for education and training specifically aimed at the unskilled. It would be fair to say, at this writing, that our publicly supported retraining programs have been beneficial. It would be equally fair to say that the nation is getting closer to the point of making a more massive commitment to an investment in its human resources. Yet there is the telling criticism made of retraining programs which observes that they cannot conceivably deal with the employment problems generated by the addition, for each of the next several years, of one million-plus new entrants to the work force or for another two million displaced by productivity improvements. This poses a task of truly staggering dimensions both from this quantitative viewpoint and from the previously reviewed qualitative view.

Our current public policy is attempting not only to generate economic growth and educate and train persons for the work demands of the future but also to help unskilled workers by providing them with a more effective public placement service. The attempt to upgrade the public employment service has been made sporadically ever since the first World War when the first attempts to provide a truly national service were made. Improvements have come slowly over the years but have never been consonant with the growth in the work force and in our manpower needs. Much remains to be done if real placement aid is to be provided to the hard-core unemployed, the poverty stricken, jobless youth, and other disadvantaged persons.

The emphasis here on government policy and program does not mean that employers are uninterested or not involved in the unskilled worker problems under review. Not at all. Many employers have found it advantageous to provide retraining for their employees and to take other constructive steps to provide job opportunities for those who are or were unskilled. Such programs are treated elsewhere in this volume.

QUESTIONS FOR THE THOUGHTFUL

This is a very brief sketch about a complex phenomenon—unskilled workers. Unskilled workers are usually undereducated, unemployed, or underemployed, and many other things. If they are unemployed as well as being unskilled, they tend to cluster among the older persons in the work force or among youth. At both polar extremes the unemployment rates are distressingly high for nonwhites. All unskilled workers deserve an opportunity to improve their economic security and their status in life. Unemployed, unskilled workers represent a real problem that must be alleviated. Not many would question these goals, but the problem is how these goals should be achieved. Without attempting any exhaustive listing here are a few challenging questions which, if answered, might point the way to the work yet to be done:

1. What kind of educational system is necessary to provide fundamental (both useful and practical) education for all persons regardless of intelligence or interest?
2. For those who are out of school and unskilled, what are appropriate rewards or penalties which would induce them into formal, upgrading programs?
3. How should the transition from school to work be effected?
4. Should our wage structure be manipulated so as to alleviate some of the constricting elements of the so-called social minimum wage?
5. What responsibilities should employers assume for training, retraining, or otherwise re-equipping the unskilled for more productive endeavor?
6. How can the unskilled who are on public assistance or in distressed areas be provided with marketable, occupational skills?

Clearly there are more questions than answers and more than enough responsibility for all who can make a contribution. Clearly, too, the paradoxical coexistence between prosperity and relative deprivation should not be allowed to continue.

A PROGRAM FOR HIGH SCHOOL DROPOUTS •

MARJORIE W. GEERLOFS

At a time when American business faces an imminent shortage of such skilled workers as trained machinists, tool and die makers, dental technicians, metal workers, electricians, nurses, auto mechanics, and dietitians—at such a time, one out of three students who enters high school fails to graduate. In New Jersey, for instance, there are 50,000 boys and girls currently out of school and out of work.

A Bureau of Labor Statistics report states that 70 per cent of these students have normal or above-average I.Q.'s, and a surprising 10 per cent are of college ability. Without a proper education, however, they find job getting a very difficult problem. High school dropouts usually are written off as academic, social, and economic liabilities. They therefore end by swelling the ranks of the unemployed and frequently becoming candidates for the relief rolls.

Why do these students drop out of school? School authorities point out that lack of motivation is the reason in many cases. If a student sees no hope of getting a decent job in a society where the new jobs being created by industry are getting further and further out of his reach, he sees no point in sweating out the long, hard grind of getting an education. One of the greatest contributions management can make to these troubled boys

---

Marjorie W. Geerlofs is Personnel Administrator, Bamberger's New Jersey, A Division of R. H. Macy & Co., Inc., Newark, New Jersey.

and girls, therefore, is to provide them with a sense of hope. Realizing this, our Personnel Division decided in the latter part of 1962 to take a direct approach to the problem.

Our first step was to look into a program for dropouts sponsored by the Chicago Board of Education and Carson Pirie Scott, a Chicago department store. Their program—christened Double *E* (for education and employment)—began in September 1961. In that year Carson agreed to hire 35 boys and 24 girls selected by summer school counselors from a cross section of the Chicago dropout population. All were between 16 and 21, and each was judged to have a "potential for success."

Jobs were not "created" by Carson especially for these dropouts. Instead, they were assigned to regular jobs ranging from stock and clerical work to gift wrapping and printing on a three-day-a-week schedule. The remaining two days a week were spent in classroom work. After a year, school and store officials declared the program an undoubted success. Thirty-nine of the original group were still at work when the pilot project ended in June 1962, and 30 of them stayed on as regular Carson employees.

Encouraged by the success of the Chicago program, Bamberger's held a series of meetings with the vocational guidance counselors in the schools of communities where Bamberger stores are located to see whether they felt a similar program in New Jersey would be valuable. With their approval, we launched our own plan in January of 1963.

Called the Diploma (or *D*) Squad Program, the plan seeks to accomplish the following:

1. To find some of New Jersey's dropouts and encourage them to finish high school by giving them adult responsibilities, earned cash, and a sense of being needed.
2. To aid in educating the public by calling its attention to the economic and social implications of the present situation.
3. To open the door for other businesses and industries to frame similar solutions to the dropout problem.
4. To sponsor a work program that provides an incentive for the dropout to stay in school and that can be perpetuated without "creating" jobs.
5. To cultivate a new source of talent by providing a training ground for the development of future full-time personnel.

All of our eight stores make available evening employment as stock clerks or messengers, as vacancies occur, to qualified high school juniors or seniors who have dropped out or who are thinking of dropping out of school. Employment is given only on condition that the individual *return to* and *remain in* school; maintain satisfactory grades, attendance, conduct, and health; and perform his job satisfactorily. Our agreement with the students and with their schools is that we are permitted to fire them immediately if they do leave school. In addition, a career in retailing is possible for any member of the *D* Squad upon graduation from high school.

Our stores operate on a two-shift schedule. They can therefore accommodate upward of 80 boys and girls in a year's time. At the outset, only those dropouts who were college material were recruited; but after an initial period of defining and redefining valid criteria for judging applicants, we decided to fill vacancies from among all those whose test scores and school records indicated they were capable of completing the work necessary for high school graduation and whom we felt we could salvage.

Initial referrals are made by vocational counselors in the schools of communities where our stores are located. We write to the placement or guidance counselor enclosing a form by which the counselor can recommend a student. We ask the counselor to indicate whether test scores and school records indicate that the applicant is capable of completing the work necessary for high school graduation. We make it clear that the student must return to and continue in school in order to remain in Bamberger's employ. We ask the reason why the student had left school.

The referrals are interviewed by the personnel manager, who rates them with respect to appearance, personality, motivation, attitude, integrity, reliability, sense of responsibility, and financial need. The accompanying exhibit is a sample of the interview appraisal form used. They must also score satisfactorily on a Wonderlic test and get approval and permission from their parents before they can be placed into positions in the stores. We send a letter to the parents which explains the *D* Squad. We enclose a form which the parent must sign to indicate his approval of the program and to give his permission for the student to be employed. The parent agrees that the applicant must remain in school in order to continue working at Bamberger's.

The employment manager in each Bamberger store is responsible for the operation of the *D* Squad. He coordinates all correspondence among parents, counselors, school principals, and so on, utilizing appropriate *D* Squad forms. In his periodic checks with the school counselor the employment manager asks him to rate the member of the *D* Squad on grades, attendance, conduct, and health, since eligibility to remain on the squad depends on satisfactory attendance and grades at school. He also reviews

Bamberger's New Jersey

Diploma Squad

Interview Appraisal--Aptitude Rating

Name _____   Birthday _____

School _____   Graduating Year _____

How does his appearance impress you?

☐	☐	☐	☐	☐
Makes very poor impression. Slovenly, unkempt, or flashy.	Somewhat careless about clothes and appearance.	Clothes & appearance are ordinary; neither shabby nor exceptional.	Creates better than average appearance.	Creates excellent appearance. Clothes neat and appropriate.

How well does he talk? Does he express himself clearly and adequately?

☐	☐	☐	☐	☐
Very good expression and speech; forceful and effective.	Good expression; talks deliberately and fairly fluently.	Average expression; talks fairly well but not with great fluency.	Poor expression; tries to express himself but does not succeed very well.	Very poor expression; talks little and doesn't express self well.

Personality

☐	☐	☐	☐	☐
Unfriendly, unsociable, or bashful.	Somewhat reserved or retiring.	Friendly but not overly expressive.	Friendly and quite expressive.	Extremely social; completely at ease with new acquaintances.

Motivation--Attitude

☐	☐	☐	☐	☐
Highly motivated. Self-starter. Has goals for himself.	Hesitant. Lacks self-confidence.	Slightly unsure.	Reasonable assurance. Has goal.	Dynamic, superior purposes and force.

Do you recommend hiring him for this job?   Yes ☐   No ☐

Comments _____

_____

_____

_____

Interviewer _____

the performance of all *D* Squad members monthly. In his review, he asks the member's supervisor to report on attendance; the quality and quantity of his work; his willingness to cooperate; his initiative, appearance, effort; and any comments or recommendations which the member's department head sees fit to make.

D Squad members have performed well in their duties. Among the first recruits were James Epp and Richard Dixon, both seniors at South Side High School in Newark. James was placed in the customer returns room and Richard in the addressograph department. Both subsequently graduated from South Side High School and are now in the U.S. Marine Corps.

We also have had failures, including a student who quit after misrepresenting the nature of his need for employment. Out-of-school training of the dropout is sometimes difficult because of his emotional block against formal learning. But the results to date have, on the whole, strengthened our belief in the program and the feasibility of similar programs in other areas of industry.

The number of would-be dropouts saved by our stores may seem to be nothing, statistically, against a backdrop of 700,000 unemployed young people. The number is certainly nothing against the 1.5 million who will be idle if current trends persist. But we feel it is important to do whatever we can. Through programs such as this, the store helps accomplish the following: (1) it validates its responsible position in the community and also furthers enlightened self-interest; (2) students reclaimed through such activities add to the economic well-being of the country; and (3) they provide a source of stable, experienced personnel who can enrich themselves and the industry in retailing careers.

Every firm, school, and parent in this country has an important contribution to make toward the solution of the problem. There is a crying need for more youth employment programs. Furthermore, a concerted effort to enlist the cooperation of every responsible segment of the community should be made, for to assist in the solution of this problem is to invest in the long-range economic health and stability of the communities in which we live and work.

SENIORITY REFORM—ONE ANSWER TO DISPLACEMENT OF THE OLDER WORKER •

BENSON SOFFER

THERE IS LITTLE DOUBT that adjustment to automation presents the major industrial challenge of this decade. It is obvious that the automation revolution will profoundly affect almost every facet of the economy, and that as in any other revolution, there are bound to be some victims. We can already see who they are going to be; it is quite apparent that older workers represent one group marked for this role—and they know it.

At the same time, we need the cooperation of these older workers in transition to the age of automation; furthermore, we can ill afford to waste their skills or take on the tangle of social problems stemming from involuntary idleness. But if something isn't done to prevent their being victimized by automation, and to reassure them about their jobs, we can count on their determined efforts to make change costly, to share the unemployment, and to tighten present seniority practices. This is only human nature; the fact that such efforts will harm everyone else probably won't sway the older workers from trying to protect themselves, because they will feel that "everyone else" is against them.

BENSON SOFFER is Economist, Research Staff, Committee for Economic Development, Washington, D.C.

It is true, of course, that automation threatens other workers, too. Why, then, should we focus our attention on the older ones in trying to find a solution to the problem of job displacement? For one reason, their problem is the most pressing. All experience indicates that older workers are much less mobile than younger ones and much less susceptible to retraining for substantially different occupations. Men who have lived and worked for many years in the same place (often at the same sort of job) have psychological and motivational blocks that make them less flexible and less capable of learning new ways. Moreover, they tend to have had a formal education inferior to that of younger workers and anyway have forgotten much of what they learned in school. In effect, they are not retrainable except at disproportionately high cost. Experience under Government retraining programs proves that such training will not benefit the older blue-collar worker. Although the retraining of older workers is theoretically feasible, in most cases the investment involved cannot economically be amortized over the short working span remaining to them.

Their resistance to drastic changes and the reluctance of employers to hire them for jobs markedly different from the ones they have been doing are hard truths of industrial life, not to be disproved by humanitarian pleas or a few demonstration projects. The system of state employment services have struggled for many years to eliminate maximum age criteria in hiring but have had very little success. The older worker is the victim of discrimination in the labor market, and an attack on this injustice is long overdue.

Let us consider a plan for seniority reform that would more realistically take the facts of automation and job displacement into account. Briefly, this plan entails the building up of broad, intercompany, interunion, special "labor pools." Besides appearing to offer a practical solution to the problem of the older worker, it has the further advantages of benefiting younger workers, saving employers money in the long run, and gaining wholehearted labor support for technological change. Before we examine this seniority revision in detail, however, it might be appropriate to see what, exactly, is wrong with present seniority systems.

Basically, the trouble with these present systems is that they assume a stable economy and a relatively stable technology. But "seniority" cuts little ice for older workers when their jobs simply vanish—when, for whatever reason, a department, a plant, or a whole company closes down. When they go job hunting, despite their considerable know-how and experience in well-paying, productive work, these older workers all too frequently find only "scrap heap" jobs—or no jobs at all. Often, the younger workers who were laid off first have moved into the type of job that the older ones can do; but if it's any comfort to their unemployed elders, the younger workers may be out of work, too, in five or ten years, when automation in due course eliminates their jobs.

To illustrate this point, when Armour's Oklahoma City plant was closed, it was discovered that the younger workers who had been laid off much earlier had promptly taken the jobs then available, so that now the older workers who had remained found themselves with a double handicap, their greater age and a dearth of job opportunities.

As for the younger workers, they may benefit temporarily from the fact that the very process of attrition often requires substantial hiring, despite the lack of growth or even decline in total jobs. But many of these transitional jobs are on their way out because of advancing technology. If a young worker takes such a job and is laid off several years later, he has lost his chance to develop skills that will be in permanent demand.

As short-lived sources of income, transitional jobs are useful to only one type of employee—the man who is going to retire before the job folds. The proposal to be outlined here entails the creation of a new, broadened seniority system for transitional jobs that would reserve these jobs for workers who are ending their careers and wall them off from younger workers who should be building up seniority in more permanent or career jobs.

Seniority arrangements as we know them are so varied—individually worked out in unique and complex bargains—that they cannot be meshed. The only way to broaden seniority without totally disrupting them is to introduce this "transitional job seniority" as an exception, which would not be applicable to the permanent complex of existing arrangements.

In itself, the broadening of seniority units is not a new idea. The automobile industry pioneered broad interplant seniority for all company plants in the same geographic area more than a decade ago, and more recently the steel, meatpacking, and glass-container industries have developed companywide and industrywide seniority for displaced employees. Unfortunately, however, when jobs decline in one plant, it often means that they are declining in the entire industry. For example, right now semiskilled manual jobs in manufacturing are declining in large absolute numbers. For unskilled and semiskilled workers at least, the protection of seniority will be meaningful only if interunion, intercompany, multilateral seniority "pools" are established, especially on a metropolitan or regional basis.

The fact must be faced, however, that whatever the merit of any proposal to alter seniority rules, many union leaders may object. This reflex is natural enough, because every change in seniority disturbs the system; the security and status of all workers become involved, and the loss of vested interests is sure to mean a battle. Even with the greatest skill and determination, getting the union to change will be a long and difficult task, though, logically, seniority should be changed as technology changes. Because the plan proposed here separates one aspect of seniority controversies from all the others, negotiations for it should be simplified. That is one point in its favor, although there are others.

First, though it may be a comment on the obvious, security in the case of young workers means something quite different from security in the case of workers approaching retirement. The older workers have only to "hang on" for a specific, relatively brief span of time. Their security is based on the pension fund in which they have attained a contractual right to a pension. Security for younger workers depends on their establishing themselves in career employment. Therefore, while the seniority rights of a younger worker in a transitional job are of negligible value to him, they are of supreme value to the older worker.

Actually, it doesn't make much difference to the older worker whether his seniority lies in a transitional or nontransitional job, so long as he has it. The aim of this proposed overall pooling of transitional jobs is to persuade him to transfer his seniority from a nontransitional to a transitional job.

Of course, this means asking the older worker to adapt to change, even though we know that as a rule he doesn't adjust easily. The adaptations required by this plan, however, are the least difficult ones, and the new jobs offered older workers would be the closest available approximations to those they had been doing before. It need hardly be pointed out that the larger the pool of these jobs, the greater the choice and the easier it would be to make the shift to another job. The reluctance of older workers to participate in the plan should be quickly dispelled, once they fully understand its advantages.

We can anticipate that management also would have some misgivings about such a plan. Quite reasonably, employers will point out that though a job may be transitional, if it is given to an inferior worker costs may be raised for a significant length of time. Furthermore, they may argue that all this reshuffling will probably entail the additional expense of training, to say nothing of the considerable personnel work involved. In reply to these objections, it should be noted that the reshuffling would be held to the minimum called for by specific circumstances, and no workers would, of course, be switched to jobs they couldn't perform acceptably.

It must be admitted, though, that while this proposal would involve adaptations that are relatively small and easy, they would require an unusual effort on management's part—a farsighted look at the labor force and jobs, and an identification of jobs that are phasing out. But this is a step that managers should take in any case, because if they do nothing to plan ahead when phasing-out jobs become unstable, the better and younger workers will quit to keep one jump ahead, thereby increasing turnover and training costs and leaving a good deal of confusion as well as these costs in their wake.

The plan proposed here would avoid this undirected reshuffling by matching up, in each plant, the workers who are phasing out—that is, approaching retirement—with the jobs that are phasing out. For example, jobs that were expected to end within three to five years would be assigned to workers over 60 who were capable of doing the work. Some reduction in earnings might result, but workers at this age would conceivably be willing to trade this in return for the extra job security it would bring. If a great many jobs were phasing out, it might be necessary to go further down the list and assign them to workers who would be eligible for early retirement by the time the jobs ended. If still more workers were needed to fill the jobs, the next group to be considered might be those who will have attained vesting rights in the pension plan by the time the jobs are phased out. Or, another possibility if there were a shortage of older workers for transitional jobs would be to raise the retirement age accordingly.

The younger workers moved out of these transitional jobs should be willing to leave them if it is clearly explained to them that there is a cut-off date in sight. Again, some might have to take a pay cut, but it should not be difficult to convince them that they will be better off in the long run. In any case, management should, of course, try to offer wages that are as close as possible to those they have been getting.

It goes without saying that there are all sorts of unpredictables in this situation. For instance, the number of older workers in the company might not match the number of job openings; or the workers in question might not be transferable to the kinds of jobs available. It must be anticipated that if the transitional job approach is to be a workable solution to technological displacement, it will have to operate on a scale that will require the cooperation of industry and the union far beyond individual plant or even industrywide contracts.

The process of broadening seniority units and providing special aids to displaced workers has already begun, both in some individual multiplant companies as well as in whole industries. Obviously, in implementing the plan proposed here, any such arrangements already in existence should be used first, and more should be developed. But it must be recognized that no matter how carefully they are worked out, seniority programs confined to one large company or even one industry could not overcome the possibility that (1) displacement may be so massive (as in the coal industry) that it would far exceed the capacity of the entire industry, let alone the individual company, to absorb it; and (2) labor may be so immobile that workers will prefer to take on other kinds of work in the locality rather than follow the migration of jobs to other areas.

Already many companies moving to new locations have found this second point to be true to an unexpected degree. The remedy here would seem to be new arrangements cutting across company and industry lines. With the handwriting of automation and its consequences clearly on the wall, all companies and unions in the locality should make a list of transitional jobs that are unfilled from their own work forces and turn it over to a centralized employment service whose function would be to set up a pool of unfilled transitional jobs and of older workers scheduled for displacement. A multilateral reciprocity agreement for specific occupational categories, in which all the companies would join, should be drawn up. Arrangements should also be made for the workers switching employers and unions to be oriented to whatever changes the transfer involves.

Under such an areawide program, steps should also be taken to insure that new employers do not have to shoulder undue costs. For example, pension benefits could be made "portable," with the original employer paying the transferred employee on retirement all benefits earned with the company before the transfer. Thus the new employer would be relieved of much of the pension burden of an older employee. The necessity to retrain would probably be minimized also, because in a large pool the matching-up of jobs and men is likely to be much more exact than in a smaller one. If substantial retraining is needed, the Federal Government stands ready to do the job under the Manpower Development and Training Act.

Of course, such a pooling arrangement would not proceed without a hitch; indeed, it would have to meet a variety of contingencies. For example, the transitional jobs may terminate sooner than estimated, with the result that the transferred workers would then be displaced before their normal retirement date. In this event, the policy should be for these workers to get first preference for other transitional job openings in the area. In other words, they would have greater *transitional* job seniority than younger transitional workers; transitional seniority would be based on age, not years of service.

Certainly this would be an improvement, from the employer's point of view, over the present expensive practice of giving an older worker whose job has disappeared large severance payments or a pension until he can collect Social Security benefits. It is possible, though, that the local pool might prove inadequate in some respects and again the problem of labor mobility would arise. If worse came to worst, these special early retirement and severance pay benefits—not becoming part of many labor agreements —might have to be invoked for the oldest workers, because both the costs of moving them and their resistance to moving might be too great.

For those displaced employees willing to move there could be special relocation allowances and arrangements made for them to retain their transitional job seniority, to eliminate the fear of landing at the bottom of the ladder in a strange community. Conceivably, whole groups of workers might be moved together, so that friendship ties would not be altogether broken, and everyone involved would feel more secure. The European Common Market has demonstrated that with proper planning such larger-scale moves can be successfully undertaken, from the point of view of both the individual workers and the employers concerned.

Of course, the safeguards already negotiated for older workers for whom there are no jobs would have to be retained for the benefit of those for whom there are no openings even under the broad multilateral program proposed here. But the expense would be negligible in comparison with the cost of present arrangements as automation affects larger and larger numbers of older workers.

This transitional job program would benefit the entire economy by reducing unemployment payments and retraining costs. Of course, it would be unreasonable for employers to expect that such a program would never involve them in added costs, but over the long pull they would benefit from having to pay less unemployment compensation and taxes to cover the cost to the government of unemployment and retraining. Employers would also be freer of labor shortages and high turnover, since they would have a larger labor pool to draw from. A sensible rationing of transitory and nontransitory jobs would mean less pressure for higher wages and supplements and would also offer a practicable alternative to the 35-hour week, which thus far seems to be labor's self-defeating answer to automation.

Under this proposed pool system, unions would be more secure because organized rather than unorganized labor would be placed in the jobs available. Both employers and unions would gain greater loyalty and appreciation from workers for minimizing the burdens of displacement, and both free enterprise and collective bargaining would thus be enhanced in the public eye. Though intangible, these are very real benefits.

Finally, let me emphasize once again that any program to meet the drastic changes involved in automation will have its difficulties, expenses, and sacrifices. The ultimate benefit of this plan would, in my opinion, far outweigh the effort and the headaches it might entail. It is not a full solution, but I think, it should help all of us to meet our responsibilities to both old and young workers alike, at the same time serving the national interest by holding manpower waste and labor discontent to a minimum. If there are holes in the argument, then a detailed examination of it may show us even better ways to make our peace with the problems of automation and get on with the job.

SECTION V

Meeting the Need for Management Talent

> *The company that neglects to provide for adequate managerial talent is courting disaster. In the years ahead, this task will be made even more difficult because of population trends which indicate a shortage of personnel in the middle group from which our future managers will come.*

THE MENACE OF MANAGEMENT OBSOLESCENCE •

GEORGE FRANK

THE OBSOLESCENCE OF FACTORY and office equipment has always received major attention from management, but the costly obsolescence of management personnel is a growing and unsolved problem in most corporations. The problem has shifted from a gnawing one to one that is alarming, considering the enormous changes and rate of change in business operations in the past decade. All about us are examples of executives struggling to solve problems of the 1960's with management tools of the 1930's.

There is the inventory manager—responsible in most companies for a very significant portion of total expenditures—who is unfamiliar with inventory models. These models have been thoroughly proved out by mathematicians in industrial applications as tools for rationalizing inventory control and costs.

Then there are the managers who have been instructed to use the expensive computers, but they follow general instructions, using them for payrolls, accounts receivable, parts inventory, and so on. Generally, they are simply transferring manual data processing to electronic data processing rather than utilizing the new aids for problem solving. In far too many cases, the computers hum along, doing arithmetic, while plant and product engineering problems are being solved by pencil-wielding engineers

Finally, there is the all too frequent case of the marketing manager who is still playing the numbers game. He takes a quick look at the profile of the market—sex, age groups, population, income—and tells the sales force, "All we have to do is increase our share of this market 2 per cent and we will increase our overall sales by 22 per cent." He neglects the contribu-

---

GEORGE FRANK is Vice President and Director, Middle West Service Company, Chicago, Illinois.

tions of the social sciences to modern marketing theory. He also neglects the newer mathematical tools for projecting results from advertising, the addition of salesmen, or other tactical factors in the program.

Similar examples can be found in every department of most companies, and they lead to certain conclusions:

1. The poles of management capability and management responsibility are moving apart at a rapid speed.
2. Management has been fulfilling its prescribed obligations, but the prescriptions are antiquated.
3. The greatest burden of fault lies with policies which nurture management obsolescence through inadequate recognition of management's role and of the importance and dangers of creeping obsolescence.
4. The problem will remain incurable until top management establishes a policy and program of management development that will help keep managers abreast of new techniques.
5. Top management must demand of its decision makers the same degree of familiarity with up-to-date tools and techniques that it does of its hourly workers.

There is growing evidence that management is becoming "imperfectly developed, atrophied, suppressed, or lacking," to borrow from the dictionary definition of obsolescence.

Our firm began a study of management in 1960. One of the purposes was to evaluate the capabilities of men in utilizing modern management techniques. At the end of three years, our sampling totaled slightly more than 1,000 managers whose salary classifications ranged from $8,000 to $20,000. Our study tools included analysis of 1,000 work histories and interviews with 20 per cent of the group. Participating in the conduct of the interviews was an associate staff member, Dr. Ingo Ingenohl. The study to date confirms a number of conclusions about managers:

1. They stop learning new ideas and new techniques virtually the day they step off campus. Beyond the initial practical experience in which they may apply some of the skills acquired in classrooms, they appear to use progressively less of their training. The influence of on-the-job training administered by immediate superiors who may themselves be using outmoded management tools makes more difficult the scientific approach to management.
2. They practice management mechanically. The lack of dynamic interest in management as a profession is almost complete.
3. They exhibit little familiarity with advanced management techniques.

The average management practitioner is about as well acquainted with new methods as he is with Sanskrit.

4. They show little appreciation of the fact that many aspects of business management are evolving toward a science rather than a seat-of-the-pants operation.

5. They barely recognize the advances made by the social sciences in such areas as communications, participation, motivation, and other humanistic aspects of the business enterprise.

In the interviews, it was clearly stated that we sought familiarity with—not technical expertness in—modern management methods such as operations research, statistical analysis, linear programing, advanced methods for measuring productivity, marketing theory, economic theory, the potential of computers, and current management literature.

The interviewees were asked, for example, what they knew about operations research. They were reminded that we were speaking about a mere appreciation of operations research, not the specialist's knowledge of the field. The few who made any response gave such answers as: "I don't believe in this." "Oh, that's just another name for what we do all the time." "We use it." Probing further, we tried to find out if there was some knowledge of some of the simpler methods of operations research such as linear programing, the Simplex method, or inventory models. The result was almost total ignorance.

Most interviewees claimed "complete familiarity" or "competence" in statistical analysis. We described two sets of variables, such as the amount of rainfall in Iowa and corn production in Iowa. The candidates were asked how the relationship of the two could be measured, not necessarily assuming cause and effect. A few were able to answer correctly that one would use a simple correlation to produce a correlation coefficient. These few were then asked, "What is a standard deviation?" Even fewer knew the answer—"a measure of dispersion around the mean." Although these are extremely elementary questions in statistics, not one person could describe the specific uses of a partial correlation in an operational situation.

Those who claimed competence in economics—including several corporate planners—were asked to define "macroeconomics." They did not know that macroeconomics involves the economics of national income accounts. Furthermore, surprisingly few were able to provide the technical definition of gross national product as the sum of consumption, Government expenditure, and investment. They did not know that net national product is GNP less depreciation. Paradoxically, it would be difficult to find a current text in beginning economics that does not treat of these subjects and their significance in industrial planning.

As a final example, we tried to determine familiarity with current literature and thinking in the management specialties of those surveyed. For instance, industrial engineers were asked to name anyone who had contributed some new ideas to the field of work simplification or work measurement. Hardly a man offered the names of Allen H. Mogenson, Ralph Barnes, or Gerald Nadler, although a considerable number acknowledged having heard of them when the names were mentioned. All persons interviewed were asked to name one or more authors in the field of general management theory. One or two named Peter Drucker but could not demonstrate familiarity with any of his writings. As a fitting climax to these observations, not one man could name the title of a book on professional management that he had read since earning his diploma. Nor did many appear to read regularly any technical management periodicals.

Lest it be presumed that we simply might have had the bad luck to come across a series of chronic malcontents or career transients whose lack of ability is the exception rather than the rule, here are a few titles of these gainfully employed executives: executive vice president, manager of corporate planning, manufacturing manager, plant manager, chief of production control, vice president of manufacturing, corporate controller, production manager, supervisor of planning, chief industrial engineer, and marketing manager.

These men were not employed by small or family-owned companies but were from companies with annual sales ranging from several million dollars to the billion class and with reputations as being among the best managed companies in the country.

Despite the axiomatic observation that true learning really begins with the completion of formal education, we find disturbing evidence that the final day of class is the final day of technical and theoretical education for most executives. Our study clearly shows that many companies are not requiring their managers to utilize techniques any more advanced than those available to them before World War II.

It is ironic that the same managements who insist on the finest tools and equipment for their hourly workers—with complex programs of proper and efficient operation and maintenance—do not put forth similar demands for modern tools of management. Many of these management tools are listed in the accompanying exhibit. It is a part of the questionnaire used by Middle West Service Company in its personnel recruiting program.

MANAGEMENT SELF-ANALYSIS

Please make a fair self-evaluation about your knowledge in the following areas. Can you apply and do you understand:

From the field of economics:

Present discounted capital?
National income statistics?
Leading and concurrent economic indicators?
Marginal productivity?

From the field of finance:

Turnover ratios?
Retirement and replacement programs?
Cost of money?
Rate of return?
Present value of money?

From the field of marketing:

The design and evaluation of surveys and questionnaires?
The design of a consumer panel?
Survey sampling design?
Market penetration analysis?
Analytical forecast of sales?

From the field of organization:

Responsibility charting?
Formal versus informal organization?
Organization planning?
Management audit?

From the field of personnel:

A design of a job evaluation system?
A wage and salary survey and wage regression curve?
Executive compensation planning?
Programed instruction?

From the field of operations research:

Linear programing?

Inventory models?
Economic order points?
Queueing?

From the field of integrated data processing:

Computer language?
Computer diagraming and flow charting?
Random access storage?
Digital versus analog computers?

From the field of statistics:

General probability, descriptive, and inference statistics?
Analysis of variance?
Product-moment correlation?
A Chi-square analysis?

From the field of industrial engineering:

A ratio delay or work sampling study?
I. E. Schematic models?
CPM and PERT?
A work simplification program?
A production cost analysis?
An evaluation of the pros and cons of process versus
product-controlled layout?
An incentive system installation?

The destructive costs of a management core virtually ignorant of current management science and techniques can be assessed directly and indirectly. A great number of decisions on expenditures are made by these managers. They are responsible for deciding manpower and inventory levels and patterns of distribution. They make decisions on the purchase of materials or equipment, product development, engineering, and make-or-buy alternatives. Certainly, these are the ones whose collective judgment prepares, or at least influences, major long-range policy decisions.

Who is paying for this management obsolescence? The managers themselves and the business enterprises which engage their "professional" services are jointly paying the costs of backwardness and ignorance. Who will suffer the most or the longest is an academic question.

Greater reliance on mechanical devices may be one consequence. This will go on regardless, but it should be obvious that those who have failed to keep abreast of changes will be among those who will join unskilled labor in the growing company of those who appear to be permanent unemployables. Managers thus face a problem similar to that which production workers face in automation.

In the meantime, however, no machines will replace executive perception and judgment in those areas of decision making, unprogramed problem solving, and creativity where business actions remain an art rather than a mechanical operation. Enlightened management personnel will remain essential in spite of certain recent expressions to the contrary.

Far more menacing to the security of such men than the machine are younger men armed with the knowledge and ability to use effectively and profitably those tools developed by science for business expansion and progress—and which today are essential to its continuation.

There is the popular lament that we have become so deeply infused with conformity that we have drained ourselves of dynamic leadership capable of perpetuating successful business enterprises. But certainly business itself is responsible for failing to develop effective leadership. It is unthinkable to suggest that in management ranks there do not exist scores of men with potential capability for greatness and leadership—especially with the new scientific tools and techniques available.

We only appear to be engulfed in mediocrity because we are overwhelmed by mediocre performance. Management is not measuring up to its opportunities. Lackadaisicalness is contributing to this destruction-by-inertia of human resources; but this waste is only part of the cost business is paying.

Corporations are also paying for the immeasurable but surely enormous waste of automation equipment. Sophisticated, highly regarded—and expensive—computers or data-processing equipment do have immense value. Yet a great many firms have not even begun to extend the usefulness of this machinery beyond such routines as computing payrolls and processing inventory data.

The situation appears to be partially based on a lack of understanding and appreciation of the gravity of the problem. Businessmen have noticed a number of apparent symptoms but haven't yet diagnosed them to be separate manifestations of the same malfunctioning. Such diagnosis is the first step to recovery.

Partly to blame, too, is the lack of understanding by some top management of the new management techniques and the lack of appreciation of the full potential of electronic decision-making aids. Another interpretation of the situation is to say that management in many cases has been "getting away with murder." A more precise interpretation is that top management is allowing management to continue performing in low gear with little cognizance by either that there are greater needs and capabilities.

A major factor contributing to the situation is the application of the so-called classical theory of organizational plans which strives for stability. Functions, levels, and responsibilities, once put in writing, become the corporate manifesto. This has been considered the way to stabilize costs, stabilize operations, and stabilize methods to achieve short-range objectives.

But the cost of stability is fixed, rigid, frozen thinking. This is no longer an age of business stability. It is an age of flux, an era of dynamic shift, swell, and change. No man ever ran the gauntlet successfully by taking calm, measured steps. Nor will any company survive the growing intensity of business pressures unless it can display flexibility and adaptability.

This is not to suggest that every orderly process of developing standard procedures would preclude the option of finding new and better methods of organization and operation. In fact, one of the strengths of standard procedures is that they do establish concrete bench marks for progress.

But organizational charting and procedures designed to eliminate the kind of error that grows out of poor memory or inconsistent judgment do have one notable inconsistency: Most do not establish a statement of policy that demands, or even suggests, that managers stay abreast of new developments—not even in their own specialty and much less in general management.

If there is any circumstance of business that is timeless, it is that top executives are generally too busy with long-range needs to concentrate on matters of the moment. Policy makers must rely on a capable management team for contributions of the soundest possible data, analysis, and recommendations in order to develop plans, policies, and objectives. Too often these contributions are inadequate for present needs because they are likely to be prepared with obsolescent management tools. Instead of being stimulated or obligated to accumulate new knowledge and facts upon which to base their judgments, many managers are locked into yesterday's thinking—frozen by static organizational charts, job analyses, job classifications, and perhaps by personal choice. The situation is likely to continue until top management discovers that better tools of management are essential and develops a clear-cut policy demanding that they be utilized.

The simple logic of organizational schemes that "what works best for the most today will work best for the most tomorrow" is no longer valid. We have already entered an accelerating cycle of dynamic change of factors influencing business operations. In the face of this volatile change, the most essential attribute of the successful enterprise will be adaptability. Rapid adjustment to changes and new opportunities will require all the skill and knowledge that can be brought to bear.

To remain in competition, and therefore to survive, companies must seek to understand the broad capabilities of the new scientific techniques of management. This must be coupled with a recognition of the fact that the top managers cannot and need not become expert in these techniques themselves. In the meantime management must at last demonstrate an awareness of these techniques and use that knowledge to develop an organization which will reward the utilization of modern tools and techniques.

The solution to these problems will not come wrapped in a tidy package. Answers must be sought by each company, basing its actions on its own operations. However, there are a few general guidelines—prepared by my associate, Dr. Ingenohl—some or all of which might be useful in raising the level of management capability. Others will surely be developed as recognition of the problem becomes more widespread.

1. We should see to it that managers are involved in decisions about their own development, with the option to accept or reject advancement opportunities without fear of reprisal.

2. We should provide the opportunity for development—at corporate expense. This should be a competitive proposition.

3. We should not look for men merely "to fill shoes." Each man should develop his own unique capabilities. He should be given increasing responsibilities. While his growth is oriented to the development of skills identified by management as necessary to his job, a certain amount of flexibility encourages self-development. He will begin to read and study material outside of the formalized training offered him not because he must, but because he wants to.

4. We must judge development on performance of assigned responsibilities and overall accomplishment, not on the ability to fit a stereotype.

5. We must see to it that training and development have a purpose. The relationship between development and its goals, applied in operational situations, stimulates effort and desire to learn.

6. In encouraging use of new methods and techniques, we must guard against the tendency to create narrow specialists, isolated from the mainstream of policy and operation.

THE INVENTORY SYSTEM AT MINNESOTA MINING AND MANUFACTURING •

LYLE H. FISHER

A RELATIVELY SHORT TIME AGO Minnesota Mining and Manufacturing Company was a small, intimate organization. The officers and owners of the company were personally acquainted with the hundred or so supervisors and managers, and the selection of candidates for a newly created position was not a difficult job. Quite frequently the consideration, evaluation, and appointment of a new manager was a lunch-table activity. A glance around the lunchroom was all the inventory taking that was necessary.

With growth and decentralization, the selection process became more difficult. Management talent was no longer concentrated in the lunchroom, and the personal acquaintanceship between president and employee disappeared.

For a while the selection process was continued on a name and reputation basis. Among the officers, one or more would be sufficiently acquainted with the available candidates to advise the president adequately as to the best selection. Since personnel records such as original applications, job

LYLE H. FISHER is Vice President, Personnel and Industrial Relations, Minnesota Mining and Manufacturing Company, St. Paul, Minnesota.

assignments, pay history, and performance appraisals were in the custody of the personnel department, the head of this unit quickly became the prime source of counsel and guidance.

Not long ago, when the president was in his early sixties and there was speculation about his replacement, our chairman of the board noted that "when the decision for a new president must be made, the problem will not be finding *a* man to fill the position but rather selecting one from the *dozen or more* capable men in our organization."

The personnel department agreed that candidates were available in such numbers, but they felt a more formal inventory of them was necessary. The inventory system thus developed at 3M is based upon three general beliefs:

1. A belief in promoting from within: The company's officers have an average of 26 years of service.
2. A belief that a company can only make development opportunities *available:* Basically, each individual has to develop himself. The rapid growth of the company, of course, affords many such opportunities.
3. A belief in management committees as a source of training. These committees, operating at both the corporate and at division levels, act as review boards and guiding lights for major activities. Members get liberal opportunities to observe and take part in running a large corporation.

In setting objectives for the development and evolution of our inventory system, we were anxious to keep it as simple as possible. We knew that good judgment dictated we should keep the cost low. The nature of the information we would gather demanded the highest degree of security to protect the individuals concerned. But perhaps the most important single objective was that of practicality. We had seen some very sophisticated systems adopted in other companies collapse because they were not practical, because their results did not justify the cost, or because the confidential information involved was not handled properly.

It took more than just a unilateral decision in the personnel function, however, to set the wheels in motion. Past practices had to be overcome. Even our "promotion from within" policy was found to be somewhat opposed to a successful inventory of promotables on a companywide basis because a manager who had staffed his operation with good men was prone to want to keep them for his own future needs. Promotion from within to him meant promotion only within his unit.

To get our plan off the ground we made a trial run in one of our major operating divisions. Working from a list of salesmen who had been designated as better than average in our performance appraisals, we accumulated all the available personal history on each man. We solicited the sales manager's appraisal of these people as to future potential. The sales manager was invited to add to the list any "comers" we might have missed and to eliminate any whom he thought were not promotable in the near future.

When we finished, we had a list which included less than 20 per cent of the men in this sales unit. Many of these were designated as needing further experience before being promotable, and our list of promotables within 24 months dropped to about 5 per cent of the total unit. Reviewing the projected growth of this unit alone and applying our experience ratio of additional managers needed in the next 24 months, we could ably demonstrate a lack of management potential within this unit.

We then followed this same procedure in another division of the company, and our results were quite different. In this division we reached the conclusion that an excess supply of management potential existed.

These experimental runs proved one of our contentions. We had hand-picked these two divisions on the assumption that a rapidly expanding unit would probably not be developing managers as rapidly as needed. A more established unit, we felt, would develop men faster than it developed promotional opportunities. The obvious need for interdivisional mobility was our greatest asset in selling an inventory on a corporatewide basis.

The results of these trials were presented to top management, and we were commissioned to go ahead in all functions and all divisions. Well-established divisions saw opportunities opening up for their good employees in the newer, more dynamic divisions, and these divisions saw a source of tried and proven manpower. We are quite proud of the increase in interdivisional transfers and the cross-pollination among our product divisions resulting, at least in part, from our inventory activities. This we feel is a plus value not fully anticipated when we established our inventory system.

Having top management's authorization to go ahead on a companywide basis was not, however, an assurance of success. To be truly effective we needed full support and full usage of the inventory by all divisions and subsidiaries. We were asking all units of the company to contribute names to the inventory and at the same time to use the inventory in locating the best man for any specific opening. Still we did not want to take away the division manager's prerogative of choosing his own staff.

All key appointments in a division of our company have been subject to the ratification of the president. He realized that his ratification of such appointments would be far more meaningful if he had not only the background of the selected man but the background information on two or three alternate candidates as well. He issued a request that division managers provide him with their first-, second-, and third-choice candidates for such openings. He further suggested that all three candidates should be persons listed in the inventory of potential managers.

The full importance of his request is not immediately obvious. Certainly it assures consideration of more than one candidate for an opening. But further than that, it could be assumed that a man *not* listed in the inventory would not get full consideration for an opening. After this acceptance and request by the president, we no longer had to pry loose potential managers. They are being included in our inventory completely voluntarily—even by managers who at first decided to hold on to good men for their own future use.

For each man listed in the inventory we have three significant kinds of documents. First, we have a running history of his regular performance appraisals, which are regularly added to his file because a new appraisal is made each year. Second, we have the personal history form, which describes what the man brought to the company when he was first employed—education and previous employment—and reflects all the assignments he has had since he was first employed. Third, we have an "estimate of potential" (see Exhibit 1), which lets us know what his boss thinks about his future. This document is renewed at least once every two years.

The key document in the inventory is the estimate of potential. This gives us some insight as to what the man is and what qualifications he has from many different standpoints. It includes, first, his obvious strengths, which may form the most tangible basis for getting him recommended as a candidate for an important opening. The interests of the individual are also explored both on the estimate and on the performance appraisal, and we encourage supervisors to be alert to all fields of interest seriously expressed by their people. We also cover possible limitations, such as health problems, unwillingness to relocate, and so on.

Further, we give the supervisor an opportunity to make specific recommendations as to the type of job or specific job for which he thinks his man is qualified. This is looked at very closely because although the immediate supervisor should be in the best position to know what a man is suited for, we sometimes find that the supervisor has little if any objective knowledge about the real requirements for success in the kind of job for which he is

Estimate of Potential - suggestions for further utilization of capabilities

Continued company growth and success depends upon the effective development and utilization of company personnel assets. This effective utilization depends first upon management's ability to recognize available manpower capabilities. Each supervisor is responsible not only for seeking out and utilizing the capabilities of his people in their present positions but also for pointing out capabilities which may be profitably utilized in other positions.

This form is designed for supervision's use in recommending those who should be considered for other positions and responsibilities for more effective use and development of their capabilities either within their own department or division or in other divisions. The form is to be completed by the supervisor for review by his superior as a supplement to performance appraisal information whenever appropriate.

Name _____ Division _____

Current Position _____ Location _____

Married___ Single ___No. of dependents___ Length of time in this position _____

1. *Indicate strong points* (including skills or knowledge not now being utilized) which suggest that other or additional responsibilities should be considered.

2. *Indicate employee's expressed interests* in other types of work, departments, divisions, location, foreign service, etc., which are sufficiently real and strong to be considered.

3. Comment on any business, personal, health, family conditions, strong preferences or qualities which might limit flexibility for change or relocation.

EXHIBIT 1

4. Recommendations for more effective use and development of capabilities (normal, reasonable changes within near future). Comment only on those items where you feel a consideration is appropriate.

Be as specific as possible.

	Ready Now	Within 6-24 mos.	*With Other Reservations
(a) For DIFFERENT TYPE OF WORK, LOCATION, DIVISION, etc.	☐	☐	☐
Specify: _____	☐	☐	☐

(b) For ADDED RESPONSIBILITY IN PRESENT ASSIGNMENT "OR TYPE" "OF WORK"

Comment:	☐	☐	☐

(c) For DEFINITE PROMOTION TO (Specify position, to supervision, etc.)

_____	☐	☐	☐
_____	☐	☐	☐

*Comment particularly on any reservations, limitations, possible further needs or questionable areas which may be important in a change. Include any other specific suggestions which may be helpful in more effective use of capabilities.

Completed by _____ Title _____ Date _____

Reviewed by _____ Title _____ Date _____

Comments by reviewer as to agreement, differences and further suggestions.

EXHIBIT 1 (Continued)

recommending his man. We try to give the supervisor some assistance in putting his recommendation into the kind of language which makes his commentary easy to code into the inventory.

In the actual inventory we carry a file folder for each man containing his personal history and all of the performance appraisals and estimates of potential that have been created on him. We have developed codes for putting the significant information on tab cards, which permit us to make ready reference to the coded inventory information. Periodically, we have a printout prepared which shows visually all of the information coded on each man in the inventory. Through the adaptation to tab cards, we can have people listed together according to the division in which they work, the type of job to which they are assigned, age, education, or any other factor which we may wish to explore.

We find, however, that a printed listing of people, sorted out by the division in which they work, is our most useful tool and that with the number of people listed in the inventory at around 2,000, the whole operation can be much more expeditiously handled by a simple visual scanning than by a more highly mechanized tabulating or computer operation.

When a visual scanning, which we call an inventory search, has been completed, a list of candidates is compiled. We then make a quick personal scan of the file on each of these men so we may screen out those who may have looked suitable from their codings but who actually are not quite qualified for the specific job in question. We might even add some names of men who might come to mind as being suited for the opening even though they may not be included in the inventory or, if they are, may not be coded appropriately for a search to turn up their names.

At this stage we also look at the number of candidates produced by a search. If the number of apparently qualified candidates is too large—say, 50 to 100—we might go back to the search requester in order to tighten up the criteria to produce a smaller final list of candidates. Conversely, if the criteria on which a search was based are so stringent as to produce only one or two candidates, we discuss the criteria with the search requester in hopes of producing a larger list of candidates, all of whom might still be realistically qualified to fill the opening. We like to have a minimum of six names and a maximum of 12 to 15 names on any candidate listing.

Since the inventory has been in operation, our major emphasis has been on identification of the promotable people and feeding them into the inventory, not only to keep expanding its usefulness but also to keep pace with the inevitable drain on the inventory.

We see a quantitative picture of our promotable group with respect to age, education, current job and pay levels, and other coded information in the inventory. We also see a very definite qualitative picture of each of the individuals who comprise this group. We also see definitely how this group has moved and changed in mix and content. We can determine the number of interdivisional moves which are being triggered by the inventory. We can determine the promotion rate for any facet of employee population. We can derive a great deal of information about retirements, such as the ratio of quits to deaths to retirements.

It is also possible for us to make rather detailed studies of supply and demand. Our supply is the summary of potential manpower in the inventory. Some parts of this supply are ready now for new responsibilities, and we call these men "probables." Others are ready to move only after additional experience on the present job or only on certain expressed types of jobs, and we call these "possibles." Still others are deemed best suited to their present responsibilities; these people, while not likely to move into new responsibilities, are nevertheless important segments of our total management talent; and it is certainly in the company's interest to know who they are and where they are.

We determine the demand side of this equation two ways: (1) simply by making a future projection of historical demand for new managerial talent and (2) by canvassing each division head to determine what specific management manpower needs he anticipates for the coming year. These two techniques produce widely varying figures for the company as a whole, and at this point we believe it is better to use both techniques rather than count too heavily on either one.

The day-to-day operation of the inventory program is carried on by a central staff personnel division for salary administration and management development. Salary administrators are assigned, on a functional basis, to division vice presidents or general managers. For example, a division salary administrator serves the entire Tape and Allied Products Group, working with the supervisory management people in the administration of salaries. His assignment includes clerical, administrative, sales, technical, supervisory, and executive employees; the facets involved are many.

The division salary administrator is encouraged to promote the inventory program at every opportunity. Normally the manager who has the opening will contact his division salary administrator and discuss the job opportunity in detail with him. He will then assist the manager in completing the search request form (see Exhibit 2), which when completed, is

```
                            - Confidential -
PERSONNEL INVENTORY SEARCH REQUEST       Date_____  #_____  _____
Position to be filled_____   Will report to _____
In Division _____       Title:_____
    Department _____
Geographic location _____          Requested by: _____
of position _____          Title: _____
```

INDICATE MOST SIGNIFICANT RESPONSIBILITIES:

Supervisory responsibilities:

INDICATE QUALIFICATIONS FOR THE POSITION AS FOLLOWS:

	Essential, required qualifications	Desired but not essential
EDUCATION: Level, degree:		
Major field(s):		
Special courses or knowledge:		

AGE:
3M SERVICE:
Min./Max.
(include if particularly significant)

SALARY:
    Position's appropriate salary classification: _____

    Those now earning up to $_____ per year could be considered.
OVER   OVER   OVER
For inventory use only:

EXHIBIT 2

given to the inventory search section. The 12 to 15 candidates turned up in a typical search are then returned to the division salary administrator concerned. Each folder contains a personal history, all previous performance appraisals, and the most current estimate of potential form. The division salary administrator examines each of the files to satisfy himself that all are good candidates.

At this point the folders must be cleared for release by the candidates'

	Essential qualifications	Desired but not essential
WORK EXPERIENCE: Types & amount:		
Supervisory experience:		
Special skills:		

PERSONAL QUALITIES of particular significance:

OTHER CONSIDERATIONS:
  Travel required:

  Special, unusual conditions:

  If there is any significant growth anticipated in this position in the near future which may have a bearing on this selection, please indicate.

List those you now consider possible candidates.	For inventory use only.

EXHIBIT 2 (Continued)

managers. Since it is entirely possible that each candidate is located in a different division, the clearance problem becomes complex. Salary administrators assigned to other divisions negotiate the necessary clearances in their areas.

No information on a candidate is released until the man's *present* superior is contacted and agrees to the release of the file for study. This is often a difficult contact, because the candidate's present superior may not think the new position is in fact a promotion or an opportunity. He may feel that the candidate has a better job where he is, or the candidate may be a key man in a move contemplated in the near future in his present department or division, or the man *really* may not be qualified for this particular position after all, even though the file states that he is. Once these clearances have been made, the files are turned over to the "searching" manager, along with the admonition that under *no* circumstance should the candidate be contacted.

Normally the division salary administrators assist the searching manager in studying the files by pointing out items of interest to him. Hopefully, the manager will be able to narrow the field to about three strong candidates, and he will normally want further information on these three. Most often this additional information is available only from the candidate's present superior, who is then contacted and who alone may grant permission for his man to be interviewed for the promotional opportunity.

The effect of a single search of this nature, involving 12 individuals, for example, is far-reaching. Twelve managers will be contacted and reminded that the company believes in promotion from within and that if this sort of thing can happen to one of their men, perhaps it can happen to them. Moreover, three men will be interviewed for the position, and normally one will be selected and get the promotion. The other two at least have had the opportunity to interview for the position, and we hope they will continue working toward another day when they'll have another chance for increased responsibility and promotion.

THE ASSESSMENT CENTER METHOD OF APPRAISING MANAGEMENT POTENTIAL •

DOUGLAS W. BRAY

THE ACCURATE APPRAISAL of managerial potential is surely one of the prime necessities of the successful enterprise. The most obvious purpose of such appraisal is the selection of those individuals with the potential to be appointed to or advance in management. Identification of them can be used as a basis for promotion and the decision to invest additional training or development activities in such individuals.

But knowing the range and depth of upward potential in the work force has further ramifications. The number of new college graduates that need be taken on in the immediate future, the selectiveness of employment standards for new noncollege employees, the opportunity that can be promised to nonmanagement people for advancement into management, the degree to which one can depend on home-grown management—these and other key manpower planning decisions depend on the accuracy of appraisals. On the development side, refined appraisals can help to develop the types of developmental experiences and courses which are most needed to maximize management ability.

Yet in spite of the importance of such appraisals, there is evidence that most management are not satisfied that they are doing a good enough job in this area. Management people who look at those around themselves at all critically are usually convinced that at least a few mistakes are being

---

DOUGLAS W. BRAY is Director of Personnel Research, American Telephone and Telegraph Company, New York, New York.

made. The many management conferences, both within and outside of organizations, that deal with appraisal problems and the plethora of appraisal methods—including forced choice, adjective and graphic rating scales, critical incident techniques, and the various methods for conducting appraisal conferences—all testify to the lack of satisfaction with the appraisal job that is now being done.

There are several factors which make the appraisal process difficult. A review of them makes one wonder how the job is done even as well as it is. In the first place, the candidates to be appraised frequently work at a variety of different jobs. These jobs differ in their duties, the skills required, the number of persons with whom interaction is required, physical surroundings, degree of stress and pressure, and so on. Professional students of human behavior are reluctant to make comparative statements about people unless they see these people in a standard situation. Yet in large organizations we try to make comparisons between people who are functioning in very different circumstances.

This problem is compounded by the fact that each appraiser sees only a small percentage of the potentially promotable men and women in an organization and frequently does not have a realistic idea of the range of capabilities which are available. It goes without saying that appraisers differ greatly in their own abilities and in the severity of their standards. In addition, the rapid rotation of people in many organizations prevents a long enough exposure for sound appraisal, and some supervisors are so harried by the actual operating demands of the job that they have little patience with any elaborate appraisal process. One can appreciate that truly adequate appraisal may be pretty hard to come by.

The Bell System's Assessment Program for the appraisal of management potential grew out of a long-term System study of the development of managers called the Management Progress Study. This study was started in 1956 with the intent of adding significantly to the store of fundamental knowledge, which is all too thin, of the development of young men in management. It is a longitudinal study in which the careers of over 400 young men are being followed very intently. As the study was planned, it became clear that it required as comprehensive a picture as could be had of these young men at the beginning of their careers in management. It was necessary to discover their abilities, aptitudes, goals, social skills, and the many other qualities which go to make up unique individuals. It appeared that the most effective way of doing this would be to assemble the subjects a few at a time and have them spend several days together going through interviews, tests, group exercises, and individual administrative work under the observation of a special staff.

The term "assessment center" appears to have become part of the language of psychology during World War II when Professor Henry Murray of Harvard University applied, to the selection of OSS personnel, procedures similar to those he had used a few years earlier at Harvard in his personality researches. The method is a procedure where several different types of assessment techniques are applied and final assessment made by the combined judgments of several assessers of the subject's predicted behavior outside the test situation. Writing in the *Psychological Bulletin* in 1959, Dr. Ronald Taft listed seven noteworthy assessment programs up to that time. All of these involved either student or military subjects. It is believed that the Bell System assessment centers represent the first extensive application of this method to the appraisal of management potential.

The first Bell System Assessment Center was, as noted above, devised as a research tool; and, at the outset, there was no plan for its eventual use in actual personnel practice. As its research use went forward, however, its promise as an adjunct to the normal appraisal process became more and more apparent. The first application of the method was made in the Michigan Bell Telephone Company in 1958. The subjects were male vocational employees selected by their supervisors as candidates for first level management.

The typical Bell System Assessment Center processes 12 candidates per week. The candidates themselves spend two and a half to three days at the center with the remainder of the week being used by the staff for report writing and rating and evaluation staff conferences. While at the center the candidate undergoes a lengthy interview, a few paper and pencil tests of mental ability and knowledge, and several less usual evaluation techniques. One of these is a lengthy administrative exercise known as the In-Basket simulating the paperwork of a real job. (It is believed that the first business In-Basket was developed in 1956 jointly by The Executive Study at Educational Testing Service and the Bell System.) Another lengthy exercise is a miniature business game, in which six candidates at a time participate, while another group problem, also for six, is a leaderless group discussion preceded by more formal presentations by the members of the group. Another technique is a partly individual and partly group exercise involving labor-management relations.

The performance of each candidate in each of the various techniques is described and analyzed in a detailed written report prepared independently for each exercise. Slightly condensed examples of such reports follow. The first summarizes the performance of a man on the In-Basket, the second of a different man in the discussion problem. The following examples of these reports are from a center assessing men in middle management:

In-Basket Summary. This man's performance was characterized by both a lack of confidence and conviction in the way he handled items and a narrow restricted approach. He saw engineering as his field, and although he willingly tackled problems from other fields, he commonly excused himself for poor handling by claiming lack of experience. As a matter of fact, however, even on engineering items he didn't have either the depth of perception necessary or any great breadth to his approach.

He tends to deal much more with material things than with people. His lack of perception would often have him in trouble. He sends papers down the line without realizing that parts of them could be quite disturbing. His lack of crispness in understanding the subtle meanings behind problems and the feelings of people involved could cause him to be wrong often enough to give his people cause to doubt his leadership. They might often feel that he didn't understand them as people either.

He was not very decisive in his actions. Too often it was possible to change his position from one side to the other and then back to the original position. He freely admitted that he often didn't know which action he would really prefer. Many of his original decisions were not good ones and had not been developed on the basis of broad consideration of alternatives.

He seemed completely at ease in the interview, and this was quite surprising because of the many weaknesses in his performance. He must have realized that he had not done too well. He did almost nothing on several items in the basket and stated that he didn't have much more than just enough time to finish and he felt that he did not work fast enough. He appears to proceed at a slow, methodical pace.

Much of this man's problem in the In-Basket was that he did not perceive the relative importance of items even when written statements were pointed out to him that would have helped greatly in the solution of a particular problem. He did not comprehend their value. His frequent mistakes in dealing with people were frequently the result of his not fully understanding how they were related to the problem at hand.

Group Discussion Summary. This man's formal oral presentation was ranked 5 (2nd highest) by the staff observers. It was ranked 4.6 by the man's peers. It was the highest average ranking for any man in the group and he ranked himself 4. He was nervous during his oral presentation. He was rather flustered because others had stolen much of his thunder. His hand shook slightly, and he played with his pencil and paid close attention to his notes. However, his nervousness in no way affected adversely the quality or overall effectiveness of his presentation. He was extremely articulate, used excellent sentences, made an extremely good choice of words. He was forceful and spoke with a well-modulated voice which commanded attention from both the observers and the other group members. More than any of the other group members, he conveyed interest, enthusiasm, and seriousness for pursuing the task at hand. He also played the role assigned to him by the problem more effectively than any of the rest.

His talk was well organized and carefully planned. He set out three operating principles and proceeded to outline his basic plan; and then, as a means of review, he listed and discussed the several advantages which his plan offered.

He was the first to speak in the group discussion; he suggested a rough plan for the utilization of time. He commanded the immediate attention of the group, and it was due to him that the other members temporarily chose to ignore one of the other participants who went to the easel. Only when our participant was ready did he and the other members turn attention to the outline the other man was trying to develop at the easel. Thus, he proved easily to be the master of any other member of the group in verbal encounters. He did not choose to compete with the participant at the easel. Instead, he viewed this participant as the discussion leader and himself as expediter. He played this role nicely—taking the structure being developed at the easel, submitting points to group discussion, and referring them back to the outline via the participant at the easel. Early in the discussion he conflicted with another man. He apparently flattered this man by calling his approach philosophical and called for a more realistic and practical solution. He easily and clearly won the dispute. In fact, he felt this man contributed to the group's effectiveness through his willingness to back down and depart from his original position. Similarly, this man viewed the participant being discussed highly—ranking him as the most effective member of the group. He also won another man over by assigning him the task of being the critic of others' ideas, that is, he said that the others would proceed toward a practical solution and that this man (with his conceptual and philosophical slant) should stand ready to examine each idea critically. Our man's superior language skills aided him greatly in overcoming any possible antagonism engendered by his impatience with other group members.

He was clearly the most successful member of the group in promoting his views and getting his ideas across while, at the same time, winning support from the opposition rather than antagonizing them or rubbing them the wrong way.

The staff conference considers each candidate in turn. The report prepared by the various staff members on the candidate's performance in each exercise are read so that all members of the assessment staff gain a complete picture of the man's behavior during the time he spent at the Assessment Center. The candidate is then rated on approximately 20 characteristics relevant to success in management, such as skill in planning and organizing, decision-making ability, leadership skills, flexibility, breadth, and so forth. After the rating process is completed the staff then discusses the candidate's potential for promotion, assigning him to one of at least three categories: "acceptable for promotion now," "not acceptable now but possible of becoming so in the relatively near future," and "not acceptable now and unlikely to become acceptable." At some later date, usually the following week, the Assessment Center director writes a descriptive report on each candidate outlining and documenting his strengths and weaknesses as seen at the center. The following is an example of such a report covering the performance of a middle management assessee:

Assessment Summary. This man entered into the assessment exercises in a friendly and energetic manner. He demonstrated some excellent characteristics along with some weaknesses. All in all, he was seen as a man of moderate potential by the assessment staff.

This man's mental ability appears to be average, or possibly slightly above, as compared to Bell System college hires. His scores on the mental ability tests given at the Center were about average as compared to this group. His quantitative ability, however, was in the second quarter from the top as compared to college hires.

Although his mental ability is not particularly high, he uses it far more effectively than many persons in tackling problems. He was given a very high rating by the assessment staff in organizing and planning. His paperwork was well organized according to priorities and his notes were in outline form showing the steps in the actions he would take. In the business game, this man made an excellent contribution in his role as an analyst. He quietly set up a comprehensive record-keeping system, and he was able to use these records to make thoughtful reports to other members of the group.

This man made an effective contribution in both group exercises. In the business game where he served as an effective analyst, he was rated as the top contributor to the success of the group by the staff observers and by his peers. The staff observers noted that had the group been more under his influence than that of others, the group performance would have been more successful. In the group discussion problem, this man was not as prominent, being seen as the third most important contributor by the staff observers and his peers. Yet he was very useful in keeping the group moving towards its goal. He was articulate and served as an effective compromiser between two very forceful men in the group. The group selected this man to represent it in presenting its conclusions to an outside group.

This man was also seen to be definitely above average in decisiveness. He firmly made decisions called for on the In-Basket, and where he had not reached a decision he was specific and positive about the further information he would need to make a decision and how he would get it. The In-Basket interviewer reported that this man was poised, confident, and enthusiastically articulate.

This man is, however, not an outstanding leader. In spite of his excellent contributions during the business game, he really did not attempt to contribute leadership to the organization. He did not appear very forceful in this exercise, and he gained his influence through excellent staff work rather than leadership skills. In a discussion problem he ran a not-too-close third to two considerably more forceful men, and he played the role of a compromiser who was articulate and smooth but not very dominant. He prefers to avoid actions which might annoy or promote friction with others. He appears to be concerned that others will see him as inexperienced and lacking in forcefulness, and it seemed that being direct and forceful requires some deliberate effort on this man's part.

This man is not a profound thinker and, in fact, is likely to be quite superficial and conventional. This was noted both in the personal interview and in the group discussion problem. He is highly conservative and conventional, and one of his main motivations is to please others and to live up to their expectations rather than any deep interest in self-development. He notes, for example, that although he believes reading is something he should do, it is something he would rather not do.

One highly specific weakness in this man, which is likely to prove irritating to others, is his tendency to be long-winded and rambling. The personal interviewer noted that once he got this man talking on a subject, it was difficult both to keep him to the point and to get him to stop so that another question could be asked. Even in the business game where he did a good job, the staff observers noted that his reports were too long and tended to encroach upon the time for taking action. In the discussion problem his formal presentation was fairly good, but he ran overtime and had to be signaled to stop. Even then he had a difficult time finishing, adding sentence after sentence and seemingly not knowing how to conclude.

Assessment staffs are made up of management personnel two levels above the level of the candidates being assessed, and thus of supervisors of the level for which the assessees are candidates. When vocational employees are being assessed, for example, second-level supervisors make up the assessment staff. Only occasionally has any member of such staffs had any previous education or experience in testing or assessment procedures. In other words, the assessment staffs are nearly always completely nonprofessional. Staffs usually undergo three weeks' training, the final week of which is a practice assessment of 12 dry-run subjects.

Assessment results are fed back to the candidate himself and to line management. Each assessee is given the option of a personal feedback, and experience indicates that approximately 85 per cent of the subjects elect to receive a report of their performance. Several methods of giving this report have been tried; the most effective appears to be a face-to-face report given to the candidate by a member of the assessment staff.

The report to the line organization has also taken several forms. Some centers have invited line managers to audit the staff evaluation conference itself; tape recordings of such conferences have been used in some instances; and in other instances the assessment director's descriptive report of the candidate has been sent to line management, supplemented by later telephone conversations where needed. Reports are seldom directed to the candidate's immediate supervisor but are fed into the line organization at a somewhat higher level.

The selection of candidates for the Assessment Center has been left to the normal appraisal processes operating in the organization. Management has been urged to send to the Assessment Center only those that in their judgment possess the potential for early advancement into management. It has come as somewhat of a shock, therefore, that well more than half of those assessed are rejected by the assessment staffs as *not* having abilities warranting immediate promotion. In fact, a substantial minority are deemed to have little potential for promotion even in the more distant future.

Rejection by the assessment staff does not, of course, mean that the candidate is absolutely barred from promotion. Local management is expected to make a careful comparison of the description of the man provided by the assessment process and the man's performance on his present job. Where there are discrepancies, it is the responsibility of management to dig into the situation to determine whether appraisal of the man's potential, as deduced from his job performance, has been off base or whether the Assessment Center has obtained a faulty impression of the man. If the evidence is convincing enough, the assessment decision can be overridden, but it can not be lightly ignored.

There are, of course, other uses for Assessment Center results in addition to aiding line management in making promotion decisions. The outline of strengths and weaknesses which is the upshot of the assessment process can afford valuable guidance as to developmental needs. This can be utilized both by management and by the candidate himself to suggest steps which can be taken to overcome deficiencies so that at least some of the rejected candidates can achieve acceptable abilities some time in the future.

The Assessment Center method as an adjunct to the appraisal process has proved extremely attractive to line management. Assessment Centers spread widely throughout the Bell System before any formal endorsement by top management. Scores of experienced line managers from every level in the business have observed the Assessment Center and have judged it to be a definite step forward in appraisal methods.

Perhaps one reason for its attractiveness is the fact that the Assessment Center does not attempt to substitute for management judgment any mechanical probability device such as forced choice ratings, critical scores on paper and pencil tests, or a predetermined pattern of abilities. Managerial judgment is, in fact, the cornerstone of the process. The members of the assessment staff are (in the case where a vocational employee is a candidate for first-level management) second-level managers—exactly that level of management which normally has a strong voice in promotions into management. Furthermore, the staff is drawn directly out of this level of management and is quite representative of the level except for the fact that they have had a period of special training. In addition, the staff is given no mechanical methods for combining their many observations into any sort of a final index. On the contrary, they are told that the weight which should be accorded to any behavior or trait will depend on their own knowledge of the job and their experience as managers. The difference in making such judgments as a member of the assessment staff rather than out on the line is that the assessor sees all candidates in standardized behavior situations and all members of the assessment staff consider the same behavior. In addition, the 20 qualities which assessment staffs must evaluate open up a broader range of considerations than they may have previously considered without forcing them to give weight to any particular one of these if in their judgment it is irrelevant.

Although no extensive study has yet been made of the later performance of those who have passed through the Assessment Center, one smaller but very careful study has been conducted by the Plant Department of the Michigan Bell Telephone Company. It compared the first 40 men appointed to management after having gone through the Assessment Center with the last 40 men appointed to management before the Assessment Center method was put into operation. A thorough review of each man's performance as a foreman was made on the basis of interviews with the immediate superior of the foreman's supervisor, the foreman's supervisor, and the foreman himself. Many aspects of job performance were rated.

An overall rating of the performance of the men in each group revealed that about twice as many in the assessed group than in the control group were doing a better than satisfactory job. The exact figures were 62.5 per cent for the assessed group and 35 per cent for the men appointed just before the Assessment Center started. One other important figure was the percentage in each group judged on the basis of job performance by their supervisors as having the potential for further promotion to at least the second level of management. The results here were similar to those previously cited; 67.5 per cent of the assessed group as compared to 35 per cent of the control group were seen to have such potential.

The first operational Assessment Center in the Bell System was, as noted above, applied to male vocational employees in the Plant Department. Since then, however, the Assessment Center method has been applied to a wide variety of candidates. Since the aim of the Assessment Center is to assess management potential and not job knowledge, nearly all centers have now become interdepartmental. Assessment Center methods are of sufficient generality so that departmental background is irrelevant. The assessment of women on an interdepartmental basis has also been undertaken with great success, and the size of the female assessment program rivals that of the male. In addition to moving out laterally, the assessment method is also tending to move up the management hierarchy. Several hundred men who have already reached middle management have been assessed and the results fed back to line management as well as to the men themselves.

THE FEASIBILITY OF MANAGEMENT TRAINING PROGRAMS •

RICHARD E. SWANSON

Gᴇᴛ ᴀ ɢʀᴏᴜᴘ ᴏꜰ ᴍᴀɴᴀɢᴇʀꜱ from different companies together, start them talking about management development, and sooner or later one of them is bound to come up with some such objection as, "A program like that is all very well for you big fellows, but we're too small; we just don't have the time or the money for such frills."

Usually, the man who makes this comment comes from a fairly new company that, thanks to its sheer technical know-how, has been able to make rapid strides in its special field. It has a top management team preponderantly made up of highly competent engineers and scientists. In the course of its rise, it may have swallowed up one or two less successful competitors. But despite its generally rosy outlook, already there are telltale signs that growth has brought with it a host of problems whose solution calls for something more than purely technical leadership.

That "something more" is professional management. After all, in every organization it's the managers who set objectives; plan how to attain them; and then select, train, and direct the employees who are to carry the plans out. If managers cannot perform these functions, then in the long run their competence in their own specialty will be of little avail.

Rɪᴄʜᴀʀᴅ E. Sᴡᴀɴꜱᴏɴ is Director of Employee Relations, Control Data Corporation, Minneapolis, Minnesota.

Certainly the experience of our organization, Control Data Corporation, offers some fairly convincing proof that even a small company can afford a formal management training program—and profit noticeably from it. We started out less than seven years ago with exactly 11 employees. Today we have nearly 6,000 employees here and abroad, and we are planning for continued rapid growth in the future.

We would not be able to sustain rapid growth in our business without being amply endowed with technical talent of the highest quality. At the same time our ability to administer this growth is in no small part due to the fact that from the very beginning the founders of the company recognized that technical talent was not enough. These men quickly reached the conclusion that if we were destined to be successful in the long run, we had to start then and there to train our key people in the skills needed to *manage* a growing enterprise. As events turned out, we grew far faster than we had hoped; but because our managers at all levels had been grounded in the philosophy of management and trained in its skills, they were able to handle with a minimum amount of stumbling the problems that have so often proved the undoing of many a company.

Today we probably have one of the most comprehensive management training programs for a company our size. It rests on the foundation of strong, professionally qualified personnel departments, generally conversant with modern management practices and particularly competent in day-to-day coaching and consulting. This is most important. No one can develop competent managers if training programs are designed and carried out by people who do not know what desirable management practices are. Furthermore, since management development must be a continuous activity that is interwoven with what the manager actually does day by day, it is equally essential that the personnel staff consist of the kind of people to whom line managers will readily turn for help and advice as they try to apply their newly learned principles on the job.

In any company where management wants to spend its time solving its most pressing problems, published policies and procedures are vital. They indicate to the entire company that certain problems have already been thought through and standard approaches have been organized. Thus the same problem is not being solved over and over again. These policies tend to be the conscience or the road map for the company's day-to-day actions with its employees, its customers, its shareholders, and the public.

To inject training as far as possible into every aspect of the line manager's daily activities, therefore, we have a series of administrative guides covering the company's policies and procedures in every area of responsibility within the organization. Each of these guides furnishes the basis of a formal training course, organized by the personnel staff in conjunction with the functional managers concerned, at which the thinking behind each policy is analyzed and discussed and the procedure for administering it is explained. In this way, sound management practices are consistently observed throughout the company, and temporary improvisations are minimized.

We have 15 divisions, each of which has its own professional personnel staff. These personnel professionals work closely with both corporate top management and the managers at all levels in their own divisions. Thus they are able to feed back to top management all pertinent data on such matters as the divisional work climate, any policy or procedure problems that may have cropped up, how individual managers are developing, and so on. In turn, top management is able to feed back through the divisional personnel staffs any changes in policy or procedure that it wishes to transmit to line management at the divisional level. It is within this generally cohesive atmosphere that the formal management training programs organized by the personnel staff are conducted. These formal courses fall into three general categories: in-company programs held during working hours, in-company programs held after working hours, and outside courses.

A three-part series on basic management topics such as understanding the management function, selecting and developing people, and human relations and productivity is conducted for all our managers, in groups of about 20 at a time. Meetings are held once a week, each session lasts two hours, and each topic takes about nine or ten weeks to cover. We use the conference method, including discussions, films, case studies, and role playing. To date, 400 of our managers have completed this series, and 50 are in the midst of it now.

We also have over 30 college-level courses taught in the evenings in our own classrooms. About half of these are management-oriented. One of the most important classes in this series is on financial management for non-financial managers. It ends with five groups competing in a five-hour management business game. Another, on leadership fundamentals, is designed for employees with management potential who have not yet attained supervisory status. No managers are allowed to attend this course.

We recognized another need and discussed it with the director of the Management Center at St. Thomas College in St. Paul. The Center has developed an executive training program specifically designed for the small and medium-sized company. Since it is difficult for us to allow a large number of people to be gone for a month or more at a time, the managers taking this executive development course attend it full time one week a month for six months. Thus far, 30 of our managers have completed it, and eight others are currently enrolled.

The well known Kepner-Tregoe full-week workshop on management problem solving and decision making is another part of our management training. We use their Apex Program for top management as well as their Genco Program for middle- and first-level management. More than 100 of our managers have completed this workshop.

To supplement these programs and to insure that our management development is a continuing process, we also urge—and indeed often require—our management personnel to attend the various workshops and seminars run by professional management organizations.

In order that top management philosophies and know-how can be shared throughout the company, the company executives are writing their own motion picture scripts on special management topics. These men give examples of such crucial topics as cost control, company planning, company policies, and customer relations on film. We have been able to film 30-minute black-and-white 16 mm. sound films for under $350.

As for the functional training courses, we have, for example, a weekly training session in administrative procedures that goes on for several months, given by each divisional personnel manager. This course covers day-to-day administrative problems, with certain sessions handled by specialists in government security, purchasing, and so on. Then we have a very thorough course in salary administration, which includes management group meetings where the general concept of salary administration is explained, argued, and discussed and local, regional, and national salary surveys are analyzed and explained. This course also explains the concept of job evaluation and outlines the steps in our highly formal appraisal program. Our appraisals are results-oriented—that is, we are interested in knowing what an employee has accomplished, what mistakes he has made and why, and just what his boss is planning to do to help him overcome his inadequacies.

We also have a training course in recruiting, thanks to which our key supervisors are able to participate actively in our college recruiting program—both on campus and in the plant—and in the recruiting of experienced personnel. This, of course, is a valuable aid to the personnel staff, but we feel that it contributes to the development of the manager at the same time. Incidentally, though we have to compete with major electronics firms from all over the country, our acceptance rate from the colleges has been averaging nearly 50 per cent as a result of the thorough grounding our line managers have received.

No management development program can succeed if the wrong employees have been hired in the first place. Quality is our first concern, but suitability is a close second—that is, we try to match the employee's professional talents and personal qualities as exactly as possible with the job requirements. This means that even after complete screening, Personnel never makes job offers without a go-ahead signal from the line manager; hence the emphasis, in our basic management training course, on the techniques of employee selection.

Our management development efforts are an attempt to make managers on all levels realize that managing is significantly different from their original functional specialties. We are making considerable headway in that attempt. Our management development program shows that size is no barrier to adequate provision for this important activity. In fact, it is our contention that a company—regardless of its size—cannot afford *not* to have such a program.

SECTION VI

Applying the Behavioral Sciences

> *Tremendous advances have been made in the behavioral sciences in this century. Many of these have been adapted or applied to management—and particularly, personnel—problems in business. A few of these applications are discussed in this section: new management theories, programed instruction, laboratory training, personnel testing, and new methods of appraisal of performance.*

THE APPLICATION OF THE BEHAVIORAL SCIENCES TO MANAGEMENT •

RICHARD A. DUNNINGTON

TODAY'S MANAGER IS INCREASINGLY exposed to the work of behavioral scientists. Publications and education programs—both within organizations and outside—communicate theories and research findings unheard of by management 25 years ago. In addition, there is mounting evidence that the appropriate application of these resources can make an important contribution to the effectiveness of individuals, groups, and organizations— effectiveness not only in terms of individual satisfaction but in activities on the job.

One might conclude that managers, as a matter of course, would extensively use the resources of the behavioral sciences. We find, however, that there is considerable variability in the degree and manner of utilization. This is currently a matter of research interest to a number of behavioral scientists. It is of practical interest to responsible leaders in a variety of organizational settings.

The logical sponsors for new behavioral science approaches to the management of human resources are personnel or industrial relations departments. Unfortunately, within many organizations we find the parameters of activity for personnel administrators restricted and defined by prior work. They are not seen as having any particular expertise which

RICHARD A. DUNNINGTON is Manager, Basic Personnel Research, International Business Machines Corporation, Armonk, New York.

sets them apart from other members of management. And, indeed, they may not possess the knowledge which would give them a special standing and professional status.

A professional role for personnel can draw much of its strength from the behavioral sciences. It is the emergence of this role and overview of the application of the behavioral sciences to management problems which will be our major concern in this chapter.

THE BASIS FOR CHANGE

The external intellectual environment is supportive of a new and innovative role for those in personnel management. This support is expressed through publications that define challenging problems of our time, such as the need to find new concepts of motivation, new approaches to organizing human effort, and the special problems of key employee groups.[1] Other publications elaborate research findings which point the way to new and creative approaches to understanding these problems. However, they frequently fall short of prescribing particular actions for particular organizations appropriate at a specific point in time.

Mathematical models and statistical analysis procedures made possible by computer technology open new vistas for the utilization of the behavioral sciences. It is now possible not only to determine the probability of certain kinds of people being successful in given jobs, but to project the work force needed for particular engineering and production schedules. These new techniques permit analysis of research data such that more variables can be handled in any particular study and consequently greater understanding derived in a shorter period of time than was thought possible 15 years ago.

Coincidental with the external supports and improved research techniques are the internal strains and perplexities which are a part of most organizations. Rapid technological change, change in the values of society which impinge on the organization, increased communications capabilities, and an expanding competitive environment thrust new and challenging problems before contemporary managers. They seek a home for exploration and resolution within organizations. Where personnel has been able to redefine its role and responsibilities and where there has been increased

[1]Watters, Albert F., "Personnel Management: Future Problems and Opportunities," *Personnel,* January-February, 1961.

utilization of the resources of the behavioral sciences, we find that it can make an important contribution to the solution of these problems.

APPLICATIONS OF BEHAVIORAL SCIENCE

Although there are similarities among organizations and individuals, there are also important differences. It is the similarities which permit the behavioral scientist to generalize. It is the differences which make the application of findings and theories difficult.

For this reason, an organization which desires to use the findings of the behavioral sciences must develop or obtain the talent necessary to translate the generalizations into meaningful terms for the particular environment. This talent may take the form of professional consultants, professional employees, or organization members who have special talents and training in the application of behavioral science knowledge.

Industrial psychologists were the pioneers in applying psychological concepts to management problems. The paragraphs which immediately follow illustrate some of the fruitful areas of cooperation between members of the psychological profession and management.

Some of the characteristics of these applications are that they make an immediate contribution to the rationality and efficiency of the organization. In addition, they are largely concerned with individuals rather than the relationships within and between groups. For purposes of this review, I have grouped a sample of these applications under the general heading *The Individual*.

THE INDIVIDUAL

Selection. The character and quality of any human organization is partly determined by those who are members of it. The matching of individual abilities, aptitudes, and skills to the job is an early and major contribution of psychology. Used initially as part of the screening process for recruits during World War I, systematic selection techniques have now become standard practice for many jobs in a wide range of organizations. As with any other personnel procedure or practice, they continue to have value as long as they are reviewed and periodically updated. A case in point are psychological tests over which a controversy has been raging. Saul Gellerman gives an assessment of these tests in another chapter in this section.

Placement. The use of systematic evaluation procedures need not stop with initial selection for employment. They may contribute to the subsequent placement of individuals into positions other than those for which initially hired. Assessment centers for the identification of individuals to go into management or highly creative jobs have gained increasing acceptance. Among the more widely known and successful applications of these assessment centers is that employed by American Telephone and Telegraph in its management development program. Douglas W. Bray of A. T. & T. describes this technique in the section on management talent in this book.

Appropriate use of behavioral science knowledge in the selection and placement process can reduce considerably the probability of job failure. It is at the point of input of human resources and the selection of individuals to move into positions of successively greater responsibility that management can exercise the most discretion with least trauma to both the individual and the organization. Management can exercise judicious control over these vital activities through the appropriate application of behavioral science knowledge.

Development. The rapid change, characteristic of contemporary society, heightens the need for means of training and retraining in an economical and effective manner. New techniques such as programed instruction, teaching machines, and closed-circuit TV are all based in some measure on the work of behavioral scientists. The task of training for many organizations is not restricted to one occupational group but cuts across many skill levels: production employees and clerical, technical, and professional employees as well as management. Among those who have adapted programed instruction to training situations in industry are the Eastman Kodak Company, IBM, and the American Management Association with its PRIME (Programed Instruction for Management Education).

Of particular interest for management development are recent innovations in the use of materials simulating the job of a manager and the environment of the organization. Through the use of computers, managers undergoing training can obtain timely feedback on the effects of their decisions. More recently this training approach is being combined with experiences in group dynamics and sensitivity training. The management simulation technique employed by the American Management Association has been in operation for several years—with a good deal of success. Sensitivity or laboratory training has been conducted by the National Training Laboratories at Bethel, Maine, the American Management Association with its Executive Action Course, Robert Blake and Jane Mouton with their Managerial Grid Program, Standard Oil Company of New Jersey, U. C. L. A., and numerous other American universities.

Evaluation. Psychologists have long been interested in developing measures of job performance. Such measures become particularly important for the validation of selection tests from the psychologist's point of view. For management, they can provide a basis for an equitable reward system.

Research findings point to the inadequacy of the traditional appraisal program in which the superior sits in judgment of the subordinate using personal trait or performance factors of a very general nature. As a result of research on the process of appraisal and counseling, programs which provide opportunities for mutual goal setting on the part of superior and subordinate followed by appraisal against the accomplishment of these goals are being established in a number of organizations. A description of a new system of work planning and review is to be found in the chapter by Edgar F. Huse and Emanuel Kay later in this section.

Counseling. Our concern thus far has been largely with the cognitive processes rather than emotional factors. Although an important component of counseling may have to do with vocational guidance, an equally important role that skilled professionals can perform is that of diagnosing emotional reactions on the job.

Certainly those who manage are well aware of the degree to which emotions, feelings, and attitudes of individuals can work for or against high performance. In some instances the source of the problem may be deeply rooted in the development of the individual, or it may be physically based. Professionals skilled in diagnosis—psychologists or psychiatrists—can assess the nature of a problem and recommend the most appropriate sources for assistance.

We have broadly sketched some of the aspects of the behavioral sciences which can be brought to bear when we consider the input, utilization, evaluation, and conservation of human resources in an organization. The work of the behavioral scientist does not end with the development of a selection, evaluation, or training application. If he and his work are to make a lasting contribution to the setting in which he works, there must be continued monitoring, review, updating, and improvement in the same fashion that accounting systems, technological processes, and marketing strategies are modified in the light of new developments, new intelligence, or a changing set of needs and relationships.

Too often it is assumed that once a program has been introduced the work of the behavioral scientist is finished and the program will operate automatically. This is usually not the case. Continual maintenance and improvement of behavioral science applications are as essential as the maintenance and development functions in other aspects of organization life.

THE TASK

The emerging field of human factors psychology is concerned with adjusting machines and work to men. It complements the process of selection and placement of individuals by studying the relationship of people to machines and work processes to insure that the design of tools, layout of the work, and the physical environment are compatible with human characteristics. Management and behavioral scientists have increased work and development in this specialty spurred by the unknowns of space travel and man-machine systems.

There is an additional dimension of the task environment which merits careful attention by management. The logic of efficiency dictates that work should be rationalized and divided into tasks which meet the requirements of a particular system, assembly, or manufacturing operation. In so doing, the employee is often allowed to contribute only a portion of his potential to the job.

There is research evidence to suggest that individuals in some situations maximize their contribution where the work they perform includes a number of tasks that enhance the intrinsic interest and meaning of the job. As with previous factors, this is directly controllable by management and those responsible for the design of work.

THE GROUP

People gain many of their satisfactions both on and off the job while associating with other people. Our American heritage stresses individual achievement and reward; thus we tend to overlook the impact of individuals as they interact with one another at work in fact-to-face relationships. Much of the research in this area has contributed to and been based on social psychological theory.

More than a quarter of a century of research has repeatedly revealed the degree to which internal work-group relationships can and do influence the level of productivity and satisfaction of group members. Although proper selection, placement, training, evaluation, and task design may be necessary for high levels of productivity, they are not sufficient. One of the important additional factors is the nature and quality of interpersonal relations at work.

This again is something which management can influence and control. The composition, size, and life span of the group as well as the degree to which the immediate supervisor gains acceptance of a common goal will influence group effectiveness. Recent studies suggest that productivity, absenteeism, and job satisfaction can be influenced depending upon the climate developed within a group. This climate is largely a function of management action.[2]

THE ORGANIZATION

Much of the new and exciting work of the behavior sciences of direct relevance to management falls under the general heading of organizational behavior. The field is broad and diffuse; therefore, we will attempt here only to touch on the highlights of what seem to be significant developments and bold experiments by staff and management groups. Underlying much of the work going on today is the concept of an organization as being a dynamic set of factors related in a systematic, on-going, interdependent fashion.

Cooperative work between behavioral scientists and management in this area follows three paths. One of them is the traditional model of research to increase understanding of the phenomenon being studied. The behavioral scientist does not look on the output of his research as having any one-to-one relationship to management action. Rather, he sees his role as that of providing new insights and explanations for organizational problems. The utilization of these insights may take place in diverse ways: providing managers with new ways of thinking about and conceptualizing old problems, establishing a base for experimentation, or rethinking old policies and developing new ones.

A second path is called at various times and places action research, organization improvement, or business effectiveness programs. This approach to cooperative endeavor between management and behavioral scientists is based on theories of group dynamics and sensitivity training. The programs encourage openness of communication on such factors as power

[2]Klein, S. M., *Work Pressure and Group Cohesion,* Unpublished Doctoral Dissertation, Cornell University, June 1963.

relationships and individual styles of behavior which block effective communication and understanding. The goal is to establish a culture and pattern of behavior in an organization which will encourage mutual trust, openness of communication, and expression of feelings such that decisions can be made more rapidly and effectively and work accomplished with minimal stress.

The third path also has an action orientation. It follows the more traditional pattern of individual consulting. A single behavioral scientist—either as a member of the organization or one based outside—works with individuals within the management structure on problems of an organizational nature. His role is that of a behavioral science entrepreneur who largely acts as a middleman, matching resources outside the company with internal needs.

I would like to dwell on the sponsorship of an internal research program by an organization since this will not be the direct concern of subsequent chapters. There have been attempts by several corporations to engage in such research: A. T. & T., General Electric, General Motors, Esso, and IBM, to name a few. A detailed account of the General Electric experience is reported elsewhere.[3]

The skilled design and implementation of behavioral science research projects done within the organization setting can serve several purposes. It can bring to bear current behavioral science knowledge on a problem of immediate or long-range import. It can provide findings which are of particular relevance to the organization and thus increase the probability of utilization. Because those doing research are members of the organization and thus knowledgeable regarding the particular culture, the research design can reflect its unique characteristics. Needless to say, the findings of such research, carefully reported, can greatly enhance the stature of the organization unit sponsoring it.

The research findings, in themselves, do not necessarily provide a definitive course of action. They do, however, increase the probability that any action taken will more directly relate to the realities of the situation.

There are additional advantages to a well structured internal research program. One of the dimensions which has been lacking in much behavioral science research is that of change over time. Longitudinal studies permit greater leverage in understanding the impact of change. If organization units are the focus of study, we then can have comparative analysis

[3]Ferguson, L. L., "Social Scientists in the Plant," *Harvard Business Review*, May-June 1964.

between units and comparative analysis over time of one unit. Such studies permit organizations to have bench marks against which they can judge their past actions and better determine the course of future activity. If particular occupational groups are the focus of study, it is possible through longitudinal studies to determine the interaction between individuals and the organization, and the consequences of this interaction for both individual and organization effectiveness. The importance of such studies has been more fully elaborated elsewhere.[4]

* * *

There is every evidence that we are experiencing a confluence of forces stemming from the academic community, the economic environment, and the internal needs of organizations. These forces are steadily encouraging management to utilize the resources of the behavioral sciences. Whether the sponsorship will rest within the realm of personnel or find its place in other parts of an organization will largely be determined by the historical role of the personnel function, how top management perceives this role, and the interest of personnel managers in expanding their sphere of influence.

[4]Dunnington, R. A., S. M. Klein, and D. Sirota, "Research for Organization Theory and Management Action," *Proceedings of the Sixteenth Annual Meeting*, Industrial Relations Research Association, December 1963.

AN EXPERIMENT IN MANAGEMENT •

ARTHUR H. KURILOFF

Non-linear systems is a relatively small company of some 300 employees in its twelfth year. Our business is the design, development, manufacture, and sale of precision electronic instruments. Most of our executives have engineering backgrounds, as one would expect.

Three and a half years ago, we decided that it was high time that we behaved like scientists and engineers—like intelligent, rational people in the management of our business. We decided to throw out the witchcraft, the old wives' prescriptions, and many of the conventional notions embedded in our culture about how to manage a business. We concluded that we would try to operate on the basis of the findings of the social scientists, industrial engineers, industrial psychologists, human relations specialists and, when appropriate, the poets and philosophers who preceded them.

The approach we adopted was the one engineers follow when they solve a design problem. They select from various disciplines those elements which are applicable to the problem at hand. They then synthesize a solution, basing it on proven knowledge and theory. In like fashion, we selected from whatever disciplines or fields of knowledge seemed indicated. We operated, so to speak, at the confluence of the disciplines. We could accept ideas from, say, Abraham Kaplan, Rensis Likert, Douglas McGregor, Paul Goodman, or anyone who had principles or data that pertained to the problems at hand. We synthesized, from these sources, answers that seemed appropriate to our own problems, our own business, and our own notions of how things ought to be done.

We saw that in any business there are four areas that have to be considered. First, the economic enterprise that we were trying to manage is an organ of society. It exists under the law and therefore has a contract with the community. In order to fulfill its contract, it has to pursue

---

ARTHUR H. KURILOFF is Vice President, Non-Linear Systems, Inc., Del Mar, California.

its course in ways that are beneficial both to itself and to the community. Second, we have the problem of departmentalization. How do we organize this enterprise to perform its function? How do we go from the concept, the original idea, the innovation, to the creation of new products, the best ways to manufacture and sell them, the best ways to collect the money, and so on? Third, we have to consider the groupings within departments. How do we dispose the groups to make appropriate departments to serve the functions of the business? Finally, we must concern ourselves with the people who make up these groups.

The last is vitally important because it can be shown that any company organizes itself on the basis of the ideas about people held by the top management of that company. Some executives consider the human beings that form the organization to be so many pairs of hands. These hands, they feel, are mutually interchangeable. If Clock Number 3,412 is missing, Clock Number 5,642 can be substituted and the work will get done pretty much as it was before. Not only are these "hands" interchangeable, but also they're not really very bright. Therefore, the job had better be cut down to its lowest common denominator, so that these "hands" can be indoctrinated quickly to serve the purposes of the production line. In addition, these "hands" really don't want to work very much. They're inherently lazy and they have to be forced, coerced, directed, and controlled into performing. And as if this were not enough, they are probably a little dishonest. As a result, they have to be monitored and watched all the time.

This is not really a very pretty picture of one man's view of another; and yet if we were to think very hard about it and examine the realities of organizations, we would confess that the picture seems to be true. What results is a form of organization sometimes called the "accounting model." It is set up essentially to detect and correct error. We have superintendents watching foremen, assistant managers watching superintendents, managers watching assistant managers, executives watching managers, accountants watching executives, controllers watching accountants, and so on until we get to the top office. The result is the kind of complex, multilayered organization with which we are familiar, replete with difficulties in communication and distortions in content as information filters up and down through the layers.

What kind of an organization would result if we had different ideas about people? If we stopped talking and thinking about people in terms of the functions they can serve, if we looked at them in the light of the psychological findings and the reality of what they are, would we get a different kind of organization? We at Non-Linear Systems decided that we would try this approach and see.

We went to work on the principle that each human being has a different set of aptitudes, talents, desires, and needs. We decided that if we could design the work situation so that these needs and aptitudes could be filled and used, we would get a more productive, more efficient, and more effective organization. We would get a healthier, happier, and, incidentally, a more profitable organization. We assumed that people are not inherently lazy, that they will exert all kinds of energy to serve their own purposes and to meet their needs, and that they have the capacity to learn if we make it possible for them to do so on the job. In a word, we assumed that people can be trusted. And a different kind of organization evolved.

Three and a half years ago we turned our organization inside out. Up to this time it had exhibited the usual pyramidal form. We had six layers in our organization, which are many for a small company such as ours. We then adopted an essentially horizontal form of organization, eliminated layers, and set up departmentalization on a horizontal line with approximately 32 departments all reporting to an executive council of eight people. Each of these eight operates in a specific area in which any business must set its goals and measure its attainments in the achievement of those goals.

Next we threw out our assembly lines. We took the department which produced instruments and simply wiped out the four assembly lines. We did this at one fell swoop. We divided the 80 people into groups of approximately seven people. Each group was run by what we call an "assistant manager," a technician with a good background in electronics, very skilled at the technical aspects of the work. We instructed these groups in the following manner:

> Now you are on your own. We will give you a model of an instrument we want built. We would like to have you build ten of these at a time. We will give you no planning. There is no central agency which will tell you how to do this work. You must use your own minds and proceed at your own pace. Trade off jobs as you will. All we want is instruments that duplicate the original model and work exactly the way the model does.

There was chaos for a while. It took us about nine months to get back to the effectiveness that we had on the old assembly lines. By that time, we began to see some fascinating things. We began to discover that the people were coming up with new and better ways to do things. Their skills were increasing. We began to see a drop in the amount of time required to assemble an instrument. We began to see improved quality and improved effectiveness. Over the long haul, we reached a point where we were something like 30 per cent more effective in the use of time than we had been on the old assembly line.

In other departments we followed similar tactics. We used the group method wherever we could in the organization. We found that people were able to satisfy many of their needs to do a job more effectively, to help support each other, and to become an integral part of the operation.

As a matter of fact, Douglas McGregor implies this kind of approach to management in the terminology he uses. He says the kind of organic management he spells out as "Theory Y" can be described as "management by integration and self-control." The objective is to teach each person in the company what his part is in the accomplishment of overall goals. Then by structuring the situation so a man can fulfill his needs, he will proceed to spend the energy required to do just that. The total operation then becomes one of the integration of the efforts of all the individuals who make up the enterprise.

To the practicing manager, an understanding of human motivation can be most illuminating. This knowledge points the way to exciting possibilities in the improvement of work and its surrounding structure, as I have so briefly indicated.

A widely accepted formulation of a theory of human motivation is that of A. H. Maslow, of Brandeis University, who synthesizes the work of previous psychologists and philosophers. Maslow says, very simply, that man is a wanting animal. His wants occur in a series of five levels, the lower of which are concerned with the physiological, safety, and social needs. Succeeding are the higher, less tangible needs of ego-satisfaction and, ultimately, self-fulfillment. All these needs in most members of our society are partially satisfied and partially unsatisfied simultaneously. As a lower need is in process of gradually being satisfied, the next higher need gradually emerges.

On the basic level are the physiological needs—that is, the needs for air, food, shelter, water, and clothing. Once this set of needs is reasonably well filled, another set arises to take its place, the needs for safety. Safety needs have to do with man's feelings about freedom from fear. He wants to be free from fear of deprivation and loss of life. He needs the ability to pursue happiness in his own way. When this set of needs is reasonably well filled, then the third set arises—the social needs. Man, being a gregarious animal, must exchange information, be close to other people, give love, be loved, give admiration, and be admired. The very human qualities that we all possess are wrapped up very tightly in this set of needs. Once the social needs are pretty well satisfied, the fourth set arises —the ego needs. The ego needs are of two kinds: the need for competence and the need for reputation. A man has to feel that he can do something very well, and he also has to have the feeling that other people recognize his competence.

Finally, when these sets of needs are reasonably well filled, the ultimate set of needs arises, the needs for what Maslow calls "self-actualization." McGregor terms this set of needs the "needs for self-fulfillment." This set of needs has to do with a man's desire to develop and use his talents, his aptitudes, and his abilities. A man will exert tremendous energy to fill these needs.

We asked Maslow how well satisfied the average man is in fulfilling these human needs on the American scene today, in our economy as it exists. He replied that, in his opinion, the average American citizen today is perhaps 85 per cent satisfied in his physiological needs. He is fairly well clothed, housed, and fed. He is approximately 70 per cent satisfied in his safety needs: Jobs being reasonably plentiful, it isn't too difficult to find a new one if a man has skill and confidence and is willing to move. His social needs are about 50 per cent fulfilled. The average job is poorly tailored to serve social needs, particularly the job on the assembly line. Here a man is essentially chained to a spot. The work moves along before him and he must repeat the same dull task over and over. With respect to the ego needs, Maslow feels that perhaps the average man is only 40 per cent satisfied. And, finally, in the fulfillment of his self-actualization needs, he is but 10 per cent satisfied.

Translated into operational terms, this means, very simply, that we are overlooking the greatest opportunities for using the talents, the aptitudes, and the abilities of people in the service of the company.

Let's put it another way. If we can set up a situation, if we can by our process of management create an atmosphere which permits the liberation of the talents and aptitudes of people, not only the company but also the people themselves will benefit greatly. We will get kind of a self-supporting and self-energizing spiral. People who learn some small amount will want to learn even more. People who acquire some skills will want to acquire even more skills. As a result, they will become better contributors, and the whole enterprise and community will profit.

Why, one might ask, should a profitable, well-operating company decide to turn itself inside out like this? One doesn't normally take an enterprise that's running along very smoothly and making money and completely revamp it. I think the answer to that lies in some of the philosophical notions intimated in the principle that man does not live by bread alone. A company has commitments other than that of just making money. It has a contract with society, as I have indicated. As a result, it owes to society a debt for its survival. The debt must be paid in the fulfillment of these obligations:

1. It must live so that it can continuously produce the fundamental wealth of the community, as it has done historically.
2. In order to do this, it must produce socially acceptable goods. This means better and better products for less and less money.
3. It must offer to the people who work a chance to earn a steady living; and it must provide a situation in which these people can learn, grow, develop, contribute more to the community, and become better citizens.

As business executives and managers, we must learn to develop and use the hitherto unemployed skills and talents of people. In this way we can best solve our present problems and face the future confidently.

PROGRESS REPORT ON PROGRAMED INSTRUCTION •

I. The Basic Concept

HAROLD L. MOON

THERE ARE SOME WHO HAVE called programed instruction "the greatest innovation in teaching since the invention of movable type." Others have said that the method will revolutionize education and training. These views may be extreme, but programed instruction holds great promise as an educational and training tool.

It is sometimes referred to as programed training, programed learning, automated instruction, or machine teaching (although a machine usually is not necessary); but all these terms refer to the same basic concept.

Programed instruction is an effective means of applying the principles of efficient learning by which students and trainees are known to learn thoroughly and rapidly. Whether the means of presenting the materials is a book, a machine, or some other device, programed instruction incorporates these principles:

1. The subject matter is presented in a sequence of small steps arranged in *psychological* teaching order, with each step building deliberately on preceding ones.
2. The trainee actively participates in the teaching-learning process by

---

HAROLD L. MOON is Director—Training Division, Stevenson, Jordan & Harrison Management Consultants, Inc., New York, New York.

completing a sentence, answering a question, working a problem, or doing whatever is appropriate.

3. In each step the trainee is informed immediately as to whether his response was appropriate. "Right" responses are confirmed, and "wrong" responses are corrected before he proceeds in the sequence.

4. The material is carefully prepared to lead the trainee into making appropriate responses.

5. Each trainee progresses at his own rate. The rapid learner is not held back, and the slower learner is not left behind in confusion.

These principles are not new. Socrates and other master teachers used them when acting as personal tutors. However, it was the work of psychologists that clearly identified the principles, and until the advent of programed instruction there was no effective means of applying them on a large scale.

THE NOVELTY AND ADVANTAGES OF THE METHOD

The novelty of programed instruction is in the structure of the series of steps (items or frames) called a "program," which simulates the one-to-one, student-teacher interaction of the tutorial process. When a program is completed, tested, and known to be effective with a given trainee population, the instructor who prepared the materials is able, without being present, to teach all who use the program.

A program may consist of a few steps or several thousand, depending on the training objectives. It may constitute the major instructional unit or be only a part of a unit of instruction, such as portions of a course that are difficult to teach by ordinary methods.

The following are some of the basic advantages of the method:

1. The instruction is uniform and consistent. Variability within and between instructors is eliminated.

2. The quality of training is high. All students usually master the subject matter although they may vary in the time they require.

3. Time is saved. Most learners complete programed material in 25 to 50 per cent less time than required by ordinary lecture-study methods. Time savings from 20 to 75 per cent or more have been reported.

4. Individuals can be trained. There is no need to wait until there are a number of trainees to justify group sessions, and fast learners can be placed on the job sooner than slower learners.

5. Training can be decentralized. In some instances self-contained programs can be used effectively at widely scattered locations.
6. Less instructor time is needed. More people can be trained without enlarging the training staff, and instructors can do creative work with students or give attention to other important matters.
7. Trainees like it. They usually are surprised and pleased as information quickly "sinks in."

Because most current programs teach topics that usually are learned by rote, some think the effectiveness of the method may be limited to this type of instruction. This is not necessarily so. There is nothing in the principles of programed instruction to restrict its use, and there is no sound reason for believing that it will not prove to be flexible enough to encompass most subjects if employed with ingenuity and imagination.

Primitive as programed instruction now is, it has been notably successful in teaching subject matters as diverse as grade-school spelling, chess, appreciation of poetry, contract law, computer programing, blueprint reading, and the principles of logical trouble shooting, as well as several levels of mathematics, some foreign languages, and numerous other rather precisely defined subjects.

SOME PROBLEMS CREATED BY PROGRAMED INSTRUCTION

Despite its many advantages, programed instruction is not a panacea for all training problems. The overall purpose of any training effort should be to improve training so that desired job behaviors can be achieved at the lowest possible cost. In most cases, the initial cost of programed instruction is high. For this reason alone it should not be used indiscriminately. Also, other methods of instruction may be as effective, perhaps even more effective for a given purpose. Decision as to which training tools to use should await careful analysis of the training problem, which includes consideration of the kind and number of trainees, precisely what the trainees are to be able to do upon the completion of a course, the location of training, the time schedule, the availability of instructors, and the budget.

The problems of administering programed instruction should be considered carefully. For example, the advantage of students progressing at their own rate can become an administrative disadvantage. What will be done with those who finish early? Can they continue other portions of training or be placed on the job without delay or without disrupting present schedules? Also, the advantage of individual training can become a disadvantage if planning does not include decisions as to where and when trainees will study.

There is another difficulty that has caused much disappointment to companies too eager to jump on the band wagon. An expertly designed program appears deceptively simple, so much so that many have assumed that good programs can be prepared with little training. In most cases the opposite is true Effective programing requires a high level of skill and a great amount of time, energy, and tenacity. It also requires a willingness to test the materials and to revise them again and again until desired results are achieved.

Although there are guiding principles and some specific techniques, programing at present is largely an art. It is hoped, and there is some indication that the hope will be realized, that programing may become a rather precise technology. Success will depend, of course, upon continued basic and applied research.

THE TWO PHASES OF PROGRAMING

Programing, to be efficient and effective, must proceed in two phases. The first is the "preparing to construct" phase. The second is the "construction" phase.

In the first phase, the programer must (1) state the major program objectives in behavioral terms—as outcomes discernible in the trainee. He must state what the trainee must be able to do upon completion of the program; (2) state the subobjectives—what the trainee must do to achieve the objectives and to demonstrate that he has achieved them; (3) analyze the subobjectives to determine precisely the relevant subject matter; (4) arrange the subject matter in the most effective psychological teaching order; and (5) provide enough example material to teach the subject matter. Programing cannot proceed without costly confusion and rework until the preparing to construct phase is completed.

In the construction phase, of course, the writing of the items (steps, frames) that make up the program is done. The attitude of the programer must be that of a teacher. His sole purpose must be to present material (stimuli) that require responses relevant to the behavior specified in the program objectives. The process of constructing a program can be described best in the form of the following advice to the programer:

1. Expect some, but not much, independent thought of the learner.

Prepare each step so that he is almost certain to be guided into making the desired response.

2. Present only one concept or operation at a time and eliminate all irrelevancies.
3. Be sure you do not write "test" items. Attempts to play tricks will defeat your purpose. Play "giveaway" with the learner.
4. Seed in review frames to keep newly learned responses active in the repertory of the learner.
5. In the final frames of each lesson, integrate all the concepts and operations taught in that lesson.
6. Have the lesson checked by a program editor.
7. Have the lesson checked by a subject-matter expert.
8. Give the lesson to several students one at a time. Observe their confusions, slowness in responding, and errors.
9. Revise the frames according to the information obtained from the tested students.
10. Have a subject-matter expert check the lesson again.
11. Give the lesson to more students.
12. If necessary, repeat the process of revision, checking, and testing until you have a valid, reliable program.

THE HISTORY OF PROGRAMED INSTRUCTION

As one might expect, programed instruction did not suddenly burst full-blown from the head of Zeus. It evolved over the past 35 years in two main channels: university research and development and military research and development.

Sidney L. Pressey at Ohio State University designed several devices during the 1920's for automatically testing and scoring. Multiple-choice questions were presented, and the machine would not advance until the student pressed the appropriate button. Pressey found that students who had been tested by his machine had, when tested again, learned significantly more than those who had not used the machines. Pleased with the results, Pressey predicted that machines of his type would revolutionize education. There probably are several reasons why little interest was aroused: Sputnik had not been launched; there was little concern about a teacher shortage; research in the psychology of learning was not as advanced as it is today; and Pressey's emphasis was on testing, not teaching.

In the military, the training demands of World War II sparked the development of several devices which were quite similar to current teaching machines, but the programs were not as well developed because the emphasis was still on testing. In the early 1950's, however, Norman Crowder, who was in training research for the Air Force, and B. F. Skinner, a Harvard psychologist, began independent development of the programing methods which underlie programed instruction as it is known today. Crowder evolved the branching (intrinsic) method, and Skinner evolved the linear (extrinsic) method.

The Crowder method employs multiple-choice questions to test the student frequently. If a correct choice is always made, the student progresses through the program in the shortest sequence. If a wrong choice is made, he is given further instruction and another chance. The programing is called "intrinsic" because the actual sequence followed by the student is determined by his responses. With the Skinner extrinsic method, the student constructs each response instead of making a choice from a set of plausible answers, and all students go through the same sequence. Steps in the linear program are much smaller than in the Crowder branching type.

Although the classical Skinner and Crowder methods seem equally effective in some areas of instruction, strict adherence to either for all purposes is awkward. Some sophisticated programers are mixing the two for greater flexibility and to give students a change of pace, and modifications of the Skinner method have become so numerous that it is no longer definitive of the field to describe only the classical linear and branching models. For example, there are now linear-branching programs which may employ both constructed and choice responses or only choice responses.

In 1958, when Skinner described his method in *Science* magazine, the time was right. Teacher shortages and demands for increased efforts to produce scientists and engineers to keep up with the Russians had created a favorable climate for the teaching machine. Interest spread rapidly in the military, the colleges and universities, the schools, industry, and government agencies. The U.S. Office of Education, the Carnegie Corporation, the Ford Foundation, and other agencies made large sums of money available for continuing research.

Within five years almost every major publisher either had published or was planning to publish programs, and about 900 programs were available from various sources. Many schools and colleges have adopted one or more programs, and many others are using programed instruction on an experimental basis. In industry, about 25 per cent of the large companies are using the method on a regular or experimental basis: Eastman Kodak, DuPont, Procter & Gamble, Quaker Oats, U.S. Steel, and several insurance and oil companies, for instance. Most, however, are keeping an eye on developments.

THE ROLE OF TEACHING MACHINES

Until fairly recently, the number of machines being developed outnumbered the programs available to go in them. This rather odd state of affairs apparently resulted from a lack of understanding by many machine developers that a program is the heart of programed instruction. A machine in most instances is not necessary and can often be a hindrance. Since it has been demonstrated that simple book materials are as effective or, in some cases, more effective than machines as presentation devices, announcements of new machines have dropped off; and since the expected market for machines has not yet developed, only a few have actually gone into production.

One should not conclude, however, that there is no role for teaching machines, now or in the future. If programed instruction is to be used for training complex motor skills, appropriate machines must be designed. Many now engaged in programed instruction also are alert to the possibilities of communicating with trainees by sensory channels other than the visual and auditory. For certain purposes, training may be maximized by providing tactile, olfactory, proprioceptive, and perhaps gustatory stimuli in machines.

Moreover, as the advantages of programed instruction become more widely and deeply appreciated, a demand may arise for self-organizing computer systems which can individually teach a large number of students simultaneously and bring each to criterion behavior in shorter time than is now possible by giving each one the precise series of items to meet his specific needs. Even if complex equipment does not increase learning speed, the problems of record keeping and economical storage and retrieval of programed materials may demand its use.

II. *Training Specialized Personnel*

W. R. MUNNS

A SURVEY IN 1962 REVEALED that 9,000 customer engineers working in the 200 branch offices of IBM were spending 30 per cent of their time in training. A total of 10,000 enrollments in that year included basic training for new service personnel and a wide variety of advanced training on new and more sophisticated equipment for experienced men. With the rate of training increasing and the demand for higher quality in each new course, it became apparent that new and more efficient methods of training would be necessary in order to reduce the burden of training for the customer engineer. Each additional course represented additional responsibility, additional time away from his home and family, and less time available to practice the training he had already received. At this time programed instruction was just beginning to make itself heard outside of the testing laboratories.

In anticipation of our growing problem, separate groups in Poughkeepsie, Endicott, and Rochester began to experiment with the programed instruction concepts to test the feasibility of using them to help solve some of the problems. In 1960 these three groups each released a program for field testing. The results of these programs were encouraging. After several more experiments to gain the necessary skills and develop workable techniques, a group of 20 people in Rochester were commissioned to program for actual use and additional testing a major portion of the existing basic program. This effort in Rochester and the four other schools has produced 46 completed programs representing 457 student hours. An additional 25 programs that represent 536 student hours are currently being developed.

W. R. MUNNS is Manager of Customer Engineering Education Planning, Data Processing Division, International Business Machines Corporation, Rochester, Minnesota.

We began our operation of producing programed instruction on the "each man for himself" basis. Each person assigned to a given program did all of the work on that program. He outlined his subject material, wrote frames, edited his own work, and saw that the program was tested. This approach was an absolute failure.

Very early in our work, we could see the need for specialists. Accordingly, five new job descriptions were created. Each position required extensive training and, where possible, experience. These positions were writer, technical editor, program editor, illustrator, and audio technician:

1. *Writer.* In our organization, hand-picked and experienced instructors are given in-house training in the principles of programed instruction and good writing techniques. This program takes from three to six months to produce acceptable writers. These men are already subject-matter experts and have proved themselves to be excellent instructors. The writer assumes complete responsibility for the training package.

2. *Technical editor.* This position has the same requirements as does the position of writer. The two positions are often rotated to relieve the boring months of frame writing. The technical editor is responsible for the technical accuracy of the written material. He also acts as an advisor to the writer when required.

3. *Program editor.* This position requires an English major with a working knowledge of our technical language. The program editor is responsible for correcting all grammatical errors as well as for insuring good formats and adherence to our publishing standards.

4. *Illustrator.* This position is filled by experienced illustrators and artists. They have a good understanding of the problems involved in illustrating mechanical and electrical devices for teaching and publishing purposes.

5. *Audio technician.* Many of our programs are released in the form of student workbooks with instructions on audio tape rather than just straight text. This position is filled by a person with a good speaking voice and an intimate knowledge of sound-recording equipment. This person also edits scripts to prevent the more stilted styles of writing from producing dull tapes.

In order to mass-produce programed instruction courses without any adverse effect on quality, it was clearly necessary to establish sound, workable routines with checkpoints at the critical stages in the program development. Our routines were divided into three basic sections: design, production, and publication.

The design section is responsible for the training package. The writer and technical editor write their detailed statements of terminal behavior based on actual job requirements in skills and knowledge. The first checkpoint occurs here. When the statements have been approved, the criterion tests are developed, tested, and placed into the existing training program. Again approval is necessary to continue. The approval is based on the results of the testing and the subjective opinions of the subject-matter experts.

At this point the production phase begins. Approximately one-half of the total time required to complete the training package has then been used up. The writer and technical expert then outline the material and determine the best sequence in which to teach the various parts of the subject. When the outline is complete, the illustrators and program editor assist the writer in the development of the actual format of the package. Again approval is necessary to continue.

The writer now starts the actual routine of developing frames, and each section in turn is approved by the technical editor and the program editor. The illustrators develop the necessary drawings, graphs, and charts. The illustrations, first-draft typing, and preliminary audio tapes (when required) are merged together to start the process of testing.

The program is first tested by instructors outside of the programed instruction group who have been previously trained in the subject matter. Revisions are made when necessary, and the program testing is then continued by instructors who are not familiar with the subject, by single or small groups of students in the school, and finally by complete classes of 12 to 18 men. After each testing. changes are made as determined by the comments of the test subjects and the results of the criterion tests and average time factors. When all concerned are satisfied with the program, approval to publish is granted.

Actual publication occurs at this time. An estimate of the number of students requiring training during the next six months is made, and the first edition is printed and distributed. During the first six months we keep a thorough record of each student's performance and opinion on the new program. The student evaluations and actual errors in the material are reviewed, and changes are incorporated into the first revision and republication. All programs are monitored periodically and revised when necessary.

III. The Economics of Programed Instruction

RALPH W. WALKER

IN REGARD TO PROGRAMED INSTRUCTION, the teacher asks, "Will it replace me?" The industrial training man asks, "Will it work?" And the first thought that comes to the manager's mind is, "How much will it cost?"

One fairly common observation among researchers is that the cost of a program is explicit and can be amortized in a straightforward manner. No longer do training programs have to be hidden in overhead; moreover, because of the great cost of programing, they probably couldn't be hidden anyway.

It will raise no eyebrows among sophisticated programers to say that programing is expensive. A cursory survey of literature on the costs of developing programed instruction packages shows that there is no common agreement. One author prices frame writing from $2.50 to $40 per frame; another somewhat more rigid individual has established $5 to $5.50 as the cost per frame. The consensus of most investigators is that the cost centers around $5 to $15 per frame. However, it must be conceded that course material of an unusually complex nature may easily carry the price tag toward the upper limit of $40 per frame. Convert these frame costs to cost per class hour, and we arrive at a figure of $400 to $3,000 with a mode of $750 per class hour.

Various reports indicate that the rate for linear frame writing ranges from 8 to 64 rough frames a day, with an average of about 33. But anyone in the programing business knows that the effort involved in writing rough-draft frames represents only 20 to 30 per cent of the

RALPH W. WALKER is Supervisor, Programed Instruction Unit, Technical Training Department, Martin Company, Denver, Colorado.

final cost. It appears that most programs are developed in final form at the rate of 140 to 250 frames per month. This includes gathering data, researching, task analyzing, organizing, outlining, frame writing, editing, typing, proofreading, validating, reproducing, binding, developing illustrations, and producing a criterion text. Few standard text-lecture courses, however, are initiated with such critical and detailed care.

Most industrial courses are subjected to a slow, evolutionary process which works out the imperfections as time goes by. A year-old course may barely resemble the initial class presentation. But before any program is even considered worthy of a serious tryout, it must be exposed to the hypercritical eye of the student and subject-matter expert.

A 1000-frame program of average complexity will consume around 12 hours of a student's time. At a cost of $7,500, it will take five man-months to develop. This represents a ratio of 70 to 1 in preparation time to class time. This is probably 5 to 10 times as great as the ratio for a standard course.

The great range in programing costs becomes evident with experience. The variables which creep into program development are both numerous and complex. The following are a few of the salient criteria upon which costs depend:

1. Length of program.
2. Complexity of subject material.
3. Dynamics of course material.
4. Experience and subject knowledge of program writer.
5. Required objectives, or desired terminal behavior.
6. Initial behavior (basic knowledge) of students.
7. Number of students served.
8. Number of concepts or program elements.
9. Technique and format of program presentation.
10. Extent of program validation and editing.

In spite of the high cost of producing a program, substantial tangible savings are realized as expenses are amortized over a period of time. The literature reports study after study where savings have run into five figures. It should be pointed out, however, that these savings are not necessarily reflected in the training department. Frequently, they are found in the operational organizations, where large numbers of personnel study programed courses during nonproductive hours. Even if there were no dollar savings involved in the autoinstructional method, there is a great amount of evidence that it produces significant achievement with a higher rate of retention than is realized with the standard text-lecture system of teaching.

The Denver division of the Martin Company employs some 11,000 people who are responsible for the design, manufacture, and production of the Titan I and Titan II intercontinental ballistic missile systems and the Titan III space vehicle. Many of these missiles have been installed in underground silos and presently stand in readiness as retaliatory, nuclear-tipped guards against aggression. Once in a readiness stage, they are turned over to members of the Strategic Air Command, who maintain them 24 hours a day.

The aerospace industry demands technical competence. The complexity of long-range missiles and all the supporting equipment is fantastic. The demand for accurate and efficient training is most critical. There is no room for error when our country's very existence may depend upon human reliability. The technicians in the armed forces must maintain a high level of proficiency in order to uphold our position of strategic missile superiority.

To help meet technical training needs, we established a programed instruction unit which varies in manpower strength from four to eight. The initial buildup of such a unit should be slow to allow for evaluation of the neophyte program writers. Even with conscientious screening and depth interviewing, the final selection criterion is a person's ability to write programs. A sudden buildup of a programing organization to meet a training crisis is almost doomed to economic failure. It appears much wiser to extend deadlines for program development to the most pessimistic date. This allows more time for making personnel changes and producing a satisfactory product.

The cost of programing is directly related to the size of the staff and the amount of programing that has been planned ahead. We believe the most economical creation of a programing group, particularly where an operation of fewer than five men is involved, entails the recruitment of individuals who can ultimately assume responsibility for the development of a total programed package from conception through final production.

We have found the best programers are those who have had experience in teaching and writing and are familiar with the subject matter. If they have had some experience or training in statistics, the psychology of learning, editing, or curriculum development, so much the better. It becomes pretty obvious in a small operation that a programing unit cannot afford the luxury of a team of professionals made up of program writers, a subject-matter expert, a curriculum-development specialist, a teacher, a psychologist, a statistician, and an editor.

Some members of our industrial engineering unit, together with our programing staff, worked out a plan for recording cost and time information. Based upon our previous experience, we broke down the program instruction development sequence into its smallest task components. We then estimated the time it would take to perform each of these tasks, using as a base a 180-frame program of average difficulty. These estimates were transposed onto weekly output report forms.

The forms were distributed to our program writers, the supervisor, and the secretary. We kept an accurate account of our applied programing activities each day for six months. At the end of this period, we analyzed our data and compared our projected time estimates with our actual times.

We have drawn the following conclusions from our individual analyses:

1. The soundest investment that can be made is in a competent program writer who is familiar with the subject matter. One of our writers found it necessary to spend a total of 18 days in the preparation of a 178-frame program. Experience in programing pays too. An experienced program writer can produce as much as 40 per cent more finished, acceptable frames than an inexperienced programer.

2. The cost of a program can be significantly reduced by by-passing classroom validation. Unfortunately, when this is done, the quality suffers and the entire programing effort may gain a poor reputation.

3. Programing subject matter which is of a dynamic nature can cost up to 50 per cent more than programing training material which remains static.

4. The error rate in a linear program can be brought down to 5 per cent and objectives still be attained. But to attempt to reduce the errors to 1 or 2 per cent may prove to be economic suicide.

5. Poorly established objectives on one program cost us at least one rewrite which would not have been necessary had the objectives been clearly developed in the first place.

6. Generally speaking, our longer programs have been cheaper to produce, frame for frame, than our shorter ones.

Our initial programing effort was devoted to the development of a

"Weapon System Familiarization" linear program, 613 frames in length, with an associate volume of 50 panels. It was in the hands of our students after three and one-half man-months of effort. This reflected a programing rate of approximately 180 frames per month, or a little less than one frame per hour. The program cost us about $5,600, which included overhead but not reproduction costs. This figure yielded a cost of around $9 per frame. The average class time to complete the program was 10.3 hours. When this time is converted into dollars, our familiarization program was produced for $550 per class hour, excluding reproduction.

An analysis of these figures shows how unreliable a cost-per-frame index is. Management is much more interested in the cost per class hour or, better still, the cost per student. Amortizing our expenses over 1,500 students, the programed instruction package cost about $3.75 per student exclusive of reproduction costs and around $5.25 with the reproduction expenses included.

Employees from our distant operational bases have been working through the familiarization program in 34 per cent less time than it would take them to attend the company's regular two-day text-lecture class. To date, they have attained achievement test scores averaging 9.3 per cent higher than those of their counterparts in the standard classroom situation. When we add the savings of instructors' travel expenses and salaries to the savings in student time, we are able to show management a significant training cost reduction of approximately $30 per student.

The subject taught by company programed instruction should be one which will remain reasonably static and be taught to large numbers of employees over long periods of time. A company should give itself plenty of time to develop the program, employ competent program writers, and distribute operating dollars very carefully.

SENSITIVITY TRAINING, MANAGEMENT DEVELOPMENT, AND ORGANIZATIONAL EFFECTIVENESS •

ROBERT F. PEARSE

SENSITIVITY TRAINING, also known as laboratory or T-group training, is a training technique developed by behavioral scientists. It is based on the principles of group dynamics. As applied to management, it brings together small groups of individual managers and through a process of discussion, special exercises, and general lectures helps the manager see himself as others see him, learn how groups operate, and apply these new insights to his job situation. Well-known examples of sensitivity training are the Executive Action Course of the American Management Association and the program of the National Training Laboratories. The Managerial Grid developed by Robert R. Blake and Jane S. Mouton is an instrumented laboratory outgrowth of sensitivity training.

For the past few years, sensitivity training has been heralded as a radically new and promising departure from traditional management development techniques. It has been seen by some as a tool for greatly improving organizational effectiveness. After being used in industry for some time, both line executives and staff training directors are uncertain as to just how effective it is. Some individual managers report important changes in on-the-job behavioral improvements. They attribute these changes to sensitivity training. However, other managers who have attended similar programs seem to have made no noticeable improvements in managerial behavior.

Sensitivity training as a tool for developing managers and for improving organizational effectiveness depends on two things: (1) the skill of the

ROBERT F. PEARSE is Senior Associate, Leadership Development Associates, Inc., New York, New York.

specialists who conduct it and (2) the overall situation within the company that is using it as a means of improving managerial performance. All training methods depend on the skill of the trainer for their ultimate success. Because the results of sensitivity training depend particularly on timing, nuance, "feel," and building in situations within the group, trainer skill is especially important to learning and change outcomes.

Unless the company the trainee returns to encourages and rewards his willingness to be more open and frank in discussing the feelings aspects of interpersonal conflict and differences, he is likely not to behave in this manner. As Chris Argyris[1] has pointed out, many if not most business organizations in America today encourage the "rational," factual approach to problems and discourage interpersonal exchange of feelings or open discussion of conflicting ideas, systems, and values. In a repressive or punitive organizational climate, the new learning wears off rapidly. Where this new behavior is "punished" in the sense that other managers in the organization are confused or anxious about the degree of frankness and openness the graduate of a sensitivity program demonstrates, the graduate is apt to feel that he made a mistake in using this new approach on the job.

Negative organizational reactions to new and more open behavior on the part of managers is most likely to occur when the bulk of the organization is suppressing, smoothing over, or avoiding open discussion of controversial matters in favor of harmony and surface agreement. It has been pointed[2] out that when key decision makers in the top management group typically employ a "produce or perish," win-lose, competition approach to managing subordinates, they want and expect obedience from these subordinates without question. Particularly when survival in the executive suite is seen as a matter of winning out over associates in a win-lose competitive struggle, it is difficult for the manager who has been exposed to sensitivity training to sell his associates on the organizational benefits of teamwork and joint problem solving. Even though team cooperation might offer more chance for both personal gain and improved organizational effectiveness than does manipulation, back stabbing, outmaneuvering, and functional and factional competitive struggles, it is not easy for one or a few individual managers to change the managerial climate within their company unless they have support from the top.

[1]Argyris, Chris, *Interpersonal Competence and Organizational Effectiveness,* The Dorsey Press, Homewood, Illinois, 1962.
[2]Blake, Robert R., and Mouton, Jane S., *The Managerial Grid,* Gulf Publishing Company, Houston, Texas, 1964.

A like situation exists when the sensitivity-trained executive attempts to convince his associates that their most cherished tactics—those of bargaining and compromise—have limitations in terms of profit, growth, and improved competitive strength for the organization as a whole. When a manager has been trained, both in school and on the job, to believe in an imperfect world, he becomes a realist and settles for less than perfection, either in productivity or in attention to the needs of the people under him. He finds it difficult to realize that both he and his company might become more effective if he were to change his managerial style and broaden his competence in interpersonal relations beyond what is required of a skillful negotiator or compromiser.

To make useful judgments about how effective sensitivity training is as a management development technique, we have to know what organizational philosophies and managerial styles are going to be the most effective in the next 10 or 20 years. The effectiveness of sensitivity training is clearly tied in with our assumptions about what type of organization will be most effective in the 1970's and 1980's.

TYPES OF ORGANIZATION AND LEADERSHIP

Many business executives are uncertain about what type of organizational philosophy and systems they should build to insure maximum profit, flexibility, and productivity in the next 20 years. They hear some management theorists advocating more sophisticated and forceful applications of traditional leadership methods and styles. At the same time, they hear about some of the newer and less traditional concepts of what makes for effective organization and individual leadership. The newer concepts hold that the day of the "power expert," the "manipulator," and the "conniving salesman" type of executive is numbered. This is assumed to be because authoritarian management produces limited responsiveness and motivation in subordinates and consequently decreases initiative and commitment to getting the job done.

Yet many large and successful corporations operate today on a tightly controlled, no-nonsense, top-down basis. And some of these organizations have very satisfactory profit and growth rates. Are times really changing for the continued success of such organizations? Have mass education, the affluent society, and the coming age of nuclear power so changed the competitive picture that such organizations will become increasingly less effective in the next 10 to 20 years? Or is the current emphasis on "participative management" merely a fad that will collapse and disappear under the hard reality of intense competition?

Advocates of strong, centrally controlling, hard-driving, shrewdly opportunistic leadership contend that "management by committee" has already proved its ineffectiveness. They feel that only dynamic, hard-hitting, practical individuals who know how to wield power realistically can expect to successfully direct the business of tomorrow in a period of intense competition and rapid change.

One authority,[3] for example, urges the development of bright, determined executive leaders who are individualists. Such men, he believes, will quickly analyze situations and push others skillfully, decisively, and effectively to get desired action results. This concept of successful leadership and managerial style highlights the aggressive, alert, ambitiously competitive manager who energizes and directs the organization to greater levels of effectiveness. Successful "action management of situations" is the hallmark of this type of leader.

Taking a related yet slightly different viewpoint, others[4] see today's effective business leader as primarily an expert in personal strategy. They define leadership as "strategy in action." Such a leader is one who is skillful in understanding and using organizational power complexes to his advantage. He exploits opportunities for effectiveness and advancement. He knows how to use timing and surprise as techniques for attaining his objectives. Adroitness in the art of mobilizing followers who will carry out his bidding is another of his important skills.

The general assumption underlying both of the above organizational philosophies is that the business organization is a collection of individuals who must be guided, led, directed, and influenced in a variety of ways in order to produce results. Under this concept, the most competent leaders are men who have the skill, ambition, and courage to get people to do what is necessary to produce. A key inference underlying this approach to leadership is that most individuals in an organization must be subjected to a combination of subtle reward and punishment pressures if they are to do their jobs satisfactorily.

The assumption is that most subordinates will tend to settle for a comfortable level of mediocrity in their work efforts without strenuous direc-

---

[3]Odiorne, George S., *How Managers Make Things Happen*, Prentice-Hall, Englewood Cliffs, New Jersey, 1961.
[4]Hardwick, C., and Landuyt, B., *Administrative Strategy*, Simmons-Boardman Publishing Corp., New York, 1962.

tion and motivation from competent and dedicated achievement-oriented superiors. Organizational theorists who support such views point to such behavior in business as restriction of output, unwillingness to take initiative, resentment at being asked to maintain high performance levels, and indifference to organizationals as evidence that the average subordinate has to be both pushed and pulled in order to get him to produce.

There are two critical questions that must be asked here. The first is whether the behavior described above is inherent in people in general or is only a manifestation of their attitudes and reactions under certain organizational philosophies and leadership styles. If the behavior is inherent, then leadership skills must include methods of getting around these blocks. However, if such behavior is only characteristic under certain types of leadership and organizational structure, then we may be able to increase motivation, satisfaction, and productivity by changing the structure and philosophy of the organization along with a change in leadership actions.

This brings us to the second question: What is the relationship between organizational philosophy and leadership styles and the motivation and productivity of employees? If new concepts of organization and leadership do produce greater motivation and productivity, then all organizations will either have to adopt these new methods or labor under a disadvantage in their efforts to compete with organizations that do use such methods.

Newer and less traditional concepts of organization and leadership operate on a different set of assumptions. They assume that organizational effectiveness in modern industrial society can be increased through (1) greater employee participation in decisions which affect their work; (2) improved interpersonal relationships among all levels in the company; (3) more team problem solving and joint conflict resolution; and (4) leadership that makes it possible for subordinates to act with greater personal initiative than usually found in more authoritarian types of organization.

In his research on the behavior of people in business organizations, Argyris contends that the behavior of people in organizations predictably results from certain consequences of management and leadership assumptions and methods. As he sees it, (1) many formal organizations encourage "rational" problem solving and discourage expression of feelings and conflicting opinions as being "immature"; (2) when executives repress feeling reactions to problems, they become less sensitive to their own feelings and to the feelings of their associates; (3) this decreased sensitivity increases doubt, suspicion, and mistrust about the true feelings of associates; (4) with increased doubt, each manager "plays it safe" and avoids risk-taking initiative; and (5) the vitality of the organization declines as managers are unable to work together except in very restricted ways.

If this thesis is correct, then sensitivity training properly applied would be a means of reversing the cycle. As managers become more aware of their own feelings and of the feelings of others as a result of sensitivity training, work disagreements and conflicts can be worked out and resolved rather than being suppressed, smoothed over, or denied as is so often the case in business organizations. As a result of increased sensitivity, more positive conflict resolution, and individual openness, team effectiveness would increase. At the same time individual doubt, suspicion, and mistrust would decrease. However, in order for this to happen, the organization as a whole must be able to adjust positively to the new awarenesses and relationships that are created. If the organization as a group of individuals shows fear, anxiety, skepticism, or resentment over frank expressions of feeling, then the cycle outlined by Argyris will be reinstated.

In their investigation of leadership style and motivation and productivity, Blake and Mouton have plotted different combinations of concern for productivity and for the needs of employees in a two-dimensional grid pattern. The individual manager's assumptions about the best way to get subordinates to produce, his typical method of handling conflict, and his consequent supervisory method can be categorized in terms of distinct positions on the grid.

Thus the production-centered manager in grid terms tends to use a "planner's plan and doer's do" and a "produce or perish" approach to those under him. He feels that employees are best motivated and led through direct pressure in a win-lose competitive situation in which the best man will emerge the victor. In contrast to this managerial style, the people-centered manager believes maximum productivity is attained by creating friendly and encouraging interpersonal relationships without too much direct pressure for production. A third leadership style, that of the team manager, emphasizes maximum concern for both production and for the needs of employees. The assumption is that it is possible to do both simultaneously and that this method will result in maximum organizational effectiveness.

More and more in today's complicated organizations, the newer concepts of leadership center on the direction and motivation of employees as members of work groups. The findings of a series of Office of Naval Research studies on leadership and interpersonal behavior that focus on effective leadership of groups indicate that groups doing assigned tasks operate most effectively when leadership is centered on the group and problem solving rather than dogmatically authoritarian in nature.[5]

In reviewing a number of management and leadership studies conducted at the University of Michigan's Research Center for Group Dynamics and Survey Research Center, Rensis Likert comes to similar conclusions.[6] He feels that the newer concepts of management are already demonstrating their superiority. In this regard, he states, "Managers with the best records of performance in American business and government are in the process of pointing the way to an appreciably more effective system of management than now exists." He considers the most effective interaction-influence system in management to be that which follows the participative leadership styles used by the managers of the high-producing groups reported on in these researches. Other authorities[7] come up with similar findings in their researches on leadership and organization.

APPLICATIONS OF THE NEW STYLE

Though many business organizations use portions of the concepts and leadership styles advocated by those who favor a participative approach, few if any use them in pure and total form at this time. In part, this is because of inertia, habit, and tradition. All managers in a company do not shift suddenly and simultaneously from one set of leadership patterns to another regardless of what training method is used. However, a growing body of research data indicates that greater organizational productivity, flexibility, and effectiveness have been reached in specific organizations through the use of these newer concepts and methods.

The management program at Non-Linear Systems in California is an outstanding example of such a changeover. This program, discussed by Arthur H. Kuriloff in another chapter in this book, is part of a total approach to bringing newer concepts of management into the organization. It includes the introduction of such psychologists as Abraham Maslow as visiting fellow. Maslow gave a series of lectures on motivation to introduce new theories about leadership into the organization.[8]

[5]Petrullo, Luigi, and Bass, Bernard, *Leadership and Interpersonal Behavior,* Holt, Rinehart & Winston, New York, 1961.
[6]Likert, Rensis, *New Patterns of Management,* McGraw-Hill, New York, 1961.
[7]Tannenbaum, R., I. R. Weschler, and F. Massarik, *Leadership and Organization: A Behavioral Science Approach,* McGraw-Hill, New York, 1961.
[8]Non-Linear Systems, *Maslow's Summer Notes on Social Psychology of Industry and Management,* Non-Linear Systems, Del Mar, California, 1962.

Alfred J. Marrow has conducted a number of experiments on interpersonal relations, joint problem solving, and motivation in his organization for a number of years.[9] His most recent book takes the executive reader inside a typical management sensitivity training program.[10] It tells about what goes on during such training and cites behavioral and attitudinal results. Going further, it challenges American business management to critically examine the assumptions about people, motivation, and productivity under which it has operated for the past hundred years.

Since all the evidence is not in yet, the sophisticated manager is likely to test out the newer concepts on a limited basis before going all the way in a complete changeover. His own confidence, personal training and philosophy, and willingness to conduct reasonable risk experiments in organization philosophy will have much to do with the results attained in trying out the newer ideas.

In some instances when sensitivity training as a management development technique for improving organizational effectiveness has not resulted in short-run improvements in productivity and profits, top managers have concluded that the training technique does not produce the results desired and they feel compelled to return to more directive leadership methods in periods of strong competitive pressure and declining profits.

Some organizations feel that their efforts to move in the direction of sensitivity training, increased frankness and expression of feeling, and improved interpersonal competence among managers has lessened their ability to hit hard. Particularly when profits decline in such organizations— even though the basic cause of the decline may be the organizations clinging to old methods—we find an emphasis on returning to the pressure type of leadership methods. Such fight slogans as "Back to Basics" and "When the going gets tough, the tough get going" are dusted off and used as motivators to impress employees with the driving need to hit harder, push harder, and reduce costs while increasing sales.

Failure of such organizations to reach successfully a "team management" position where strong emphasis on production is equalled by strong emphasis on employee participation results in what Blake and Mouton refer to as the "wide-arc pendulum" shift in leadership style. When profits are down and competition strong, this type of organization cuts costs, streamlines overhead, and in general gets tough. During this period, the predomi-

[9]Marrow, Alfred J., *Making Management Human,* McGraw-Hill, New York, 1957.
[10]Marrow, Alfred J., *Behind the Executive Mask,* American Management Association, New York, 1964.

nating managerial style is production-centered, produce or perish, win-lose. When profits improve and affluence returns, management swings from production-centered to people-centered leadership. There is a decreasing emphasis on hard-hitting production goals, costs—particularly overhead costs—go up, and rosy dreams are indulged in without a realistic appraisal of their value or lack of value. What such managements miss is the possibility of so integrating production and people values that a continuous high level of organizational effectiveness results.

PROBLEMS OF INDIVIDUAL ADJUSTMENT IN THE CHANGEOVER

Individual managers who have been trained to accept orders without question and to follow authoritarian direction automatically tend to avoid taking initiative or risking new methods for fear of being punished for deviating from the wishes of their bosses. Such men naturally have a difficult time shifting from the behaviors learned after having worked many years for a company that has had this type of leadership to those required by a more team-centered or participative approach to management. If all their lives they have been rewarded, praised, protected, and promoted for being good followers, they cannot help but experience some difficulty in a situation that requires them to plan, take initiative, and run risks.

One aspect of this difficulty is emotional. Under pressure, the manager trained in an authoritarian organization wants the reassurance that the men above him are calling the shots. He is not happy with too much freedom to use his own ideas. Likewise, he becomes anxious and uncertain if his subordinates show too much freedom or independence. These subordinates, in turn, like children in a family controlled by dominating parents, may freeze if given too much leeway and freedom to act on their own.

Equally difficult are the skill adjustments required of managers in a company that is moving from one type of leadership to another. It is doubtful if a few weeks of sensitivity training (or any other type of training for that matter) will give a manager trained in an authoritarian organization the skills with which to operate smoothly and confidently in a more participative setting. Caution has to be exercised in such transitions to make sure the manager does not fail—not because the new concepts of motivating and leading people will not work—but rather because the manager simply lacks the skill required to operate effectively in the new setting.

Making the shift from one type of management to another is particularly difficult for the manager whose organization has overlaid an essentially authoritarian leadership style with a paternalistic disregard for insisting on high levels of productivity. In the past, some business organizations with high gross profit margins have been able to produce a high net profit without really insisting on high individual productivity from employees. As a rule, such managements were more concerned with the personal satisfaction with their self-image as benevolent autocrats than they were with really facing up to unpleasant decisions and deep organizational problems.

Line supervisors in such companies were often delicately chided if they asked for consistently high levels of productivity from the men under them. A tacit policy of not pushing employees for too much production lest they become unhappy and resentful tended to favor the supervisor who showed deference to his bosses, while being a "nice guy" to men under him.

Since the 1950's, a number of such organizations, pressured by the profit squeeze and obvious inefficiencies in their operations have switched over to a new philosophy and now operate on a more profit-centered basis. Many of these companies lopped overhead, cut indirect labor, and expected much more in the way of effort and results from those who remained. Layoffs of men with 10 or 15 years of seniority and the initiation of early retirement programs were common features of such shifts in overall managerial philosophy.

Both the emotional and the skill adjustments of managers in such organizations are difficult. A whole new way of life has to be developed. However, when managers are interviewed after such changes have taken place, particularly when the emphasis on increased production has been accompanied by the adoption of the newer approaches to leading and motivating subordinates, they often state they feel much more satisfied with the new situation. One reason is that they have more job security. Many companies that went through such transformations were faced with going out of business because they could not operate profitably. Improved organizational effectiveness may mean more work, initiative, and responsibility. But it also means that the organization is becoming more profitable and that it is growing. Therefore, while the adjustment problems of individual managers in organizations which shift from one style of leadership to another are great, the rewards are potentially greater.

SENSITIVITY TRAINING AS A METHOD FOR TEACHING THE NEWER CONCEPTS

Declining net profit margins have been an unpleasant reality for many large and successful corporations during the last ten years. Different organizations have taken different approaches to solving this problem. Some have expanded their research and development activities in the hopes of acquiring new product lines that hold higher profit margins. Other companies have attempted to expand through growth or acquisition or merger in an effort to reach the same ends. Still other organizations have hired consultants to help them reduce costs and streamline operations. In some cases, this consolidation has eliminated an entire level of operating management with comparably dramatic shifts in staff personnel ratios.

If the newer approaches to leadership result in significantly improved motivation, productivity, and organizational effectiveness, then more organizations may be forced to adopt them in order to operate profitably. Where organizational effectiveness is hampered by employee apathy, limited interest in organization goals, and indifference to doing more than a minimum of work, the newer approaches to leadership offer promising opportunities to improve the company's overall organizational position, particularly in regard to its effectiveness.

Organizations that are in the process of shifting from an authoritarian to a participative type of management find their internal interpersonal stresses temporarily increase. This is natural because two quite opposite sets of philosophy and method are operating within the company at the same time. Managers schooled in one approach are not always able to understand or to practice the other approach with comfort and confidence. When one department or division of a company is undergoing such a leadership style change and the other parts of the organization continue on with the old styles, doubt and confusion and uncertainties tend to arise between the two groups.

For this reason, psychologists and other behavioral scientists working on organizational change stress the importance of total organizational change as a key factor in installing newer leadership philosophies and methods. The attitude of the top decision makers toward such change is a key factor in its successful adoption. Unless these men are willing to make the emotional and skill adjustments required, it is unlikely that management philosophy or methods changes will take root and flourish at the middle management level.

Management development to date has largely been indoctrination in the attitudes, assumptions, methods, and skills associated with authoritarian management. Much of it tends to perpetuate past practices rather than encourage new experimentation. Moreover, its assumptions that improved managerial effectiveness automatically results from skill training and indoctrination is open to question. One authority[11] points out that adequate managerial performance, particularly in motivating and leading others, is at least as much a matter of attitudes as it is a matter of knowledge and specific skills. Comparing the philosophy underlying some contemporary management development methods with the coercive persuasion associated with Chinese Communist "brainwashing," he argues that attempts to force a man to change through giving him negative feedback in performance appraisals may make him less rather than more effective. Unless the subordinate is emotionally ready to listen to such feedback, he only hears (through his blocks and anxieties) that his boss is displeased and wants him to change in some vague way. Until the subordinate can recognize and emotionally accept awareness of inadequacies present in his current managerial behavior, he makes only general and superficial attempts to change.

Schein's second major point[12] is that firms interested in the creative growth of managers may discourage such growth if they go about the process of attempting to change the man in the wrong way. Unless *self-development* is used as a major part of the process, candidates spend most of their time and energy figuring out the system that seems to be currently operating in the winning of company promotions. Then, as Schein states, "they will adopt essentially a political orientation of trying to please those who make the key promotional decisions."

The executive's main job is to get results through other people. Though he must be able to make technical decisions, he is paid primarily for organizing, motivating, and measuring the results of those under him. When getting results through others is seen primarily in terms of manipulation, coercion, persuasive selling, or political power plays, the superior needs only development in becoming a more effective manipulator, coercer, or political salesman in order to improve his executive leadership skills.

However, if motivation and productivity in periods of intensive competition require new types of management—in which interpersonal relations skills, joint problem solving, and the creation of self-actualizing motivation in associates and subordinates are extremely important to executive success—then management development will center around a much broader range of interpersonal skills.

Reviewing the current interpersonal orientation of business executives,

[11]Schein, E., "Management Development as a Process of Influence," *Industrial Management Review*, May 1961.
[12]Schein, E., "Forces Which Undermine Management Development," *California Management Review*, Summer 1963.

two experts[13] found four main types. "Stars" are managers primarily concerned with the interpersonal aspects of organization. "Technical specialists" are men primarily concerned with the task aspects of people at work. "Social specialists" are executives who are greatly concerned with the people and dependency side of work. A fourth category of managers, the "underchosen" are men primarily preoccupied with themselves rather than with the job. Of the four types, the "stars" are those most concerned about management as a series of skills in dealing with subordinates on a free give-and-take, interpersonal-relations basis.

Sensitivity training—with its emphasis on understanding feelings of oneself and of others, on more effective communication, and on free give-and-take in resolving conflicts—is a management development technique well suited to improving the interpersonal relations skills of executives regardless of their present managerial orientation. However, if the new skills are to take root, the organization must support the changes involved.

SENSITIVITY TRAINING AS A TECHNIQUE FOR IMPROVING INTERPERSONAL COMPETENCE

In our society, self-understanding and self-awareness are rare qualities. It has been pointed out that in order to play the highly specialized role of the business executive in our society, we are often either forced or encouraged to forget about ourselves as individuals and to become a sort of semi-mechanical problem solver.[14] While specialization in job roles is a requirement in every society, our business culture encourages us to shut off from awareness large parts of ourselves that do not relate functionally to our work.

Since many businesses have emphasized authoritarian, win-lose competition in a way that discourages expression of feeling and open resolution of conflict, skill in sensing the needs and feelings of others has been confined primarily to gathering intelligence information on their intentions which we can use for our own offensive or defensive purposes. Since our associates are often engaged in similar activities, there is little ground for collaboration and cooperation for the ultimate ends of the organization. Rather, power clusters and factions develop as individuals seek to ally themselves with like minded or like interested associates.

[13]Moment, David, and Zaleznik, Abraham, *Role Development and Interpersonal Competence*, Harvard University Press, Cambridge, 1963.
[14]Jourard, S., *The Transparent Self*, D. Van Nostrand and Co., Princeton, New Jersey, 1964.

For this reason, sensitivity training offers a method of improving our skills in both understanding ourselves and in understanding others. Although there is a wide variety of applications, sensitivity training today centers around theory discussion of motivation and behavior, skill exercises in communication and problem solving, and leaderless group interaction. Alfred J. Marrow's *Behind the Executive Mask* gives a clear-cut summary of how these three techniques are combined in actual sensitivity training programs for executives.

Executives can expect to become more skillful in communications, have greater awareness of themselves, increase in sensitivity to the feelings and needs of others, and become more conversant with the methods of building group effectiveness and commitment to follow through on decisions as a result of their training in sensitivity programs. How effectively they will be able to use this training to improve their personal leadership skills depends on their personal ability to apply such learning *plus* the organization's readiness to accept open discussion, expression of feelings, and resolution of basic problems.

During the past several years, the trend has been to send members of an organization to public programs rather than to conduct in-company sensitivity training. The public program has some distinct advantages. Direct exchange of deep feelings with strangers is less likely to leave negative reactions that have to be worked out within the company structure. Therefore, risks to an individual's self-esteem and possibly to his relationships with others on the job are less. Also, if strangers tell a man that he triggers certain feeling reactions within them, he is more likely to listen to their feedback than if he thinks his associates are merely renewing their usual negative reactions to him.

With increased sophistication on the part of sensitivity trainers, a number of promising and successful in-company programs are being developed. Successful in-company programs offer the advantage of moving the entire organization along at a comparable rate. Moreover, even slight gains among individuals and in intragroup cooperation are directly translated into increased organizational effectiveness in solving everyday work problems. As the demand for large-scale change in organizational philosophy and leadership style increases, it is likely that both public and in-company sensitivity training programs will increase.

If successful business leadership of the future requires greater skill in interpersonal effectiveness, then sensitivity training will continue to become an even more important tool for management development than it has been in the past. Continued pressure on profit margins will force industry to use any and all techniques for increasing organizational effectiveness. Such profit-reducing blocks to effectiveness as win-lose competition, factional infighting, personal manipulation, and suppressing basic conflicts about policy and method will have to be removed or the organization will have to pay the price for letting them remain.

Within the next five or ten years, we can expect to have definite comparative productivity and profit figures on the relationship between different management styles and motivation, productivity, and profit. If these figures clearly indicate that increased interpersonal competence of managers is a requirement for organizational effectiveness, we will see a great increase in the use of sensitivity training as a tool for management development.

PERSONNEL TESTING: WHAT THE CRITICS OVERLOOK •

SAUL W. GELLERMAN

PERSONNEL TESTING FINDS ITSELF on the defensive today, largely because of the publication of widely selling books that have openly challenged its value.[1] On balance I think this criticism is a good thing, even though the authors of these books have given an unrealistically frightening picture of the way selection tests are used in industry.

In the long run such critiques will stand or fall on their own merits. Rather than attempt a detailed reply to them here, I should like to consider the central question they raise. It is a very blunt question: Is personnel testing so loaded with faults that we should discard it entirely?

It is common knowledge among psychologists and personnel managers alike that tests have been widely misused, that not enough attention is paid to their limitations or to the qualifications of the people who interpret them. The literature of personnel management has for years been full of warnings about the need to use tests more cautiously, to develop better ones, and to continuously check their validity. Unfortunately, this attempt to set our house in order by preaching to each other has not tidied it very noticeably.

Perhaps, then, the pressures generated by outside criticism will be more effective in stimulating the much needed modernization and reform

---

[1]For example, see B. Hoffman, *The Tyranny of Testing*, McGraw-Hill, New York, 1962 and M. L. Gross, *The Brain Watchers*, Random House, New York, 1962.

SAUL W. GELLERMAN is Manager of Personnel Research, IBM World Trade Corporation, New York, New York.

of testing practices in industry. What we have to guard against, of course, is the fact that some of the critics are advocating not reform, but abolition. It is by no means inconceivable that their views might prevail, given enough alarm on the part of their readers and an uncertainty on the part of personnel people as to whether there is, indeed, anything in testing worth saving.

Though many of the criticisms that have been leveled against testing are true or partially true, the critics have sidestepped the basic question—is there any suitable alternative to it? That is, given the massive screening jobs that industry, universities, and governments face every year in connection with recruiting and job placement, is there a procedure other than testing that can do as helpful a job as tests at a reasonable cost but without so many disadvantages? I think all the available evidence indicates that the answer is no.

Consequently, apart from all the sound and fury of arguments for or against testing, the practical problem we face is not whether testing is worthwhile, but how we can make the best possible use of these admittedly imperfect instruments until their imperfections can be corrected or better instruments can be developed to take their place.

This is a complex problem, and it has a complex answer. In order to arrive at that answer, we must first tackle several preliminary questions:

- What is the nature of the recruitment process, and how does testing fit into it?
- Under what specific circumstances, if any, do tests help to improve the results of recruitment?
- What is a valid test?
- Are any tests valid?
- Must a test's questions be job-related and "nonfakable" to be valid?
- Is validity necessary?
- Are valid tests useful?
- Finally, are useful tests necessary?

Only after we have threaded our way through these fundamental questions can we give an informed and dispassionate answer to the challenges now being made by testing's critics.

Let's begin by taking a broad view of the recruitment process as a whole. Every recruitment decision involves three variables that can seldom be defined exactly: the available supply of candidates who are willing to take the job for a salary the company can afford, the actual requirements of the job in terms of human abilities, and the actual capabilities of the available candidates. The basic problem facing the personnel manager is to reduce the uncertainty in all three areas, so that his final decision is based as much on fact and as little on faith as possible. To do this he has specialized techniques, and one of these techniques is testing.

Here we encounter a very important rule of interaction, which is that effective control over any one of these areas of uncertainty reduces the need to control the others. For example, if the personnel manager could somehow get access to a good supply of highly talented, highly motivated candidates, it wouldn't really be necessary for him to have a highly sensitive testing and evaluating program. All he would need is an attractive "employer image" that lured these outstanding people into his company in sufficient numbers to meet his needs. These men would all be very likely to succeed, and it would be pointless to try to use tests for making fine discriminations among them.

Regrettably, such a glut of high-potential candidates is one problem most personnel managers don't have, and so the uncertainty in the selection process usually has to be reduced by evaluating both the individual and the job. Consequently, any process—including tests—that can help to identify the most promising candidates in a market where promising candidates are rare pays off in the selection process.

A careful job evaluation can help to reduce our dependence on methods of evaluating people, since it gives us a clearer idea of the minimum standards to look for in our candidates, and surer guidance in tapping the available pool of candidates. But once again, accurate job evaluations are all too rare. So we can say of personnel evaluation methods in general that they derive much of their importance from our deficiencies in the skills of recruiting and job evaluation, and that if we made progress in those skills we would not need to lean so heavily as we do on our admittedly imperfect instruments for evaluating people.

There are a number of ways of evaluating a man's qualifications besides tests; for example, interviews, reference checks, biographical data, and work samples. It doesn't make much sense to seek one method that is "better" than the others, since they all tend to be sensitive to different aspects of the individual. Also, none of them (tests included) is so reliable that a forecast based on it would not gain accuracy by being supplemented with other methods. As a practical matter, therefore, the most realistic question to ask about tests is not merely whether they accurately predict performance in themselves, but whether they add any greater accuracy to the predictions we make using nontest methods.

In certain circumstances tests *do* add to predictive accuracy, and in all other circumstances they do *not*. Tests, like any other evaluation method, will increase the accuracy of a forecast only when there is a lasting, significant relation between test results and performance results—or, to use the psychologist's term, when the tests are valid—and when the tests are measuring aspects of the individual that other methods do not measure or do not measure so well.

THE CONCEPT OF VALIDITY

The concept of validity is crucial for tests and every other selection tool. Hence it is worth noting some features about validity that are sometimes overlooked when the value of testing is being scrutinized.

First, *validity is a statistical concept; it refers to large groups, and not to individuals.* This means that a test is valid when, in a large group of tested individuals, test scores correspond to job performance more often than they would be expected to by chance alone. It also means that a test can be valid generally and still be dead wrong in the case of any given individual.

Obviously, then, tests are useful chiefly as a means of screening large groups and are less useful in distinguishing between small numbers of individuals or in making a prediction about a single person. (This is true regardless of whether the tests are scored mechanically or interpreted individually by a psychologist.) Even the most valid test tells us, basically, only one thing about an individual: his apparent chances of success.

Second, *a test doesn't necessarily have to be very valid to be useful.* This fact was demonstrated more than 20 years ago by H. C. Taylor and J. T. Russell, but it is not widely known.[2] One of the main advantages of having a highly valid test is that it is possible to define a score above which nearly everybody succeeds on the job and below which nearly everybody fails. However, if the validity of the test is low, it is harder to pinpoint the right cut-off score, because too many potential failures will be above any score and too many potential successes will be below it. Nevertheless, if the personnel manager is in a position to be very selective he can still confine himself to the *very* high scorers.

Though this procedure is admittedly wasteful of good men who get low

---

[2]Taylor, H. C., and Russell, J. T., "The Relationship of Validity Coefficients to the Practical Effectiveness of Tests in Selection: Discussion and Tables," *Journal of Applied Psychology,* October 1939.

scores, it still enables the manager, by being fussy with a small proportion of the men who take a test of low validity, to hire as many successful men as he could by not being fussy with a large proportion of the men who take a test of high validity. In other words, a test of low validity can do a useful screening job in an abundant labor market.

Third, *tests are often more valid than we can prove them to be.* There are two main reasons for this. One is that most job applicants who obtain low test scores are not hired; hence their job performance is never known and cannot be included in any calculation of a test's validity. In effect, validity usually has to be estimated on the basis of a narrow range of high scores. The formula used to compute validity is sensitive to this restriction; the result is a lower correlation figure than would probably be obtained if a wider range of scores were included.

The second reason why a test's validity is often greater than it seems is that the yardsticks with which we measure job performance are frequently unreliable themselves. Performance evaluations by supervisors are notoriously subjective; yet often they are the only practical criteria we have for "validating" tests. For example, a study in a large oil company showed that test scores that had an unimpressive correlation with supervisory ratings at the time they were given were actually better predictors of ultimate success than the performance ratings. The proof of the pudding, of course, is in the eating; but since human careers take years to reach fruition, we have to make do with more immediate yardsticks, such as performance ratings, in estimating a test's validity.

Fourth, *a test can be valid even when the test questions are not pertinent to the job.* This fact has probably caused more misunderstandings about tests than any other. The point to bear in mind is that if the test score gives a reliable indication of job capability, then it doesn't really matter whether the score was attained through knowledge, guessing, or even deception. For this reason, we can make good use of tests that ask questions on subjects that the testees know nothing about, as well as tests that are transparently easy to beat.

For example, the "general information" type of test covers a very wide spectrum of knowledge and therefore favors the man with a broad-ranging curiosity and the ability to reason his way to answers he doesn't necessarily know. It is, in other words, a measure of "applied intelligence" and can be quite a useful addition to selection programs in which *all* candidates can be presumed to be intelligent, but not all are necessarily inquisitive or clever in their use of their intelligence.

Furthermore, many interest and personality tests that lend themselves rather easily to simulation by the testee can also be useful for selection purposes, because a certain degree of posturing and concealment of motives is not only normal, but often a necessity for effective social relationships. In effect, such a test shows whether the individual is sensible enough to portray himself in a reasonably acceptable manner or whether he is so naïve as to be overly candid or (in the case of the test faker who gets carried away with his deception) clumsy enough to present an unbelievably sterling self-appraisal.

The important point is that it is not an indication of "true" interests or personality that the test is seeking, but rather (in this case) a sample of common sense, naïveté, or clumsiness. Going a step beyond that, we are less interested in this particular sample than in knowing whether the candidate is at least as sensible as he must be to do the job—which is an estimate that a valid test enables us to make with at least some degree of confidence.

Even though validity can take some strange forms, we are well aware that not all tests or test batteries are valid. When validity exists at all, it is a highly specific thing: A particular test may be a valid predictor of performance for people doing a particular job in a particular company at a particular time, using a particular minimum score as the cut-off point. But the same test may not be valid in any other context.

The "Validity Information Exchange" in *Personnel Psychology* (a quarterly journal) has for years published validity data on various tests with various employee populations, and the files of company psychologists and consultants are probably full of similar demonstrations that particular tests are valid in particular instances.

But there is no such thing as general validity for any test; its usefulness as a selection instrument has to be proved for every job in every company in which it is used, and periodically reproven, as well. It is precisely here that some of the greatest shortcomings in industrial testing practice have arisen. Too many companies have installed tests that had proved to be valid elsewhere without troubling to revalidate them locally. I will go so far as to say that failure to validate locally with established, time-honored tests probably causes more misclassification of human beings than all the charlatans and smooth-talking test merchants put together. Honest oversight, in other words, can cause a great deal more mischief than dishonest or incompetent testing.

Now, even if a test is valid, is it necessarily useful? Not always. Some tests are valid with only an uneconomically small proportion of the people who take it; for example, a very difficult test on which scarcely anyone gets a high score, though nearly all high scorers succeed on the job. Other tests may be valid but take too long to administer, or cost too much, or probe more deeply than some believe an employer should. Still other tests, particularly those using projective techniques, are sometimes valid and sometimes not, since their interpretation is more of an art than a science. Some tests are valid for most people but invalid for a critically important minority, such as exceptionally bright or creative people taking multiple-choice intelligence tests. Finally, a test may be valid but essentially duplicated by a cheaper, shorter, or less controversial test.

In general, therefore, the usefulness of a valid test depends on whether it adds enough predictive power to the test battery to be worth its added cost in time, money, and potentially unfavorable reactions. There is obviously no pat formula to guide us here, but it is a sobering fact that by combining two or more valid tests into a battery we usually get only a modest return in added predictive power. This is simply because valid tests tend to overlap; that is, they measure essentially the same characteristics.

WHEN TO USE TESTS

The next question we must ask is, even supposing a test is useful, is it necessary? Are there situations in which tests can, in fact, give an accurate, economical forecast of job performance but aren't really needed? There certainly are. We use tests to predict job performance, but sometimes we already know perfectly well what it is, as in the case of experienced personnel who have handled comparable jobs with a demonstrated degree of competence.

In such cases the person's job history may be as reliable an indicator of future performance as a test and possibly more so, since it is by no means uncommon for people who are already successfully holding down a particular job to score poorly when they are given a selection test for a comparable position. Obviously, there is little sense in testing experienced people "just to be sure" they can do what they have already shown themselves capable of doing.

There is a practical difficulty here, though—how to determine whether the previous job is truly comparable to the one under consideration. Jobs that carry the same title or are superficially similar may actually have very different requirements, and here, of course, a man's employment record may be an unreliable predictor. Plainly, the comparability of jobs must be carefully weighed before it is assumed that competence can be transferred from one job to another, but this is no reason for the ritual of insisting that *all* candidates be tested, regardless of experience. As it works out, this means that testing will usually be appropriate with young applicants or with older ones who lack relevant experience.

Another needless use of valid tests, though often resorted to, is their administration to applicants who, for reasons unrelated to their test scores, are definitely not going to be hired anyway. Companies often give tests in such cases, either to make the applicant feel that he has had a thoroughgoing evaluation or with the secret intention of putting the blame for the rejection on the test results. It need hardly be said that such deceptions are an abuse of tests, and, far worse than that, an abuse of people, too.

TESTS FOR TESTING

On the whole, then, I think it fair to conclude that testing, despite its imperfections, is clearly worthwhile in certain circumstances and probably valueless in others. It follows that a sophisticated policy in this area will be based on an awareness of the circumstances in which tests can be most helpfully employed. From the above analysis, we can pinpoint 11 conditions that should be met to enhance the probability that testing will be worthwhile in any specific instance:

1. A high proportion of the available candidates is unlikely to meet the performance standards of the job.
2. Alternative methods of evaluating candidates are not equally valid or do not measure the same attributes as tests or do not measure them as well as tests or are less convenient, acceptable, or economical than tests.
3. The test in question has been shown to be valid (that is, significantly correlated with an independent measure of job performance) in a recent study of a sizable sample of the present employees of the specific company in which it is being used.
4. It is understood by those who will make the selection decision that test results, no matter how they are expressed or interpreted, are always an actuarial estimate of the likelihood of job success for all

persons attaining similar scores and never a specific prediction for a specific testee.

5. The test results are therefore treated as only a part, and by no means an infallible part, of the total information on which the selection decision is to be based.

6. The personnel manager is mindful of the relation between the validity of the tests he is using and the available supply of qualified candidates and moves his cut-off point up or down in order to minimize both the selection of unsuitable candidates and the rejection of suitable ones.

7. Where "fakable" tests or tests with questions that are unrelated to the job are used, there is statistical evidence that these characteristics do not seriously detract from the tests' validity, range of usefulness, or acceptability to the testee.

8. The tests are valid for at least the majority of persons who are likely to take them, including "significant minorities," when there is a need to identify these reliably.

9. The tests are economical of time and money, in relation to the importance of the job being filled.

10. Reliable information on the applicant's performance in a job comparable to the one he is being considered for is not already available.

11. The applicant is a genuine candidate who may actually be selected for the opening.

While these are rather formidable conditions, before we say that they are *too* formidable we should expose all other available methods of evaluation (interviews, reference checks, and so on) to an equally rigorous appraisal. If this were done, I think it would be apparent that tests are a considerably more effective procedure, when used in appropriate circumstances, than their detractors would have us believe, despite all their criticism.

I would insist, however, that where any of these 11 conditions is not present, there is a very good chance that testing is *not* worthwhile. So rather than waste further time anxiously inquiring whether the last 40 years of industrial psychology have been one huge mistake, I believe we should busy ourselves with the more practical task of using tests as appropriately as we can and moving ahead much more vigorously than in the past to refine and improve them.

IMPROVING EMPLOYEE PRODUCTIVITY THROUGH WORK PLANNING •

EDGAR F. HUSE

and

EMANUEL KAY

THERE CAN BE NO DOUBT that the past 20 years have witnessed increased interest in the use of various methods and techniques for appraising an employee's performance and communicating the results of that appraisal to him. Most companies have formal performance appraisal programs of one kind or another, and some large decentralized firms use several different approaches. Such programs are designed to achieve certain objectives and do so with varying degrees of success. It is often suggested that these programs provide:

1. More systematic and objective measures of performance than would otherwise be available.
2. A convenient method for correlating performance with pay and thus for getting positive motivation from salary rewards.
3. A procedure to insure that each person receives "knowledge of results" so that he knows what he has done well and where improvement is needed.
4. A source of data which can be of use when making decisions concerning promotion, training, reassignment, discharge, or other management action directly affecting an employee's career.

Amidst the high interest and enthusiasm for performance appraisals, there has appeared lately a growing body of criticism and dissatisfaction. Analysis of the performance appraisal process by many experts has sug-

---

EDGAR F. HUSE is Consulting Psychologist, Small Aircraft Engine Department and EMANUEL KAY is Personnel Research Psychologist, Behavioral Research Service, General Electric Company, Lynn, Massachusetts.

gested a number of negative effects. Professor Rensis Likert, director of the University of Michigan's Institute for Social Research, summed them up nicely when he observed: "The fundamental flaw in current review procedures is that they compel the superior to behave in a threatening, rejecting, and ego-deflating manner with a sizable portion of his staff."

A searching look at our various experiences with performance appraisals in the General Electric Company a couple of years ago also led to the conclusion that things were not all what they might have been. There were indications of reluctance on the part of many supervisors to conduct appraisals. Employees often approached the interviews with more dread than enthusiasm or even curiosity. Rather strong control measures were needed to keep the appraisal programs going. The question arose as to why supervisors were resisting a technique that was designed to help get improved performance from employees—and why employees obviously resented a system devised to help them improve and get ahead.

To gain fuller understanding of the appraisal process, a study was conducted to examine some of the psychological effects of performance appraisal interviews and performance improvement planning discussions between supervisors and their subordinates. The study was conducted at the General Electric Company's Small Aircraft Engine Department plant at Lynn, Massachusetts, which was known to have a well-administered appraisal program. Supervisor-subordinate pairs were observed in regularly scheduled performance appraisal and goal planning discussions. The subordinates were interviewed before and after the discussions to obtain their reactions to the interviews and to get other before-and-after measures. For half of the group, supervisors were instructed to permit a high level of subordinate "participation" in performance improvement planning, while, for the other half, supervisors were instructed to use a nonparticipative approach. A follow-up check was made 12 to 14 weeks after the performance appraisal and goal planning discussions to determine the degree to which performance improvement had been achieved.

Briefly, the findings of the study were as follows:

1. Most subordinates felt they deserved more favorable appraisals and greater salary increases than they actually received.
2. Criticisms of performance typically resulted in defensiveness on the part of the subordinates. The more criticisms or "improvement needs" the manager cited in appraisal discussions, the more likely the subordinate was to be defensive and to reject the manager's help.

3. The *more* criticism and defensiveness observed in the appraisal discussions, the *less* performance improvement was noted 12 to 14 weeks later.
4. The use of praise had no measurable effect on employee reactions to criticism or on subsequent job performance.
5. Appreciable improvements in performance were realized *only* when specific goals were established with time deadlines set and results measures agreed on. Regardless of how much emphasis the manager gave to an improvement need in the appraisal discussion, if this was not translated into a specific goal, very little performance improvement was achieved.
6. Subordinate participation in goal planning resulted in improved subordinate attitudes pertaining to man-manager relations, but little difference in degree to which goals were achieved.

This research study shed some light on the problems associated with the appraisal process. It appeared that attempts by the supervisor to help the employee by criticizing his performance and pointing out areas where improvement was needed underlay most of the difficulty. Employees tended to resent and reject such criticism, with the result that the appraisals were not always pleasant or productive of improved performance. Little wonder that supervisors resisted this activity. Not only did they have to face unpleasant interviews, but they had to do so with little expectation that they would obtain improved performance as a result.

Following this study, management at the Small Aircraft Engine Department asked for the development and evaluation of an appraisal method which would primarily be concerned with performance improvement. The research on performance appraisal had clearly demonstrated that no one technique could achieve all of the performance appraisal "objectives." Therefore, it was agreed that other objectives normally associated with the performance appraisal process—such as justification of salary decisions, personnel development, and documentation for personnel files—should be dealt with separately and by other means. This chapter, therefore, will concentrate on the development and use of the work planning process to improve the productivity of exempt employees.

HOW WORK PLANNING AND REVIEW WAS DEVELOPED

In order to get work done, there is always some form of work planning going on. Every supervisor gives task and work instructions to his subordinates. Every supervisor has some sort of system to check the work of his subordinates and make sure that work is being done properly. Nearly every subordinate will, at times, ask questions about work assignments or offer suggestions to his supervisor. Most supervisors and subordinates spend a fair amount of time together in the normal course of the daily work, and they can discuss job duties and job tasks with each other. However, because of certain difficulties inherent in the supervisor-subordinate relationship; because of operating problems, pressure of business, and "crash programs"; because of the well-known problems in communication—because of these, few supervisors make optimum managerial use of time spent with subordinates.

At the same time, most subordinates want to do a good job. Most of them often feel that they do not fully understand what it is that the boss wants. They want a better feel for how they are doing. Almost every subordinate wants to have feelings of accomplishment, interesting work, and additional responsibility. They want to be able to offer suggestions upward and to have these suggestions weighed carefully, even though they may not be accepted. In other words, supervisors want to do a better job of managing, and subordinates want to improve their own work performance. The question is, "How do we set up conditions whereby people can be helped to do a better job?"

We had hoped that our performance appraisal process would help in this respect. Research indicated that it did not. We found that the biggest problem was the self-conflicting role of the supervisor as a counselor and the supervisor as a judge. Because performance appraisal was so closely tied to subsequent salary action, the supervisor was being forced to play the role of judge with regard to salary action, while at the same time and in the same place he was expected to play the role of a helper in terms of advising the employee on how to improve his work performance. These two roles are incompatible. For this reason, in the new approach, they were separated. The next step was to ask "How can we provide a climate in which our managers can act as helpers to improve work performance?" The answer was *work planning and review.*

WHAT IS WORK PLANNING AND REVIEW?

The work planning and review process consists of periodic meetings between a man and his supervisor. The meetings are oriented toward the daily work and result in mutual planning of the work, a review of progress, and mutual solving of problems which arise in the course of getting the job done. The process does not involve formal ratings. Rather, it provides the basis for the man and manager to sit down informally, discuss the job to be done, and then (1) agree on a plan and (2) review progress.

The process was designed to take advantage of known principles which relate to certain conditions necessary for subordinate motivation and job growth. They are not exhaustive but do include the essential ingredients which must be present for best manpower utilization. The three basic motivational principles are:

1. An employee needs to know what is expected of him.
2. An employee needs to know how he is doing.
3. An employee needs to be able to obtain assistance as needed.

Exhibit 1 diagramatically shows how these principles apply to the job. Let us now explore how work planning and review fits these principles.

An employee must know what is expected of him. This principle can be subdivided further as follows:

1. Work performance is appreciably improved when the man knows what results are expected. Work planning and review sessions provide the man with information regarding the results expected, the methods by which results will be measured, the priorities, and the resources available.
2. Work performance is appreciably improved when the man knows how he can appropriately influence the expected results. The process is sufficiently flexible to permit the man to have some say about the results expected, the methods by which results will be measured, and the priorities. The degree of influence exercised by the man will vary according to the situation.

An employee needs to know how he is doing. This is the most important (and basic) of the three principles. Learning (job improvement) takes place most effectively when the man has the opportunity to compare his performance (successes as well as problems) against agreed-upon measures. There are several important corollaries to this principle:

1. Knowledge of results must be as precise and specific as possible. Work *planning* develops specific, measurable goals. Work *review* allows the man and manager to review results against the specific goals.
2. Knowledge of results must be as immediate and relevant as possible. The flexibility of the process enables the supervisor to have review sessions when most appropriate, and the discussion can be limited

to *only* those items of performance which are relevant to the on-going situation or have just been completed.

3. Knowledge of results which comes from the man's own observations is more effective than knowledge of results obtained from someone else. When the goal measurements have been made specific, the man can more objectively evaluate his own progress. In addition, the supervisor can use the flexibility of the process to encourage this.

In summary, the work planning and review process is specifically designed to give knowledge of results which is objective, timely, and flexible enough to permit self-assessment. Either the man *or* his supervisor can schedule a review session when either feels it is most appropriate, thus allowing for *immediate* knowledge of results.

An employee must be able to obtain assistance when and as needed. For the employee to improve job performance, he must be able to obtain assistance, coaching, and guidance as needed.

First, the employee must feel free to request assistance when necessary. Employees will ask for assistance *only* when they are not "punished" for such an action—for example, when this is not seen as an admission of weakness or as ultimately resulting in criticism.

Second, the supervisor must feel free to offer assistance as necessary. At times, every supervisor sees a need to give assistance to a subordinate. This may come in the form of pointing out mistakes, suggesting a different approach, or in any one of a number of ways. To be most effective, this *must* be done in a constructive rather than threatening fashion. He must avoid causing a defensive reaction from the employee which would only reduce his effectiveness.

Third, to establish this climate, the supervisor must act as a *helper* rather than a judge. In work planning and review sessions, the emphasis shifts from the judging implicit in appraisals to concentration on accomplishing mutually acceptable goals. The emphasis is shifted from the weaknesses of the man to a job-centered operations approach. A climate is established for the employee to receive assistance when and as needed. In other words, work planning and review is a process which establishes a climate of *mutual* cooperation. Instead of stressing or accumulating past mistakes or successes to justify a salary action, the man and supervisor should use the review sessions as opportunities to learn how to improve future work performance. Instead of dealing in subjective opinions, praise, or criticism, they should mutually search for better measurements of mutually acceptable goals. The subordinate is a partner not a defendant.

HOW DO YOU DO WORK PLANNING?

Experience with the work planning and review cycle has demonstrated that supervisors typically go through a process of experimentation before they settle on a method of doing work planning which is most effective for themselves and their subordinates. Because concentration is on the basic concept rather than on any particular technique, such experimentation is encouraged and fostered. In other words, the specific technique should not transcend the *basic purpose*—improving work performance. To this end, supervisors are encouraged to experiment and modify the process so they can do their own best job of applying the three basic motivational principles.

However, discussions with supervisors applying the concept indicates that some simple do's and don'ts considerably shorten the process of experimentation. As Exhibit 1 illustrates, the first motivational principle requires developing mutual understanding between the man and his supervisor as to what is expected. This consists of two closely related parts, (1) outlining the job to be done and (2) outlining achievement measures or yardsticks to determine when a job has been done well.

The job to be done. The job to be done stems from two different but related sources: the job description and company needs. The job description usually changes infrequently. It summarizes the overall responsibility of the job and the individual. On the other hand, company needs are constantly changing. This is reflected in the changing tasks that individuals must do.

The supervisor has a twofold responsibility in defining the job to be done. He must be sure that specific tasks and projects contribute to company needs. He must also make certain that he and his subordinate develop the fullest possible understanding about the job to be done. One good method of increasing understanding between employee and supervisor is to have the subordinate prepare a list of suggested goals and commitments prior to the planning session. Then, in the session, the two can discuss the goals and make whatever changes may be necessary to reflect the supervisor's ideas.

Here are some do's and don'ts in outlining the job to be done:
DO:
- Insure supervisor-subordinate agreement on major plans and tasks.
- Make plans specific rather than general.
- Relate work plans to business needs.

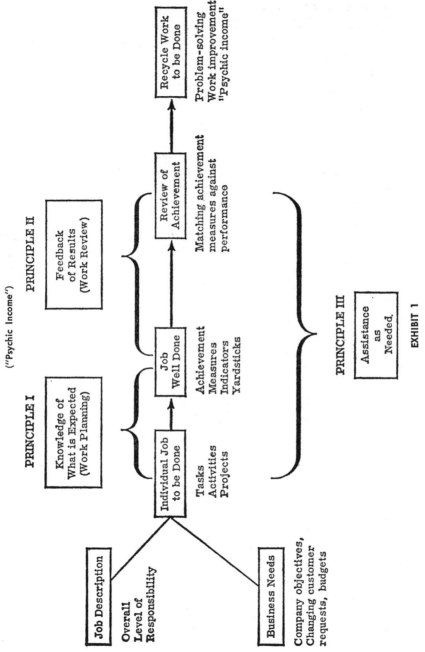

WORK PLANNING AND REVIEW

("Psychic Income")

PRINCIPLE I

Knowledge of
What is Expected
(Work Planning)

PRINCIPLE II

Feedback
of Results
(Work Review)

PRINCIPLE III

Assistance
as
Needed.

Job Description

Overall
Level of
Responsibility

Business Needs

Company objectives,
Changing customer
requests, budgets

Individual Job
to be Done

Tasks
Activities
Projects

Job
Well Done

Achievement
Measures
Indicators
Yardsticks

Review of
Achievement

Matching achievement
measures against
performance

Recycle Work
to be Done

Problem-solving
Work improvement
"Psychic income"

EXHIBIT 1

- Change work plans to conform with changing business needs.
- Have the subordinate develop his own work plans when he is capable.
- Keep it as informal as is practicable: Jot down work plans rather than have multiple carbons made.

DON'T:

- Try to set work goals too far in advance.
- Make activities, responsibilities, or tasks too broad.
- Become overinvolved in completing forms; instead, concentrate on mutual understanding.
- Be inflexible about changing work plans in response to need.

The job well done. Identification of the specific goals, tasks, or activities is only the first part of implementing the principle of "knowledge of what is expected." The second part is to develop achievement measures or success criteria.

These measures help both parties to determine when a job is done well and to outline areas where improvement in work performance seems needed. These measures must be outlined in advance so that both participants can agree with them. Developing achievement measures is easier said than done. They must be carefully designed to answer the question for supervisor and subordinate, "How will we both know whether the job has been done well?"

The yardsticks, or success measures, should be specific to the task and should be as objective as possible. However, good judgmental, subjective measurements are better than poor objective measures. Time deadlines are, of course, one type of measurement, but they should be used alone only when they are the only factor of job success. If the subordinate develops his own work plans for the supervisor's review, he should develop the results measures at the same time.

DO:

- Be sure the measures cover the whole project.
- Make certain that achievement criteria are spelled out clearly before the employee starts the task.
- Make sure that supervisor and subordinate agree on the yardsticks *before* the job is started.
- Make measures as specific as possible.
- Make measures as objective as possible.
- Be willing to change measures if the task or conditions change.
- Approach from a positive, rather than negative, direction.
- Identify factors that can be used to improve job performance.

DON'T:

- Use time deadlines only. They are only part of a job well done.
- Develop the measures as a way of "trapping" the subordinate.
- Make the yardsticks too broad or general.
- Become overinvolved in completing forms; instead, concentrate on mutual understanding of what is expected.

In summary, the steps in work planning are:

1. Have the employee develop a set of work goals *and* measurements. (The supervisor may omit this step if he wishes to do this himself.)
2. Schedule a planning session.
3. During the planning discussion, insure that supervisor and subordinate come to a *mutual* agreement on tasks, due dates, and measures of achievement.
4. After the planning session, write down the finally agreed-upon goals and yardsticks. The supervisor and the employee each keep a copy.

HOW DO YOU DO PROGRESS REVIEW?

As Exhibit 1 illustrates, work progress review involves implementing the second principle, "feedback of results." It is an integral part of the job cycle. After the project is finished, subordinate and supervisor go over their previously agreed-on goals, measuring performance against the yardsticks which were established in the work planning session.

To the extent that the work planning was done well, progress review is easy. The secret lies in developing good achievement measures. When these are done well, the review process follows almost automatically. In fact, the subordinate usually has a pretty good idea, before the review, how the supervisor will feel about his work. When the achievement measures are poor or consist only of time deadlines, the review stage cannot contribute to increased motivation or improved performance.

It is extremely important that the work review session not become a judging session. Instead, the emphasis should be placed on an objective, job-centered discussion of the extent to which goals have or have not been met, and the reasons why. Overemphasis on rigid measurement and goal attainment will destroy the mutual problem-solving climate. In these sessions, the supervisor must act as a helper, not a judge.

On the basis of the review, corrective action can be taken when needed, goals can be reset, and new goals established. This completes the work planning and review cycle. In brief, the review steps are as follows:

1. Several days in advance of the review session, the employee should be asked to review the goals and measures of achievement and be prepared to discuss progress, problems, solutions, and possible new goals. Concurrently, the supervisor should be doing the same thing.
2. In the discussion, the employee should be encouraged to summarize his progress, status, problems, and solutions. The supervisor introduces his own comments as appropriate. A discussion of both points of view should be encouraged so that there can be complete mutual understanding of progress and what the next steps should be.
3. If the discussion uncovers major problems of development needs, these should be stated in the form of new written goals.
4. At the meeting, update and add new goals as necessary.
5. Remember: the review session is not a performance appraisal. It is a review of progress with an emphasis on the joint solution of problems involved in getting the job done.

DO:

- Use review to improve performance.
- Use review time to discuss achievement against the performance measures.
- Use review time to recycle and replan work.
- Use an informal, rather than formal, approach.
- Use review to encourage rather than criticize.
- Use review to provide assistance in improving performance.
- Review work whenever appropriate, rather than at fixed periods such as at the completion of a project or specific tasks.
- Encourage subordinates to initiate their own reviews if they feel confident in this role.
- Establish a climate in which supervisor and subordinate can mutually agree on results accomplished, problem areas, and future needs.
- Remember that the purpose of a review is to obtain mutual knowledge of results for the purpose of improved performance.

DON'T:

- Approach in a punitive, rather than encouraging, manner.
- Put off reviews to predetermined fixed dates.
- Always try to review the whole job at a time. Review specific activities.
- Discuss personal characteristics. Concentrate instead on the job and ways to help improve job performance.
- Conduct reviews in a formal, stilted manner. The object is to help improve performance, not to lecture or patronize.

A WORD ABOUT DETAILS

The exact timing of work planning and review sessions is determined by the individuals involved and the exigencies of the job. Work planning should take place often enough to insure mutual understanding of what is expected. Review should be done often enough to insure that both parties agree on the results. Participants most likely will want to talk about specific projects or tasks from time to time, rather than about the total job. Some tasks have a very brief time cycle and might call for fairly frequent informational sessions. Other tasks or projects may have a fairly long time cycle and will be discussed at less frequent intervals.

In other words, the specific timing of review sessions will vary with the situation, the job, and the individual. As the supervisor becomes more relaxed in his approach, he will find himself jotting down plans and achievement measures during regular daily and weekly contacts with his subordinates.

Forms were developed in General Electric as a guide for use in work planning and review. Some typical ones are illustrated in Exhibits 2, 3, and 4. These forms were developed as an aid to help supervisors get started

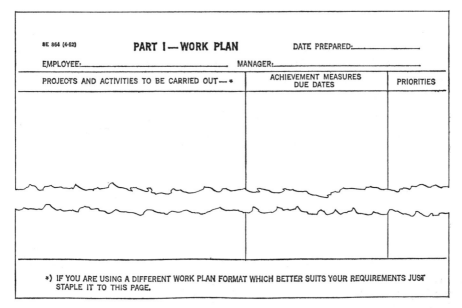

EXHIBIT 2

SE 865 (4-62)	PART II-A — PROGRESS REVIEW	DATE:_____
PROGRESS TO DATE	PROBLEMS	SUGGESTED ACTION TO BE TAKEN

(CHECK ONE) MANAGER'S COPY————
EMPLOYEE'S COPY————

EXHIBIT 3

on work planning. Experience has shown that many supervisors prefer to develop their own forms or to modify a form already in existence, and this practice is encouraged. Forms are not a major factor in work planning and review, but they are useful as recording devices. In general, best results are achieved when supervisors are given wide latitude in the type of form.

The purpose of work planning and review is to improve productivity. In order to achieve such additional supervisory objectives as justification for salary decisions, personnel-file documentation, and person-centered development discussions, separate procedures have been developed and implemented apart from the work planning activity.

The fundamental concept of the work planning and review process is contained in the three basic principles outlined above. To the extent that work planning is implemented without regard to these basic principles, it becomes less effective. In other words, techniques should never be allowed to transcend the basic purpose. A rigid and unsympathetic approach, hasty implementation through managerial edict, slavish allegiance to forms—all these are evidences of overemphasis on "technique" and will surely cause work planning to fail. Therefore, implementation should be preceded by a careful re-reading of the do's and don'ts.

WHAT ARE THE BENEFITS OF WORK PLANNING AND REVIEW?

At the time that work planning and review was developed and implemented at the Small Aircraft Engine Department, management also asked for an assessment of the program. It was felt strongly that the installation of

SE #66 (4-62)   **PART II-B — REVIEW SUMMARY**

1. FOLLOWING ITEMS REPRESENT SIGNIFICANT ACCOMPLISHMENTS

2. FOLLOWING MAJOR ITEMS WERE NOT ACCOMPLISHED AS PLANNED

3. FOLLOWING PROBLEMS HAVE BEEN IDENTIFIED AND ARE COVERED IN THE WORK PLAN

4. ADDITIONAL COMMENTS

REVIEW BY_____ DATE_____

EMPLOYEE_____

EXHIBIT 4

a costly personnel program should be accompanied by the research necessary to assess its value.

The benefits of the work planning and review program were determined by comparing it with the annual comprehensive appraisal then still in effect through much of the Department. Prior to any change, a large and representative sample of the exempt nonsupervisory employees in the Department completed and signed attitude questionnaires. This survey provided baseline data against which to evaluate attitude changes. The work planning and review program then was introduced in half of the Department. Fifteen months after it was introduced, some 150 employees were selected at random and interviewed, and the original questionnaire was readministered to them. Those interviewed were selected from the same group (1) who had previously completed the signed questionnaire, (2) who had held the same job, and (3) who had the same supervisor. Slightly more than 41 per cent of those interviewed had made the switch to work planning; the rest still were being given the traditional annual summary appraisal.

Both groups were found to be equal in all respects on the "before" questionnaire. However, they showed marked differences on the "after" questionnaire. Generally, the results show positive and significant gains by the work planning group as measured by the questionnaire. The performance appraisal group showed no change in any of the areas measured. The results for each area measured by the questionnaire are as follows:

1. Help received from manager in doing present job better. This area encompasses one of the basic objectives of the annual comprehensive appraisal. The work planning group showed highly significant (in a statistical sense) positive gains in employee perceptions of the amount of specific help given by the manager (supervisor) in improving employees' performance on the present job; the acceptance by managers of new ideas and approaches; the expertness of managers in planning work; help received from managers in making better use of their ability and experience; and increase in challenge and stimulation of interest in their subordinates by the managers.

2. Mutual agreement on job goals. On the first questionnaire, department employees reported that while many of the goals for their jobs were about what they ought to be, *some were not what they should be.* Thus there frequently was a situation in which an employee lacked complete identification and involvement with what he considered to be the goals and requirements of his job. On the second questionnaire, the work planning group moved in the direction of greater identification and involvement, with most reporting that the goals for their jobs were very much what they, individually, thought they ought to be.

3. Future improvement and development. Another of the major objectives of the performance appraisal program was to lay the groundwork for future improvement and development. In this area the work planning group reported positive and significant increases, specifically in regard to knowledge of specific future improvements expected of them and help received from their managers in planning their future development.

Two interesting points stem from these results: (1) future job development and future improvement were highly interrelated and tended to be seen as one and the same, and (2) work planning did appear to deal with future job development even though it was designed primarily to deal with shorter-range job activities. Thus work planning resulted in significant gains toward a goal usually associated with the annual comprehensive performance appraisal program, while the appraisal program itself had no effect in this respect.

4. Participation in job-related decisions. Previous research in General Electric on the performance appraisal interview indicated that any change in the manager's practices regarding subordinate participation in planning job goals following a poor appraisal resulted in poorer job performance. Thus it seemed important for the manager to be consistent in his practices relating to subordinate participation. In this study, the work planning group reported a slight increase in participation in making job related decisions. Therefore, it appears that work planning did not, in the eyes of the subordinates, bring about any major changes in the manager's approach to managing. This indicates that work planning can be implemented successfully under a wide range of managerial styles.

5. Attitudes toward performance and appraisal discussions. The work planning program was adopted to avoid some of the problems associated with the attempt to provide an opportunity for the manager and subordinate to discuss performance in a constructive manner through the comprehensive performance appraisal discussion. Some similar problems might be anticipated, nevertheless, since the work planning program does not eliminate all discussion of performance results. The review-of-progress part of a work planning session would seem to be, in effect, a type of performance appraisal discussion. Therefore, one of the basic considerations in evaluating the work planning and review approach was to examine reactions to discussions of performance results.

Members of the work planning group showed positive and significant improvement in their attitudes toward discussions of performance. Specifically, they reported increases in their appraisal of (1) the skill of their managers in discussing job performance; (2) the value of these discussions as a means of helping them to improve their performance; (3) the fairness of these discussions; (4) the extent to which the discussion permits a good exchange of views and opportunities to reach a clear and mutual understanding of where improvement is needed; and (5) the desirability of performance discussions. Review discussions associated with the work planning approach appear to have taken on increased value with subordinates in the direction for which the annual summary appraisal was intended.

6. *Evidence relating to performance improvement.* During the follow-up interview, persons who had switched to work planning were asked:

1. In thinking of your most recent work planning and review session, what were two or three of the things which you and your manager felt could be done to improve results?
2. What action have you taken along these lines?

Persons who had been using the annual appraisal were asked:

1. What were the two or three major criticisms brought up by your manager in your last appraisal discussion?
2. What actions have you taken to improve in these areas?

For interviewees in both groups, an attempt was made to elicit evidence of specific actions that had been taken to improve performance. The result of the comparison follows:

1. Both groups recalled about the same number of required improvements.
2. The needed improvements mentioned by the work planning group referred, in almost every instance, to specific improvements in job performance, whereas improvements mentioned by the performance appraisal group were more general and referred more to personal characteristics—for example, "be more aggressive" and "get along better with people."
3. The work planning group could cite specific actions they had taken to improve performance on 70 per cent of the improvement needs mentioned, while the performance appraisal group could cite specific actions to improve on only 40 per cent of the items.

In other words, in addition to the dramatic changes in employee attitudes toward supervisory practices, the work planning and review process resulted in a significant improvement in the specific actions taken by employees to improve their performance.

Evidence from this study showed the work planning approach to be significantly more effective than the annual comprehensive performance appraisal interview in improving employee attitudes concerning the help the employee receives from his manager that makes him more effective on his present job; mutual agreement between man and manager on job goals; plans for future performance improvement and personal development; and the constructive nature of man-manager discussions of the employee's job performance.

While the effects of the program on job performance were not measured as precisely as were attitudes, evidence was found to show that significantly greater action to improve performance was taken in response to work planning than was taken under the annual appraisal program. Based on this evidence, and a 15-month direct experience with the program, management decided to install the work planning and review program across the entire department.

* * *

As has been noted, an employee needs to know what is expected of him, obtain feedback of results, and get assistance as necessary. Work planning and review is a flexible way of establishing and continuing the job cycle necessary to get the work done, integrate the efforts of individuals and different components of the business, and increase individual motivation. It is a method whereby man and manager can *mutually* establish the objectives of the job, plan what is to be done, insure that the work is done, and evaluate the results and re-set the goals. In short, work planning and review provides the following advantages:

1. A constructive climate for the man and his supervisor to mutually solve the problems involved in getting the job done.
2. A means of assuring that business needs are translated into specific work items for the individual.
3. A practical way of quickly changing the direction of individual work plans to meet changing needs of customers and the business.
4. Assurance that the employee's abilities, skills, and interests will be reflected in the work he does and the way he does it.
5. An increase in the help employees receive from their supervisors in planning their future development.
6. Dramatic positive changes in attitudes and morale.
7. Significant increases in specific actions taken by employees to improve their performance.

SECTION VII

Equality of Opportunity

The demand for equal opportunity on the part of the Negro and other minority groups is one of the major social problems today. What management has done, is doing, and can do in the future is summarized in this section.

THE DEMAND FOR EQUAL RIGHTS •

GEORGE SCHERMER

A MERICAN BUSINESS AND INDUSTRIAL management has a tremendous stake in the struggle for equal rights and opportunities now being waged in the United States. Thoughtful people are deeply concerned about the ethical considerations. Many others are more conscious of the overall economic aspects of the problem. Those who close their eyes to both the ethical and economic implications often find themselves confronted by Government contract requirements, fair practice laws, or consumer pressures and boycotts.

The manager who limits his moral concerns to the operation of his own enterprise may be persuaded that he has no obligation to extend actively and affirmatively the opportunities available to members of disadvantaged groups. However, if he is a responsible citizen as well as a manager, he will readily recognize that the American free enterprise system can prove its social worth only if it serves the needs of all segments of the population, including those that have been barred in the past from equal participation.

Those who possess some imagination and a broad grasp of economics will have no difficulty recognizing that the 22 million plus nonwhite Americans have the potentiality of becoming either a tremendous asset or an economic liability. The nonwhite population of the United States is larger than the total population of Canada. With adequate education, training, and opportunity, it can be a major force for productivity and an extremely lucrative market for goods and services. Without training and without opportunity, it is certain to become both a burden and a threat to the safety and welfare of the nation.

GEORGE SCHERMER is Director, George Schermer Associates, Philadelphia, Pennsylvania.

EFFORTS TO DATE

There may be a few in management today who recall that as long ago as the 1920's representatives of the Urban League were timidly approaching employers for opportunities to place qualified Negroes in what are now called "nontraditional" jobs. More probably, those who have been in management for 20 years or more will date their first awareness of the problem to 1941, when President Franklin D. Roosevelt issued the first executive order requiring equal opportunity in employment on Federal Government contracts and establishing the first President's Fair Employment Practices Committee.

That order was inspired by the announced plan of several national Negro groups, led by A. Philip Randolph, to "march on Washington." The wartime need for national unity, for a maximum production effort, and for an unblemished world image required that that march be avoided if possible. The Executive Order was issued as evidence of the Government's good faith in promoting equal opportunity.

While efforts to enact a Federal fair employment practices law have been unsuccessful to date (the Civil Rights Act is being debated on the floor of the Senate as this chapter is being written), each succeeding president has considered it appropriate and necessary to issue continuing executive orders, extending the principle of equal opportunity on Government contract work.

Beginning with New York in 1945, a total of 21 states and several dozen cities, embracing over 60 per cent of the nation's population, have adopted fair employment practices laws and have established commissions for their administration and enforcement.

While the executive orders and fair practices laws have been useful instruments for extending opportunities, the rate of improvement has not been fast enough to catch up with the problems and needs that have been accumulating for a hundred years. The population shift from rural to urban areas, the massive concentrations of Negroes in the cities, and the growing self-awareness and articulateness of the Negro population have required more rapid adjustment than governmental procedures could produce. While patience and apathy have long characterized Negro behavior, militancy and determination have emerged in the past decade and direct action is being tested in many communities throughout the nation.

Negro consumer pressures to enforce demands for extended employment opportunities are not new. Locally organized boycotts of merchants catering to the Negro market have been applied effectively from time to time in a few Northern cities from the 1920's to the late 1950's. Beginning in 1958 some 400 Negro ministers in Philadelphia, operating without formal organization, led their flocks through a series of boycotts against commercial bakeries, soft-drink distributors, petroleum companies, grocery chains, and newspapers. (The Negro leadership entitled the movement the "Selective Patronage Program." The term "boycott" was never used.) The demands of the ministerial leadership were not excessive so that genuine victories could be achieved and claimed. Only a few actual boycotts were necessary since many firms acceded to the demands of the group before boycotts were instituted. In addition, many firms—particularly those most vulnerable to the Negro consumer market—instituted affirmative measures to extend opportunities for Negroes even though no direct pressure was indicated or applied.

While it is impossible to measure the results of such a campaign, the most conservative estimates indicate that several thousand Negroes were employed or upgraded as a result of the direct and indirect pressures of the Selective Patronage Program in the Philadelphia area. Consumer pressures and boycotts have been applied with varying degrees of effectiveness in several dozen other cities throughout the United States.

Pressures upon employers are coming from many sources other than the Negro groups. Governmental officials, religiously motivated groups, and civic leaders view the Negro revolt of the 1960's as a national crisis and hold that a morally defensible solution is essential to the security and welfare of the nation. Although the solutions advocated include many elements, economic opportunity is generally considered the most important. Negroes and other ethnic minorities must be fully integrated into the economic system and the time schedule is short.

DEMANDS UPON MANAGEMENT

The sum of the laws, executive orders, and direct pressures demand a great deal from management. Much more is involved than a neutral policy of not refusing to hire a qualified person because of color or ancestry. Employers are expected to plan and act affirmatively to *include* Negroes and other ethnic minorities wherever and whenever feasible, at every possible skill, in every operating unit and at every level from labor through skilled operations, in the office and in supervisory and administrative capacities.

This does not mean that fair-minded and serious people are advocating such crude measures as quota hiring or the assignment of Negro bodies to jobs they cannot perform. No procedure would be more self-defeating than artificial assignments to give the appearance of fair hiring. Admittedly, the demands of some direct action groups sometimes confront an employer with few alternatives other than hiring unneeded manpower. It is the purpose of this chapter to suggest how such a dilemma can be avoided through sound planning, orderly procedures, and good public relations. The underlying objective of the presidential orders, the fair practices laws, and the more thoughtful and practical leadership among direct action groups is to enable increasing numbers of Negroes and other minority groups to develop and apply the skills and competence to place them on a competitive footing more equal to the rest of the population.

REQUIREMENTS OF FEDERAL LAW

By the time this is published the Civil Rights Act may have become law. Whether or not Title VII, pertaining to equal opportunity in employment, will have been included as originally passed by the House cannot be predicted now. The principal provisions of the bill as passed by the House are as follows:

1. Coverage: Firms with 25 or more employees, employment agencies, and labor unions engaged in industries affecting interstate commerce are included.
2. Prohibitions: The following acts or practices—if based upon considerations of race, religion, color, sex, or national origin—are prohibited:
   a. Failure or refusal to employ a qualified applicant.
   b. Discharge of an employee.
   c. Discrimination in terms, conditions, or privileges of employment.
   d. Failure or refusal to refer for employment.
   e. Refusal of union membership, segregation within a union, or any discrimination in privileges or opportunities of union membership.
   f. Printing, publishing, or otherwise indicating preference, specification or limitations in terms of race, and so on,
3. Administration: An Equal Employment Opportunity Commission is established and empowered to administer and enforce the Equal Employment Opportunities provision of the Act and to promote and conduct educational programs.

The bill provides for the following procedures:

1. Complaints or charges of unlawful employment practices will be received in writing from either aggrieved individuals or from a member of the Commission.
2. If after investigation the Commission determines that the charges are true, the Commission shall attempt to correct the practice by persuasion. Written commitments to cease and desist from such practices may be a part of a negotiated settlement.
3. If persuasive efforts are unsuccessful, the Commission may bring a civil action to prevent the respondent from continuing such practices.
4. If, after a specific time, the Commission has not undertaken such civil action, the complainant may do so with permission of any one member of the Commission.
5. Each United States District Court has jurisdiction in such suits. The courts are empowered to enjoin the respondent from continuing the unlawful employment practices and to order the respondent to take such affirmative actions as are appropriate, including hiring or reinstatement of the complainant with back pay.

Employers are required to post such notices and to maintain such records as the Commission may prescribe, providing they are relevant and necessary for the enforcement of the Act. The Commission shall have access to such records and information as are required and is given full investigative powers.

REQUIREMENTS OF STATE LAWS

The provisions of state fair employment practice laws vary considerably in detail from state to state. Space will not permit an enumeration of the differences among the states. Many state laws exempt employers with fewer than ten employees.

The prohibitions of state laws compare generally with those in the Civil Rights Bill mentioned above. Administrative procedures vary widely. The provision that complaints be adjusted and practices be remedied by persuasion before enforcement measures are undertaken is common to all of the laws. In most states a commission makes a determination as to whether there were unlawful practices and imposes an order upon the respondent. It must bring an action before an appropriate court for enforcement of its order. Usually, the laws do not provide for the court to go into the facts. The court must accept the findings of fact of the commission but is empowered to review the proceedings to determine whether due process was observed and to modify or set aside the order if it appears unreasonable.

GOVERNMENT CONTRACTS

Presidential Executive Orders 10925 and 11114 require that all Federal Government contracting agencies insert into government contracts specific clauses to prevent discrimination and to assure equal opportunity in hiring. Also, in several states and cities there are requirements defined by law or executive order for the insertion of similar clauses into state and city contracts.

The prohibitions against discrimination contained in such clauses are not dissimilar from those contained in fair employment practice laws. However, a contracting agency may appropriately require affirmative actions as conditions of a contract that would not normally be imposed upon persons or employers not engaged in governmental work. The contractor agrees in advance (1) not to discriminate in any way with respect to employment, upgrading demotion or transfer, recruitment advertising, layoff or termination, rates of pay, or selection for training or apprenticeship; (2) to post prescribed notices and to place in recruitment advertisements that the company is an "equal opportunity employer;" (3) to notify labor union representatives of these contractual commitments; (4) to comply with the rules, regulations, and relevant orders of the President's Committee on Equal Employment Opportunity; (5) to furnish all information required by the President's Committee on Equal Employment Opportunity; and (6) to include similar clauses in every subcontract.

The responsibility for obtaining compliance rests with each contracting agency. If two or more agencies are contracting with the same firm, arrangements are made between them for only one to conduct compliance operations. The principal compliance procedures include the following:

1. *The compliance report.* The center of the compliance program is the compliance report. The contractor must file such a report 30 days after the contract is awarded and annually thereafter. In it, the firm must supply comprehensive statistical data showing the distribution of employees by race, sex, and occupation. Other sections of the report require descriptions of policies and practices, the assignment of responsibility for compliance, how the company recruits personnel, the nature and provisions of union contracts, the racial patterns and practices of labor unions, information subcontractors, and the like.

Blank forms for the report are supplied by the contracting agency or the President's Committee on Equal Employment Opportunity.

2. *The compliance review.* Unless the compliance report shows a favorable picture with respect to nondiscrimination, the contracting agency may institute a compliance review. This review is a comprehensive examination that goes into many aspects of recruitment, hiring and assignment, labor union involvement and practices of the labor unions, internal practices of the company pertaining to seniority systems, promotional charts, personnel instructions, supervisory manuals, and job classifications. The review may also go into factors outside the firm such as housing available to employees, whether local educational facilities are doing all that is necessary to educate and train minority group young people, and the extent to which the entire community is helping or hindering equal opportunity.

3. *Complaints.* Applicants and employees who believe they have been subject to discrimination are encouraged to file complaints with the President's Committee. Such complaints are promptly investigated and corrective measures instituted.

PLANS FOR PROGRESS

The President's Committee fosters a program of voluntary cooperation called "Plans for Progress." The prestige of the president's office has been used to persuade some of the largest corporations in the country to prepare and put into effect their own plans for implementing equal opportunity. While these plans vary in detail from company to company, the basic essentials are as follows:

1. The company announces a policy and transmits the policy in writing to all members of management. All employees are informed of the policy through regular channels.

2. Specific instructions are issued to all appropriate staff, and responsibilities for carrying out the policy are assigned.

3. The company agrees to notify its sources of recruitment of its policy and takes all other appropriate measures actively to seek out and employ qualified minority-group personnel.

4. The company agrees to review and analyze its personnel requirements and to make certain that eligible minority-group employees are encouraged to apply for and are considered for advancement.

5. The company agrees to open its apprenticeship, trainee, and work-

study programs to qualified minority-group applicants and cooperates closely with the schools and community groups to make sure that minority-group young people are encouraged to apply.

6. All facilities such as cafeterias are operated on a nonsegregated basis; employee recreation and management clubs are encouraged to formalize nondiscrimination policies and to make sure that they are carried out.

7. The company institutes periodic checks to assure that the policy and objectives are being carried out.

COMPLIANCE PROCEDURES OF STATE AND MUNICIPAL AGENCIES

State and municipal fair employment practice commissions have issued fairly consistent regulations prohibiting racial and religious specifications in help-wanted advertisements, pre-employment inquiries as to race or religion, and requiring the posting of notices. All the agencies rely heavily upon the receipt and investigation of complaints as a means of gaining compliance For many years most of the commissions were preoccupied with legalistic enforcement procedures and the application of the letter of the law. They held to the rigid view that the fair employment laws required a completely color-blind policy. Under such a doctrine an employer was prohibited from taking affirmative measures to remedy the long-existing patterns of exclusion of Negroes and other minorities, because to do so was interpreted as "discrimination in reverse." This narrow and legalistic approach tended to freeze existing discriminatory patterns rather than alter them.

In more recent years this philosophy has been modified. Increasingly the state and local commissions are taking the view that it is the intent of the law to *remedy* the long-standing patterns of discrimination rather than to establish a disinterested referee.

For example, the Commission on Human Relations in Philadelphia in 1961 distributed a "Notice to Employers" which stated that the Commission was more interested in the demonstrated intent to implement the purpose of the law than in the mere compliance with the letter. The Notice set forth six criteria by which the intent of the employer would be measured. This Notice was followed by industrywide investigations, conferences, and plant inspections. The venture was largely an educational and consultative process since the legal grounds for enforcing "intent" are precarious. However, the consultative process produced more actual hiring and upgrading in one year than the legalistic processing of complaints had in ten years.

THE EFFECT OF DIRECT ACTION

Direct action has taken several forms. The most common and effective where employment is at issue is the boycott. However, marches, picketing, sit-ins and lie-ins are not uncommon. The better-organized and responsibly led groups usually precede direct action with requests for negotiations and customarily withhold action unless negotiations break down or fail.

Negotiating with a direct action group is likely to be difficult. The Negro protest movement tends to be indigenous and symptomatic of a mood, rather than a well-organized or planned strategy. No one organization is strong enough to support a claim to be representative of or a bargaining agent for the entire Negro population. Therefore, to be sustained, a direct-action program must be based upon a loose coalition of several groups. There is much jockeying for leadership, and the demands are often a rather inconsistent combination of both arbitrarily specific items and generalities. The negotiating committees lack the sophistication and experience of union bargaining agents and labor lawyers. The corporation executive who attempts to apply the customary rules and techniques of collective bargaining to this new situation will find himself confused and frustrated.

Because the negotiating committee is often not unified and each member is fearful of being charged with compromising or settling for too little, one of two tendencies is likely to develop: (1) the committee becomes intransigent and refuses to negotiate on any terms other than its own or (2) what appear to be verbal understandings at the bargaining table quickly evaporate as the committee reports back to its membership. (The same thing often characterizes the management side in those instances when not just one corporation but a loose coalition of merchants and businessmen are sitting on the management side of the table.)

Suggestions for the guidance of management in such negotiations are outlined at a later point in this chapter. Before that is discussed, however, it seems advisable to suggest how to prevent matters from reaching the direct action stage, or at least how to come to the bargaining table with clean hands.

PREVENTION THROUGH SOUND POLICY

It is assumed in this chapter that management is fully committed to both compliance with the law and to the principle of equal opportunity. It is also assumed that management must, of necessity, adhere to sound personnel practices, that it wishes to maintain good faith with the labor unions, and that it wants to avoid image-destroying conflict with civil rights demonstrators.

In this era of racial unrest and conflict there can be no sure formula for achieving such a nice balance. Even the best intentioned or most progressive company or community may find itself in the path of the brush fires that have been set off in so many places. However, there are many positive aspects to the general situation. There is still time for most forward-looking companies to set in motion the processes that will substantially reduce the risk of serious difficulty.

The first step is to develop a sound and positive policy at top level. The policy in its general aspect should be clear and firm. There can be no compromise with the principle that color, religion, or ethnic origin must not be a barrier to any job. Equally important is recognition of the fact that existing patterns possess tremendous inertia and are not likely to be altered unless management makes change a priority item.

Maneuverability. Beyond those firm top-level understandings there must be considerable room for creative planning and maneuverability. Hard, inflexible decisions and fixed procedures are likely to be unproductive.

The manager who says "We'll hire any person that meets our requirements, but we won't deviate from our standards" probably will not succeed in changing the pattern very much. There are many Negroes with potential, but not many have had the specific cultural background, the early exposure in the home and the neighborhood, and the pre-work and work experience to cast them into the precise model around which the standards have been molded. Managers may believe the above viewpoint to be a morally and legally defensible position, but it won't get enough Negroes sufficiently distributed through the work force to show evidence of good faith.

"We will make a thorough study of our manpower needs and promotion charts to determine what opportunities there are and then actively search out as many potentially qualified Negroes as we can find to fill them" is a more positive and creative approach. All personnel so selected must be able to perform satisfactorily on the job although there should be allowance for some special guidance and on-the-job training. No clearly unqualified person should ever be assigned, but the person selected may not always be the one best qualified at the moment.

Even this limited degree of favoritism may run counter to the established order of labor and management relations and the neat ethical concepts by which personnel managers have been guided for the past half-century or so.

A degree of injustice may indeed appear to exist where there are two or more candidates for a particular job. Those who are troubled should remind themselves that the injustice which American society has perpetrated against Negroes begins to function from the very moment of birth. Both morality and the practical fact of the social revolution that is upon us dictate that these injustices be remedied. The firm that refuses to face this fact may find itself confronted with even less palatable alternatives at another time.

"We would like to extend more opportunities to non-whites who are qualified, but we are so committed under our union contracts and in our employee relations that we can't do a thing. Negroes will have to come in at the ground floor like everyone else" may sound like good sense to many. However, if Negroes are not already reasonably distributed in the several operating units and at many skill levels, it is not likely to be convincing to those who are demanding change. If the firm has no government contracts and is not sensitive to public opinion or consumer pressures, it may get by with such a position. If it is sensitive to public pressures, it may have to do more.

How to handle the situation will depend upon the particular unions involved, the history of employee relations in the firm and local community factors. With careful soundings of union sentiment and employee opinion, management may discover that good planning and skillful consultation can produce more positive results than may appear possible at first thought.

It cannot be stated too often that neither government nor responsible civic groups are contemplating any permanent or continuing preferential treatment for any group, white or nonwhite. What is being advocated is that the traditional log jams be broken up so that nonwhites can be placed on a competitive footing with whites. Once that has been accomplished and a genuine merit relationship has been established and accepted in a given company, no further special consideration should be accorded to any ethnic group.

Overcoming inertia. Government-compliance officials and others who have had some success in overcoming exclusive hiring practices, are agreed that inertia is the greatest single obstacle. To a large extent the reasons commonly advanced for lack of progress are themselves symptomatic of inertia. "Plateauing" is observed in many of the firms that have given the problem attention for only a limited period. In one city a large bank made a special effort to employ Negro personnel when a fair employment practice law first went into effect. Within a year's time it had brought its white-collar Negro personnel up from zero to three per cent. Ten years later it was still three per cent. Progress leveled off immediately after management ceased to give the matter special attention.

In another city a large publishing firm announced a policy of equal opportunity and issued general instructions to staff. However, no specific responsibilities were assigned. Having issued its policy statement, management gave the matter no further attention. Six years later management became concerned about impending demonstrations and was shocked to discover that Negroes had not risen above the semiskilled level anywhere in their company. Under top-level prodding 62 nonwhites, about one-fourth of those employed, were upgraded within a period of a few months.

In the plant-inspection program conducted by the Philadelphia Commission on Human Relations about 22 per cent of the firms inspected had nonwhites well distributed throughout the work force. The remaining 78 per cent had either few or no Negroes at all or employed them in particular departments or on lower skilled levels only. There was no symmetrical curve from poor to good patterns among the several companies. Instead there were two peaks, one at each end of the spectrum. There was no mystery as to how this occurred. In the "good" companies, management had established a policy and made certain it was carried out. In the other companies, management had not given the matter special attention.

Recruitment difficulties. Next to inertia the most difficult problem appears to be recruitment. Companies that have set out to implement an equal opportunity program often experience great difficulty in recruiting nonwhite applicants to meet their specifications. Negroes have been excluded from skilled clerical and other white-collar occupations to such an extent that there is a decided scarcity of well-trained and qualified persons. Many of those who have potential, particularly the young people, are unaware of their potential, uninformed concerning the opportunities, or too timid to apply. These are barriers that must be overcome. There are several approaches to the problem:

1. For management and technical trainee positions, the colleges and universities with significant numbers of Negro students offer the best source.*

2. For clerical and administrative functions, specific instructions to private employment agencies may help. There tends to be a concentration of competent and experienced Negroes working in local, state, and Federal government jobs. Many of them applied for such

---

* Calvert, Jr., Robert, *How to Recruit Minority Group College Graduates,* Personnel Journal, Inc., Swarthmore, Pennsylvania, 1963.

jobs under competitive civil service because government was viewed as less discriminatory than private employers. It will be a healthy development all around if many of them can be enticed into private employment. However most of those so employed are fairly secure and are not actively seeking work. Active recruiting and incentives will be required to cause them to change jobs.

3. Careful and intensive recruitment at the high school level in search of young people with potential for work-study, trainee, and apprenticeship programs should produce a number of good prospects. In addition, the mere fact that industry is actively searching for qualified young people will serve as a morale builder among the Negro young people.

Private employers, through industrial relations councils, personnel associations, Chambers of Commerce, and so on are becoming increasingly concerned about this problem and are cooperating with public and vocational schools to encourage Negro students to become better prepared. This is extremely important. For generations, Negroes have been led to believe that because of discrimination, training would be of no value. Employers must demonstrate in every possible way that employment *is* available to trained and competent people.

STEPS TOWARD A POSITIVE PROGRAM

While fixed formulas are inadvisable, the following well-tested steps have proven their value on many occasions.

A. *Policy*

1. The president of the company issues an explicit and firm policy statement that all personnel operations—including recruitment, hiring, training, assignment, promotion, use of facilities, and privileges—are to be conducted on a merit basis without limitation or restriction on the basis of race, color, religion, or ethnic origin and that appropriate steps are to be taken to implement the policy.
2. The policy is issued in writing. It is specifically directed to those with responsibilities for implementation, and otherwise disseminated through regular communications channels.
3. Briefing sessions are held with labor union officials and appropriate management personnel in advance of general distribution of the statement.

    4. Responsibilities for implementing the policy are clearly defined and assigned.

B. *Inventory*

An inventory of existing personnel and manpower requirements is made. The inventory includes the following:

    1. The distribution of nonwhite and other minority-group personnel by operating unit and level of skill.

    2. Present upgrading potential of minority-group employees.

    3. Chart showing where vacancies now exist or are anticipated.

    4. Matching of upgrading potential to actual anticipated vacancies.

    5. Job categories for which on-the-job training would contribute to upgrading minority-group personnel.

C. *Recruiting*

    1. Inform all recruitment sources of the firm's policy and desire to employ qualified members of minority groups. Cover all sources without exception.

    2. Include those colleges, schools, referral agencies, and public employment services known to have concentrations of nonwhites and other minorities.

    3. Beam the recruitment program directly to Negro audiences so they understand they are included. Use pictures showing Negroes on the job.

D. *Hiring*

    1. Brief employment office personnel concerning the policy, making sure it is thoroughly understood.

    2. Train employment office personnel to apply standards fairly and objectively. Make sure that unconscious biases in the application of tests are overcome.

    3. Conduct periodic checks on application of standards. Analyze samples of rejected cases.

    4. Conduct sight surveys for analysis and control.

E. *Internal practices*

    1. Conduct informational and educational programs for all management and supervisory personnel, and as many of the general personnel as is feasible, to interpret the policy and full meaning of equal opportunity programs.

    2. Insure that all in-service training, company-sponsored educational assistance, and other employee development programs are open to all personnel.

3. Provide counseling to nonwhite employees to encourage them to seek advancement through training.
4. Encourage all employees to voice their complaints of discrimination through appropriate channels. Give prompt attention to all complaints. Clear the air of misunderstandings. If the complaint is not justified, give as much attention to clarification as if it were justified.
5. Make all facilities such as cafeterias, rest rooms, recreational rooms, and the infirmary equally available to all without segregation.
6. Feature Negroes along with others, without special contrivance, in employee publications, recognition ceremonies, and the like.
7. Make every effort to include Negroes in all of the starting jobs to insure long-range distribution throughout the personnel structure.

F. *Administrative control and feedback*
1. Establish a system of reporting concerning equal employment, recruiting, hiring, training, upgrading and the like.
2. Ask for prompt reporting of unusual problems and experiences, especially until the policy has been fully implemented.
3. Include equal opportunity progress as a regular item on staff meeting agendas.
4. Conduct annual evaluation of equal opportunity progress.

ORIENTING THE WORK FORCE

There is difference of opinion concerning whether the established work force should be especially briefed and prepared for the acceptance of nonwhite co-workers. This issue is less and less important as the general inevitability of equal hiring practices becomes accepted. A company that has never employed nonwhites at all, or only in lower skill levels, certainly should make its policy known sufficiently well in advance so that the appearance of nonwhites does not cause shock and surprise. Administrative and supervisory personnel should be fully instructed in their responsibilities. Management should be ready to discuss the matter with union and employee groups at any time if necessary. The appearance of a "moral crusade" or of a tough "take it or else" attitude should be avoided at all costs. Candid discussions backed up with firmness should be all that is required in meeting employee resistance.

Overt opposition to the minority group newcomer is less likely than ostracism, lack of helpfulness, and other subtle devices for discouraging and excluding him. Another problem often arises when the numbers of both Negroes and whites is sufficient for the employees to group themselves on a racial basis. Common symptoms of potential trouble are racially segregated tables in cafeterias, or segregated locker arrangements where voluntary selection of locker space is permitted. These developments may appear harmless at first; but racial cliques, suspicion, and hostility often emerge because intraracial communication is being cultivated while interracial communication breaks down. Management should be alert to these problems at all times. The matter should be a subject of periodic consultation with supervisors and foremen. Self-segregation in locker rooms can often be avoided by a locker-assignment system that precludes voluntary selection or transfer. Candid discussion of the problem with small (interracial) groups of employees, skillfully led, is probably the most wholesome and effective measure.

INDUCTING THE NEW WORKERS

The new worker may need some moral support at the outset. Much will depend upon the individual. Employers should avoid "talking down." Nothing is more pompous and patronizing than a speech such as this: "You are the first of your color here. You must be better than anyone else on the job. We want you to be a credit to your race." Yet just that kind of lecturing occurs again and again.

Whatever instructions are normally given to any worker should, of course, be given to the nonwhite employee. In addition, a little encouragement might be given, in an off-hand way, such as: "Look, as a new man you might have some questions or problems for the first few days. Don't be afraid to ask for information or help. We want you to get the right start."

COMMUNICATION AND PUBLIC RELATIONS

While public relations should not be used as a substitute for sound policy and practice, the best possible practices can be unnoticed, misunderstood, or misrepresented unless the facts are skillfully interpreted to the employees and to the community at large. There are several distinct audiences which the company must reach:

1. The company's own employees.

2. Its customers.
3. The general public.
4. The minority public.
5. Concerned civic leaders and organizations.
6. Government compliance agencies.

The more sophisticated companies will usually have well-developed facilities and channels for communication. These can be used effectively with respect to the equal employment opportunity program. There are some who believe that public discussion of racial issues and policies does more harm than good. It is, indeed, possible to overplay the matter. However, there is even greater danger in secretiveness or defensiveness. Candor in the area of race relations is usually disarming and by far the best policy. Concerned civic leadership and government agencies will be favorably impressed with an open door and a readiness to supply information upon request. The customers and the general public are not likely to have a great interest in the racial policies of the firm unless unusual problems exist. If such problems arise, an honest statement of policy and practice are recommended.

In this era of social unrest, the minority public is especially sensitive. Minority groups with a grievance tend to be suspicious of the information channeled through the regular news media. Special efforts to reach the minority audience are in order. Many companies have made the mistake of believing they were communicating with the minority public by meeting with a few ministers and group leaders. Such person-to-person communication never goes very far; or if it does, it is unreliable.

For its own protection the company must present a positive image (assuming such an image to be founded upon truth) to a broad cross-section of the Negro and other minority publics. This is not difficult, but it does require an investment of time and money. The message can be carried through the minority-group press and the special radio programs that are beamed to the minority audience; by presenting meaningful educational programs to school and parent-teacher groups, providing cooperative assistance to civic and religious organizations, sponsoring training and scholarship programs, and in every way possible demonstrating that the corporation has an interest in the affairs and welfare of the minority group community.

The company that adopts and implements a sound policy of equal opportunity and takes reasonable care to interpret the policy to the public can be fairly certain that it will not be a target of either governmental compliance procedures or direct action by protest groups.

However, in the event that a company is confronted with a negotiating committee of a direct action group, it should be prepared to meet the group from a nondefensive position.

The first principle is for the company executives to display a readiness to meet and confer. Nothing is more likely to generate hostility and intransigence than a closed door.

The committee selected by the civil rights groups to represent them in negotiations carries a heavy responsibility from the viewpoint of the people it speaks for. In some respects the committee members are as much concerned about recognition as they are about their specific demands. According them courtesy and respect, even if their demeanor seems belligerent at the outset, costs little and can ease the negotiations a great deal.

The company should have its own plan for an orderly implementation of the equal opportunity program. However, the company spokesmen should be sensitive to the psychological and status needs of the negotiating committee. The committee should be encouraged to present its case and its proposals. The company will gain no advantage by defensive argument. If some of what the committee says is true, that much should be conceded. If some or all of it is not true, the company spokesmen should simply say, "We are sorry these misunderstandings have developed. We know you are reasonable men. We would like you to examine the facts." If some of the specific demands of the group are not out of line with the company's own program, there will be an advantage to conceding those items in a manner that suggests that the committee members have achieved that much by their own efforts.

Whatever the committee demands that is unreasonable or unfeasible should be candidly discussed. The company should be prepared to offer feasible alternatives. Much harm can result if the company makes concessions under pressure that cannot be made to work. The company is far better prepared to know what will or will not work than the delegation is. However, the company should try to sense the urgency that is felt by the delegation and should be sincere in seeking solutions to ease the situation.

It should be kept in mind that the negotiating committee needs desperately to go back to its constituency with some achievement. It is always possible for the achievement it carries back to conform with the company's own plan. Certainly the company that has made a thorough inventory of its own situation and has devised its own plan before it is confronted with direct action is far ahead of the one that waits until confronted by a delegation.

SECTION VIII

The Expansion of Overseas Operations

> *The general growth of worldwide trade and the industrial advances of the developing countries have led to expansion of overseas operations and, as a result, unprecedented personnel problems. What these problems are and how they can be handled are discussed in this section.*

OVERSEAS OPERATIONS: THEiR PERSONNEL IMPLICATIONS •

SPENCER J. HAYDEN

IT HAS BEEN ONLY ABOUT TWENTY years since most American industries awakened to the remarkable opportunities that lie overseas in worldwide markets. True, American companies were investing abroad long before World War II, but except for a few major oil companies, business tended to treat its overseas operations as a stepchild.

Then just before and during the 1950's, American companies were forced to expand their horizons by the pressure of a combination of unexpected economic developments. In industry after industry, profit margins at home began to shrink as costs in the United States climbed faster than prices and domestic markets neared the saturation point. At the same time, foreign producers began penetrating markets all around the world and stepping up their exports to the United States.

American executives, pushed by costs and competition into a search for new strategies for survival, became aware that in many cases their companies' earnings abroad, although relatively small, were on the rise and thus warranted more management attention, more capital for expansion, and more employees. As a result, the movement toward a new kind of American *multinational* company had its beginnings. Since then—in fact, during the past 12 years—American direct investment abroad has climbed to a book value of over $36 billion, three times the American holdings in 1950.

Americans are concentrating on three main markets for their foreign ventures: Western Europe, Canada, and Latin America—in that order. Europe has exerted a special attraction for American businessmen. The European Common Market and the emerging Free Trade area encompass

SPENCER J. HAYDEN is President, The Spencer Hayden Company, Inc., New York, New York and Professor of Management, New York University.

the great bulk of Western Europe. These markets have a population of about 250 million. Eventually, through economic integration, they will comprise the single most populated industrial and consumer market in the free world with a forecasted total gross national product in 1970 of over $400 billion—which is approximately the United States level now.

However, unqualified optimism about international opportunities is no longer justified. Robert Theobald, in an AMA Research Study (No. 62, *Business Potential in the European Common Market*) painted a sobering picture. He says that the accelerated pace at which American companies ventured abroad during the 1950's and early 1960's appears to have slackened and that the potential for investment in Europe has been grossly oversold to American companies in recent years. He feels that only in exceptional cases will a medium-size or small American firm be able to find a valuable opportunity in that area of the world. The reason is that both economic and political trends have combined to limit the profit prospects for the American company in Europe. For the first time since World War II, growth in Europe depends primarily on the ability to sell goods rather than to produce them. This fact has initiated a severe profit squeeze whose dimensions are further aggravated by rapidly rising wage rates. Thus Theobald concludes that the prospect is for continued evolution until economic conditions in Europe are similar to those in America.

THE IMPLICATIONS FOR ORGANIZATION

International growth means more problems for top management. The employee relations department, of course, is directly affected. S. D. Bechtel, chairman of the engineering construction company, Bechtel Corporation, points out that "each country presents its own set of problems—taxation, labor laws, currency regulations, and so on. In these matters, management must have the same thorough knowledge of each foreign country as it has of U.S. laws and that means keeping a staff of managers who will gain that knowledge."

Businesses that used to be parochial are becoming multinational. Says George R. Cain, chairman of Abbott Laboratories—a $145-million-a-year pharmaceutical company with plants in 22 countries—"We are no longer just a U.S. company with interests abroad. Abbott is a world enterprise and many major, fundamental decisions must be made on a global basis."

Companies organize in various ways to become truly "international." One highly promising approach is to integrate all domestic and overseas operations by giving worldwide responsibilities to the various vice presidents for manufacturing, marketing, finance, research, and personnel.

Procter & Gamble Company has eliminated its old overseas division and replaced it with four new international divisions, two with headquarters in Cincinnati and two abroad. Among them, they have divided their world markets outside the United States into three regions, with the fourth division handling primarily exports and special operations.

One aircraft manufacturer set up a separate company in 1959 to handle all its overseas business but found that this restricted the opportunities of its United States divisions. This has been changed so that the international company works basically as a consultant to the other divisions, helping each market its own products overseas. In practice, then, each United States division has become a multinational company with profit responsibility for worldwide operations.

COMPENSATING FOREIGN-BASED EMPLOYEES

More questions are raised by personnel directors on the subject of compensating foreign-based employees than on any other topic. Almost all United States firms that have American employees working and living abroad provide special compensations for them. The most common measure is a cost-of-living allowance to employees who are placed in areas where costs exceed those in the United States.

Many methods are used to estimate the cost differential. Formalized ones (the State Department indexes, the United Nations index, and individual company indexes) are based upon some statistical technique and are favored by companies employing a substantial number of Americans overseas. Companies that have relatively few American employees overseas rely on informal methods, such as whatever general information is available on the cost of living, comparisons with other companies' allowances, executive recommendations and observations, and individual reviews.

Housing facilities or a housing allowance of one type or another is supplied under certain conditions by most companies. When the employee is in a remote area, the trend has been toward supplying housing facilities free of charge. Allowances are usually provided in areas where the company believes that housing costs are excessive. In such cases the company bears part of the housing cost. A general rule is to allow a bachelor 60 to 75 per cent of the allowance given to a married man. The cost of educating children abroad is another compensation allowance in many companies.

It is common practice to reimburse the employee for any income tax paid abroad in excess of such taxes paid in the United States. Many companies permit the employee to benefit when the foreign tax is lower than at home.

The majority of companies pay salaries in two currencies, the local currency and United States dollars. Allowances for living costs are normally paid in local currency.

Most companies pay a higher base salary to their overseas employees than to their employees in the same positions in the United States. The most common premium is around 25 per cent of base salary. Other special allowances cover recreational facilities, initiation fees and dues to clubs, and expense accounts.

The accompanying exhibit illustrates the variety of policy that is possible in sending American executives abroad. It compares, point by point, the approaches of two actual companies that are experienced in these matters. Company *A* is a large engineering and construction firm with temporary staffs in Europe, while Company *B* is an oil firm with American personnel permanently stationed there.

Top management generally has to make many key decisions on its compensation program for its foreign employees. This subject can be particularly ticklish if the company provides many attractive allowances for its overseas personnel that are in sharp contrast to the provisions for those at home. Among the many key questions that arise on the topic are the following:

1. How should the base salary of foreign nationals be established?
2. What shall be done in the case of nationals on a local pay scale who work next to higher-paid Americans who perform the same kind of work?
3. How can headquarters benefit programs (insurance, retirement, allowances) be related to foreign or local ones? Should they be so related?
4. What can be done to instill company esprit de corps in foreign employees?
5. How can an ethical American company cope with the traditional tax-evasion practices in some foreign locales?
6. What percentage of employees should be Americans and what percentage foreign nationals?
7. When should the top management overseas be made up of local men?

The program for foreign nationals of Northwest Airlines shows how one company approaches these matters. Northwest employs nearly 400 local nationals in six countries in the Orient. The largest contingent is in Japan.

It is the policy of Northwest to pay the going rate in that country for each classification of work. With the exception of the Philippines, all of their local national employees are noncontract; this leaves with Northwest the right to establish rates of pay and benefits. Northwest's method of paying employees in the Orient has developed separately from the method of compensating employees in the United States.

Prior to World War II, the basic pay of an individual was not the most important part of his total compensation: Extra allowances greatly outweighed the basic pay of the individual. Many of these practices have thus been incorporated into the pay structures of Northwest in these locations. In addition, it is common in these countries to have rigid government standards of sick leave, legal minimum holiday and vacation provisions, plus the types of labor legislation that we are accustomed to in the United States. For instance, in Japan an employer of 50 or more employees must subscribe to the Government's health plan with premiums shared on a 50-50 basis between the employer and the employee.

Northwest has a policy of retirement at age 65 throughout the company, overseas and domestically. However, a local national in Korea, upon retirement at age 65, is entitled to receive retirement pay on a *lump-sum basis* of one month's pay for each year of service because it is the practice of retired workers in oriental countries, upon receiving this lump-sum payment, to set up little shops of their own. In fact, the economy partly revolves about this system. Northwest supports this tradition.

SELECTING OVERSEAS EMPLOYEES

Many controversies rage on the subject of selecting overseas employees. Some companies, for example, believe in hiring right out of college young men who are willing and able to adjust to permanent overseas assignments. Other firms prefer to offer transfers to loyal and proven men who have been with them for some time. Circumstances and objectives will dictate the appropriate policy on this.

Whatever the policy and procedure, the financial implications are considerable. Standard-Vacuum Oil Company estimates that costs of its extensive college recruiting program approximate $1,500 per man hired. Subsequent training costs before overseas assignment are then about $100 per training day, with training programs running from three months to one year

OVERSEAS COMPENSATION POLICY

	Company A	Company B
I. Leave and vacation allowance:		
1. Home leave in U.S.	No allowance is made for home leave beyond regular vacations. (Executives usually fly back to U.S. at least once during a 2-year period and take their regular vacation in U.S. Unless trip is an extended one, dependents' travel is not paid. If middle management or junior employees want a vacation in U.S., they usually pay their own way.)	30 calendar days per year taken at end of 2-year period. First-class ship or plane for employee and dependents; travel costs paid by company.
2. Station leave in Europe	Regular vacation allowance	7 days a year in addition to home leave. Employee pays own way. 10 months needed to qualify.
3. Sick leave	No specific provision. In case of serious illness, company allows indefinite sick leave with full pay.	After 10 years, employee accumulates maximum benefit of 26 weeks with full pay. Travel expenses for employee and dependents handled on individual basis.
4. Emergency leave	No specific provision. Company would probably pay transportation for employee and dependents to place of emergency.	For serious illness or death of employee's spouse or child, 14 days with pay allowed.

II. Other benefits and allowances:

	Company A	Company B
1. Education of dependents:		
Elementary	None	$500
High school	None	$500 local ($600 nonlocal)
College	None	1 free round trip a year
Graduate	None	None
2. Travel costs:		
Employee and family	Full	Full
Incidentals	$100 maximum	Full
Stopovers	Reported expenses	Per diem
3. Resettlement costs:		
Baggage allowance	Reported expenses—2 weeks	Per diem up to 3 months
Return of terminated employee	All required to establish home	No limit
	Company pays	Company pays

III. Direct compensation:

	Company A			Company B		
1. U.S. base salary	$10,000	$20,000	$30,000	$10,000	$20,000	$30,000
2. Foreign service premium	2,100*	2,000	3,000	2,000	4,000	4,000
3. Cost-of-living allowance	2,420	4,400	6,600			
4. Per diem allowance	3,650	3,650	3,650			
5. Total foreign pay	$18,170	$30,050	$43,250	$12,000	$24,000	$34,000
6. Per cent that total foreign pay exceeds U.S. pay	81.7	52.5	44.2	20	20	13.3

* Company A's foreign service premium for employees earning $10,000 or less is based on practice of paying such employees an average of 10 per cent of base salary for overtime plus 10 per cent of that total amount for foreign service.

in duration. After overseas assignment, salary costs may be three to four times more than comparable United States costs because of local tax structures and other cost-of-living factors. Total staffing is thus quite expensive.

Most companies begin any foreign venture by sending one of their American executives to run it for a few years with the understanding that it's his responsibility to train a management group of local nationals from whom his replacement can be selected. (Presumably, he will use the same care and screening procedures in recruiting a local staff that he would follow in the stateside organization.) However, Vice President Donald H. Robinson of Procter & Gamble explains: "We never appoint a man simply because of his nationality. A Canadian runs our French company, a Dutchman runs the Belgian company, and a Briton runs our Italian company."

A wide range of selection methods are generally used by the American personnel director in selecting the "right" man—and family—for overseas assignment. The personal characteristics of candidates frequently mentioned as important are as follows:
1. Technical competence; good job knowledge.
2. Flexibility, adaptability.
3. Wide range of interests.
4. Emotional and social maturity; stability.
5. Sense of humor.
6. Tolerance of other religions and mores.
7. Good health.
8. Good marriage adjustment and family teamwork.
9. Independence; "inner resources."

All of these qualities are difficult to assess, except in extreme cases. Some are more important at one company post than at another. Selection is clearly no simple matter. A few tests have proved to be at least partly valuable to psychologists in selecting American employees for assignments abroad. They are as follows:
1. *The F Scale*—a measure of ethnic flexibility and adaptability.
2. *The Allport-Vernon Study of Values*—a measure of personal convictions and values.
3. *The Guilford-Zimmerman Temperament Survey*—a questionnaire type of comprehensive personality test.
4. *The Individual Background Survey*—a multiple-choice measure of, among other things, early acceptance of responsibility.

In addition, intelligence tests appear to be helpful in selecting men who have enough "learning ability" to adapt easily to new ways and problems.

Selection mistakes in employment usually result in lowered productivity and increased costs of training and supervision. Such mistakes are more serious, however, when made in relation to overseas employment because there must be added the cost of transportation and family allowances as well as diminished company and national prestige. It is advisable therefore in selecting personnel for overseas work to take every precaution to insure getting the right man for the right job.

A number of progressive companies are beginning to study the foreign-service selection problem as they would any other business matter involving risk. The purpose of such study is to (1) determine what specific differences, if any, exist between individuals who successfully adjust to overseas work at company installations and those who fail or quit and (2) develop valid and practical methods which might be administered by the company to better select employees for all overseas posts. Four approaches, described below, are both practical and advisable. They can be taken separately, in any order, or together and will prove rewarding in terms of more effective staffing.

Employment records. A personnel executive or consultant examines and analyzes the employment records of foreign-service individuals considered by their superiors to have turned out to be "poor risks"—that is, they resigned or were dismissed relatively early in their employment. Such records are then compared with those of individuals hired at about the same time who remained on the job and proved to be successful—the "good risks."

Some of the employment-record items to check include age at the time of going overseas, marital status, number and types of jobs held before going abroad, place of birth, years of schooling, academic standing, medical history, test scores, earnings, and so on. This study provides valuable information on the discrimination value of individual items on the employment application form and may suggest practical additions or changes.

Standardized tests. An experimental battery of tests and questionnaires, based on the experience of psychologists in employee selection, can be assembled to estimate such factors as personality rigidity, emotional maturity, personal biases, inner resources, and motivation. These tests can be mailed to all current employees in overseas posts with instructions for answering them and returning the completed forms to the headquarters office or psychologist for analysis.

Concurrently those being tested should be rated on their performance and acceptability by their superiors in order to provide the research team with a criterion against which to measure test results. The specific tests which are found to discriminate among the superior, average, and inferior personnel can then be put together into a single battery for subsequent use by personnel departments for screening future job applicants.

Depth interviews. To supplement information collected by the first two techniques and to gain a better understanding of the personality intangibles and dynamics involved, specialists can conduct interviews and administer more penetrating psychological tests to company employees as they are rotated home for vacation. This provides a check on the information collected by the other means and frequently reveals some aspects of problems not brought out before. These depth interviews of the "best" and "poorest" employees can be conducted at the overseas locations when the time factor is deemed important by the company.

Special questionnaires. Valuable information can also be obtained from a questionnaire sent to (1) those who have successfully adjusted and stayed overseas and (2) those who have quit their overseas jobs. They can be asked to answer (without identifying themselves) a series of questions about their *expectations* regarding overseas conditions—that is, whether they (or their wives) expected the company to provide comprehensive orientations, attractive houses, special recreational facilities, and so on; whether these expectations were realized when they arrived overseas; if they found conditions radically different from what they expected; and, finally, whether they found the discrepancies to be frustrating.

Some men expect relatively little of their overseas jobs; others expect a great deal but can accept less with equanimity; while some react to unfulfilled expectations in a resentful, hostile, or defeatist manner. A well-prepared questionnaire can reveal significant differences in the expectations and reactions of "quitters" and "stayers" to overseas conditions. Such tests and interviews, of course, would include special portions devoted to the expectations and reactions of wives and children to the overseas situation.

The approaches outlined above will yield highly practical information. For one thing, the employment application form and interpretations of it will be based on the company's own needs and actual experience with its overseas employees. A validated set of tests would then be available for administration to all applicants for overseas jobs. Finally, future employment interviews would be directed at those specific aspects of the applicants' background and personality that have been revealed by research to play a real role in their job adjustment. Employment hunches will thus begin to give way to empirical facts.

TRAINING OVERSEAS EMPLOYEES

Except in the case of a few experienced international firms, American companies seem to be doing very little to prepare employees and their families for going overseas or for improving job competence after they arrive. One rather promising development in the form of a pilot study is one company's efforts to put on long-playing records a wide range of orientation information helpful to the man and his family about to be sent overseas. Two types of albums are involved; one contains fairly stable, permanent information on each country's history, laws, mores, literature, climate, recreational facilities, and language; another contains materials that have to be periodically revised, including statements of the company's goals and policies in doing business abroad; descriptions of local economics, civic problems, and political leaders. If prepared well, these records—no substitute for more lengthy, formal, in-depth training—at least serve in emergencies to alert personnel (and their families) to many aspects of the new environment about which they might ordinarily be told nothing.

If American companies often fail to do a good job of preparing people who are to be transferred abroad, they tend to do even less when it comes to the need for a continuing training and upgrading of their employees abroad. Part of the fault may be in a lack of a foreign tradition of management training. In 1959, this writer conducted an in-depth study of 431 supervisors and executives (local nationals) in a group of large Italian companies. Though the men in this study held positions of considerable responsibility, they had never been exposed to *any* sort of management training. The following courses were found to be needed most (in the order indicated):
- Principles of organization and management.
- The company's economics.
- Planning.
- Merit rating.
- Human relations.
- Accounting, balance sheets, costs.

- Cost control.
- Company policies.
- Selection and employment of personnel.
- Job analysis and job evaluation.

AMA, through its International Management Association, is pioneering in Europe and South America in attempting to meet these needs. American executives, however, must take a stronger stand on providing better educational facilities for their foreign staffs—if for no other reason than to keep their local representatives from feeling neglected and taken for granted.

LABOR RELATIONS ABROAD

Many aspects of labor relations as it must be practiced abroad differ radically from our American experience. One example is classical: the severance limitation. Under the social legislation of many foreign countries, the indemnities to workers who are laid off are so high that employers are practically handcuffed in adjusting to short-term fluctuations in demand. In some countries workers must be given 90 days' notice of intention to terminate them, and government approval must first be obtained.

There may also be government requirements for a fixed ratio of apprentices to journeymen in the plant or for the employer to provide housing for all those who work for him. These requirements cause headaches and high fringe costs for companies operating abroad, although such state protection has produced relatively docile and cooperative labor unions, quite unlike most found in the United States.

Joseph Patrick Carey, who specializes in management-labor relations of American companies doing business abroad, asks the following questions as keys to understanding the labor problems at each foreign post:

- Is your organization a member of any employer association?
- Do you participate in any industrywide collective bargaining?
- At the local or plant level, does your organization conduct formal collective bargaining?
- What is the duration of the collective bargaining contracts?
- Are any officials of the union in the employ of the affiliate company?
- Is there any representative of the union comparable to a shop steward?
- Does first-level management deal regularly with union representatives?

- Are there provisions in the collective bargaining contract applicable to the handling of grievances?
- Is binding arbitration or anything comparable available to the parties?
- Does the affiliate utilize the services of any labor attorneys or other specialists in labor relations in the country where located?

PROBLEMS OF MORALE

In a study of the anxieties and complaints of a large sample of Americans serving abroad, the present writer identified *eight* major causes of distress—some serious enough to make the employee ask to be shipped home. In order of frequency, they were as follows:

1. *Isolation from opportunities.* "Job offers and promotion plums go to the stateside boys."
2. *Language problems.* "My wife and I don't have an aptitude for languages, and we're cut off from our environment."
3. *Insufficient technical or staff support.* "There's no one to call on for help."
4. *Overall dependence on the company.* "I can't be cocky and answer employment ads any more. . . . Big Brother now has me trapped."
5. *Professional staleness.* "I can't talk to smart men in my field or attend seminars or go to association meetings."
6. *Family separation.* "My children had to be sent away to school; there are no good facilities here."
7. *Social.* "My usual leisure-time activities are impossible: I miss the theater, friends, sports."
8. *Legal and political.* "We have to fill out too many local papers; we always feel like interlopers here."

Also cited were occasional physical dangers—diseases, climate discomforts—and the feeling that company allowances were not as generous as the situation warranted.

Most of the foregoing can be dealt with once the anxieties have been identified by top management. Such identification may result from letters of complaint, conversations reported by traveling executives, or even formal "attitude surveys."

Attitude questionnaires, here in the United States, have proved extremely helpful in identifying sore spots in management-employee relations. Yet very few companies have tried them out abroad, probably because of lack of good translations for the foreigners and some uncertainty about how such probing might be received by Americans working abroad. These doubts are not really sufficient justification for failing to obtain adequate and organized information on what employees are thinking and what bothers them on the job.

One company with 20 years of experience in conducting practical employee attitude surveys in the United States has recently authorized the translation and adaptation of its excellent questionnaire for use in Europe. This questionnaire effectively and cheaply collects employee opinions on such key topics as general management policy, compensation, communication, supervision, working conditions, opportunities for advancement, training, and safety and benefit programs. It can be used with both Americans and foreigners abroad.

Management in this country is often surprised and gratified to learn of employee appreciation for its efforts to run an effective company and conversely can profit from any storm warnings that may be found in survey reports. The attitude survey is thus a valuable added channel to the communication exchanges, all the more important when the parties are geographically separate.

* * *

Staffing a company's overseas operation can cost a lot of money—and waste a lot, too. For it's not unusual for a United States or foreign national to leave an overseas company within a short time—the departure often coming during or after exposure to a costly training program.

These departures may occur because the United States national abroad cannot adjust to differences in economic conditions, compensation structures, tax systems, rates of economic exchange, or overall cultural patterns. The foreign national, on the other hand, may feel that he is not given a fair chance to demonstrate his ability to produce—and that his capacity to grow is limited.

It is for reasons like these that personnel managers of companies operating overseas need to be top-notch and highly motivated. They must have at their fingertips practical know-how on the hiring, testing, and placement practices of many local communities, the attitudes of nationals toward unions, the types of compensation factors that are considered proper, and the amount of training and management development that is necessary or desirable. The new breed of personnel manager is going to make or break the company's venture overseas; and he is going to advance or tear apart our national reputation as a vigorous and respectable people.

PRACTICAL ADVICE FOR THE OVERSEAS PERSONNEL MAN •

L ET US SUPPOSE THAT YOU, the reader, are a personnel man of experience and standing. You have shown in your work in the domestic company that you are a good man—the kind the international division feels it needs to bring order into the apparent chaos of personnel practices and relations abroad and to make them intelligible to top management.

Top management has confidence in you; and fortified by it, you are quite self-confident. From what you hear, personnel matters are handled in the foreign branches and subsidiaries of the company in rather backward ways. You have dealt with situations requiring straightening out before. You feel you will know how to do just that in this new, rather exciting assignment. Maybe you will. The chances for it are best, however, if you start out by not being too sure of it.

Compare your situation with that of the engineering manager, the manufacturing specialist, the sales manager—all those of your fellow managers from the domestic organization who are moving into the foreign operations and whose jobs are centered mainly on the company's product line. If these managers run into problems, the chances are they can turn for advice and help to the domestic organization. "Nuts and bolts" tend to be pretty much the same all over the world—they are exportable, and so is the information on them.

This is why the manufacturing man who arrived with you in the foreign metropolis is already at work in the local plant as if he had been there for years. He has sent off a cable to the home office for a shipment of a certain size widget and received a reply telling him how easy it would be to modify those on hand at the plant. This is being done, and everybody is enthusiastic about it—and about him.

MARK PRICEMAN is Manager, Education Programs, IBM World Trade Corporation, New York, New York.

You did not hit it off so well. The local plant manager talked with you very cordially but somewhat vaguely about how delighted he was to have you help his personnel department make improvements for which there was always room. You mentioned a few specific programs you were anxious to get under way, but his reactions suggested that these programs did not have too much meaning for him. He agreed with you wholeheartedly that human relations were at the heart of the business and turned you over to his personnel manager, with whom you are conferring.

The personnel manager looks like a pretty good man, but of course his English is rather halting, and you don't know whether it is his English that keeps him from being more informative or whether what comes out is all he has to say. You would like to have his frank reactions to things you have written to him about and which you are trying to nail down; you find him very agreeable but not specific at all.

You try to take up the agenda item by item. First, the recruiting program: You have inquired repeatedly in your letters about the ratio of graduate students to undergraduates your recruiters would normally interview during visits to the campus. You don't understand why this should be such a difficult question to answer—until you realize, the unsuspected cause of your host's embarrassment: The words "graduate," "undergraduate," "campus" don't have any meaning for him because the whole educational system in his country is different, and the same institutions simply do not exist. He is embarrassed because he is not familiar with our American educational institutions. But you make a mental note that it might be a good idea to acquaint yourself with the essential features of the foreign system before your next visit.

As you dig deeper, you discover that it is really a matter, not only of understanding the words you and he are saying to each other, but of being able to visualize each other's world. Once you have achieved understanding with him on what college graduates, graduate degrees, and campus are, you discover that the recruiting program that looked so plausible at home is out of place here. The local "campus" lacks the facilities and above all the interest and general atmosphere for our domestic practice of college recruiting. There don't seem to be many B.A.'s around. Everyone who has a degree calls himself a doctor; yet there are very few of them, and they do not flock to employment interviews. Incredible though it seems, few are interested in a career in marketing.

As you take a second look at the actual recruiting situation in the foreign subsidiary, you find that given the sources which can be tapped, the local people have not done nearly as poorly as it looked from a distance. Later you learn about an additional limitation they have to contend with. Not everybody qualified and desirable is necessarily willing to work for a foreign employer.

This, incidentally, is something worth your continuing attention, thought, and study: What really does it mean to employees abroad to be working for a foreign, an American employer? It can mean a great many things, depending on who is concerned. On the positive side, it can mean pay and benefits sometimes considerably above the local average; opportunities to become competent in a technology or kind of business which is locally behind in development; the exciting challenge of adapting to the local environment the "hardware" and "software" coming from a foreign culture which are potentially beneficial and needed —but need to be made actually so by people who can distinguish between what is exportable and what is not and what can be exported "as is" and what has to be made exportable.

There is also a negative side to being a foreign employee of an American firm operating abroad. It affects particularly those in managerial and professional positions. It is not too difficult to see the disadvantages once they are pointed out, but they often have to be pointed out because the chances are the company's philosophy makes no distinction between its employees at home and abroad. They are all "one family." This is a noble credo to have, but some of the foreign employees feel that if they belong to the family, they do so as poor relations.

With some, this feeling may be due to different pay scales from country to country. These differences reflect actually different standards of living. When in Rome, do as the Romans do. When abroad, abide by pay scales which will not disrupt the local labor market. The principle is sound, but it does not keep the local employee who works in close contact with Americans from being dubious about the exact meaning of "equal pay for equal work."

Some such attitudes are petty and unrealistic. The realities which give rise to them cannot be changed, but there should be an awareness of their existence. These attitudes can be affected by word and deed— often inadvertently. As a matter of fact, stress on the company's egalitarian philosophy—we all belong to the company, the company belongs equally to us—may aggravate the resentment that some abroad may have over real, but inevitable, inequalities. If it is true that all the

Americans the company is keeping abroad are in effect doing more responsible or exacting work than those around them who are paid at lower rates, then the company is in good shape and need not pay much attention to petty carping.

But equality is not exclusively, or primarily, a matter of remuneration. Equally important are status, the "weight" one carries, career possibilities, and the chance for being oneself and fulfilling oneself in one's job. In these respects, a foreign employee will seldom feel entirely the equal of an American in an American organization. For an American in an American business, it goes without saying and without his needing to be conscious of it, that things are done the American way. All he needs to concern himself with is whether they are done the right or the wrong way. His foreign counterpart cannot remain unaware for long that things are done the American way and that some ways he considers right are under suspicion of being wrong because they are not American. Often the requirement for his success is that he learn to do things the American way, indeed to "think" American. Few Americans have ever made this adjustment in reverse, and most have difficulty grasping how taxing it is.

This circumstance is very relevant to your encounter with the local personnel manager. Consider what he has to do to satisfy both you and the requirements of his job. He has to listen to your message—say, on recruiting. He has to strip it of all the specifics which you tend to think are applicable everywhere but which are not. How can he "always maintain close contact with the placement officer at colleges" when in his country there is no such officer? He has to work out an answer which makes sense in his environment and to make you accept it as such. You must realize that it is a burden which you could lighten by making it your business to become more familiar with his environment. On the other hand, you can make things very difficult if you just can't see things the way they look from where he sits.

Seeing things from a foreign national's point of view is difficult because it involves not only environmental differences but mental ones. Not only is his part of the world different, but his way of viewing the world is also to some extent different. His thought processes are organized in ways which may seem bizarre because this is not in all respects the way you were taught to think. Even someone who is as close culturally as a European seems to be has a tendency to line up a problem differently from the way an American was taught to do and to go about solving it in different ways. To realize this is sometimes quite a shock, and the almost irresistible temptation is to consider the alien way of thinking inferior. You are in a position to assert your way of thinking, and you are not forced to penetrate and comprehend any other. But he must adjust, which may be putting him under considerable strain. The less aware of this you are, and the more inflexibly you assert your ways of thinking and acting, the greater the strain.

This strain may result in a form of chronic, conscious or half-conscious, resentment which might be called "cultural alienation." When there are morale problems among foreign employees, particularly managers and others who are in contact with the American management of the company, the chances are they reflect cultural alienation. It means that the foreign employees find the actions of their American management bewildering and communications with it frustrating. They feel that they are not getting through, that they are not appreciated for what they would expect to be appreciated for in their own culture, and therefore that they do not fully "belong."

Even the manufacturing man, apart from dealing with widgets, is also dealing with people, and he too has to cope with language differences, different habits of thought and action, and unaccustomed sets of conditions in general. All this may prove quite bewildering to him at different times, and to those with whom he has dealings abroad, to the point of jeopardizing his success. And when he runs into these kinds of difficulties, as he almost certainly will, it is the business of the personnel division to help him find his bearings. After all, his main responsibility is getting the widgets out; your main responsibility is insuring that people work well with people. So you must not only learn to take care of yourself in the foreign environment, but help others to do it; and what is worse, unlike others, you cannot turn to the domestic organization for guidance on most of your new concerns. Human engineering is not exportable the way mechanical engineering is.

This statement and the reasoning behind it are not easy to accept. It seems to imply that most or much of what you have learned in years of personnel work in the domestic environment is without value, that you cannot consider yourself a professional, and you have to go back to school all over again. This would be overstating the case, but there is enough truth to it to make anyone in your position feel uncomfortable. What you have learned in years of personnel work is not wasted, but the experience can no longer be relied upon the way it was back home. The practices and possible responses to human situations learned in one environment have to be compared with those abroad and as often as not adapted to the new environment. The more you become adept at differentiating between the universal and the culturally relative, the more the experience in your background will come again into its own. But if you try to ignore the fact of environmental distinctiveness and treat the whole world as if it were culturally homogeneous, then your repertory of practices, procedures, and techniques will be misapplied and prove indeed of questionable value.

In a sense, it is true that you must go back to school—at least there is much you have to learn, most likely without the advantages of a school setting. Everybody who enters international business without preparation for it has much to learn; and since the personnel man may also have something to do with providing the teaching, there is special urgency for him to keep ahead of the others.

You should consider what it is you want to learn because at first sight it seems so overwhelming that you have to be selective about it. You may already have asked yourself how you could possibly learn all about the customs, practices, and traditions of the peoples in the world and brush up on their languages in a short lifetime. The answer is that you cannot, but fortunately less than that will do nicely. No one ever knows everything about any one thing, but on some things it is important to have enough knowledge to enable one to cope with problems regardless of the areas of ignorance you have to live with.

The strategic knowledge needed, because it makes understandable the basic problems in international operations, is a clear conception of what culture is and what culture does. Do not reject the word culture because it does not seem to fit into a businessman's vocabulary. A personnel man should become used to the concepts and terminology of the behavioral sciences. Culture is a concept which is central to a specific discipline of relevance to international business—cultural anthropology.

It is not difficult to define culture—any dictionary will help—but it is difficult for most of us to become excited over it for this reason: Most of us are born and raised in one culture and do not come into contact with a foreign culture until our perceptions and thought processes have been completely molded by our particular culture. We have been taught to think and feel and act in certain ways which we have never questioned and which seem natural to us. The more steeped we are in our culture, the less aware we are of its relativity. By the time we encounter ways which are different, we perceive them not as culturally different but as unnatural. Unnatural, of course, has an emotional, negative connotation. The purpose of understanding culture is to develop the lost ability to see the different without perceiving it as unnatural and to substitute a rational view for an emotional reaction. The importance of this lies in the fact that as we deal with people from different cultures, our relations with them are affected by our initial inclination to consider their ways as unnatural. Actually, they are culturally relative and have their rightful place in their respective cultures. It helps our relations greatly if we see it that way. The peculiar ways of culture, incidentally, do change, and changes can be promoted and precipitated under certain conditions. But he who wants to promote cultural change without knowing that that is what he is up to will more often than not come to grief.

If understanding culture has its practical importance when considering a worldwide personnel program of almost any kind, then what is there about it that can be studied, outside of taking all the existing cultures in which a man may have to move and studying them? In a sense, there is no substitute for that, but there is at least a short cut, thanks to the studies of specific cultures made by others and to the comparisons which were made and which precisely led to the modern anthropological concept of culture: A culture is not behavioral chaos (which is the way a foreign one seems to the unprepared on first impact) but a systematic structure of recognizable patterns of behavior. The purpose of learning about culture, stated more specifically, is to see structure and pattern behind seemingly "unnatural" or "wrong" behavior. Once that is learned, there will be a feeling for where culture is relevant even when it is not known precisely how a given culture will affect a specific activity.

A general culture-consciousness has further uses. It helps one to understand, and can help prevent, a phenomenon known as "culture shock." Culture shock is a condition which often results from the immersion of the unprepared in a foreign culture. It may be as severe as a mental breakdown, but more likely it will manifest itself as a depression of varying severity or as lowered morale, lowered efficiency, and so on. The likely victims are people who move abroad or move from abroad, as well as their wives and children. Life adjustment in a foreign country is nothing but learning to function satisfactorily in a foreign culture. Some people need more help for this than others; some are more likely to succeed than others. Cultural understanding is needed to provide the necessary help and to estimate the chances and the advisability of international transfers.

Cultural shock, incidentally, is not relevant exclusively to life adjustment. It can also be suffered, and inflicted, at work. A foreign employee may suffer shock from finding it impossible to function as he is accustomed to in the work environment which has been created for him. He may suffer this shock without quite realizing what is happening because it is happening in his own country. A case in point are training programs which seem entirely "natural" to you but are utterly alien and confusing to foreigners. Too much of what is taught and how it is taught may be against the foreigner's cultural grain, resulting in an inability to absorb, self-doubts, and depression.

In this connection there is, of course, a cultural factor which stands out: language. The chances are the foreign employee has to take his training in English—a foreign language for him. Unless you have yourself acquired command of a foreign language and have had to function in it, it is difficult for you to see its implications. It adds a difficulty which is more than mechanical. It is not just like switching from Gregg to Pitman in shorthand, for languages are not mere interchangeable codes. Each is part of a culture, a reflection of that culture, and one of its instruments. Languages differ not only in form but in content, just as the cultures themselves differ.

There should by now be no doubt in your mind that there will be serious questions to be resolved as you go about your new job in overseas personnel management. You will have to find your own answers, but you do not need to do so in the dark. If you want to find out more about culture, you can. Many books and articles on the subject have been written. Clyde Kluckhohn's *Mirror for Man—the Relation of Anthropology to Modern Life* lives up rewardingly to its title. *The Silent Language,* by Edward T. Hall, connects with the preceding. It will add to your perception of cultural phenomena and their practical implications. You don't have to buy all of the author's hypotheses. *The Overseas Americans,* by Cleveland, Mangone, and Adams, is a comprehensive examination of a highly relevant problem. One periodical that may put you on to some significant articles is *The International Executive,* published four times a year by John Fayerweather.

Your job will hardly permit you to become a bookworm, even if it were your inclination. You will have to be doing things, and you will be gaining a great deal of experience. Experience, to be useful, must be organized. What you may feel inspired to read will be of some help in organizing your experience.

INDEX

INDEX

H

I

J

K

L

M

U

V

W

X

Y